# Pentax K1000 P30N/P3N and P30T

**Note on the Pentax P30T**

As this book went to press, the Pentax P30T was introduced to replace the P30N. The main difference between the two models is that the split-image focus indicator in the focusing screen of the P30T is arranged diagonally, whereas it is horizontal in the P30N screen. The advantage of a diagonal split-image indicator is that it makes it possible to focus on either horizontal or vertical outlines in the image without having to turn the camera round.

HOVE-FOUNTAIN BOOKS

David Kilpatrick

# Pentax K1000 & P30N/P3N

**(In the USA and Canada the P30n is designated the P3n)**

First English Edition September 1990
by David Kilpatrick
Series Editor: Dennis Laney
Technical Editor: George Wakefield
Typeset by Icon Publications Limited, Kelso, Scotland
Printed in Germany by Kösel GmbH, Kempten

ISBN 0-86343-330-8

Published by
HOVE FOUNTAIN BOOKS
the joint imprint of

Fountain Press Ltd
45 The Broadway, Tolworth
Surrey KT6 7DW

&

Hove Foto Books
34 Church Road, Hove
Sussex BN3 2GJ

UK Trade Distribution by
Fountain Press Ltd

# Contents

*The author wishes to thank the staff of Pentax (UK) Limited and their associates for all the assistance rendered in providing information for the preparation of this book, and his wife Shirley for doing all the other work which was supposed to be happening at the same time.*

*Photographs other than illustrations of equipment are by David Kilpatrick except where otherwise credited.*

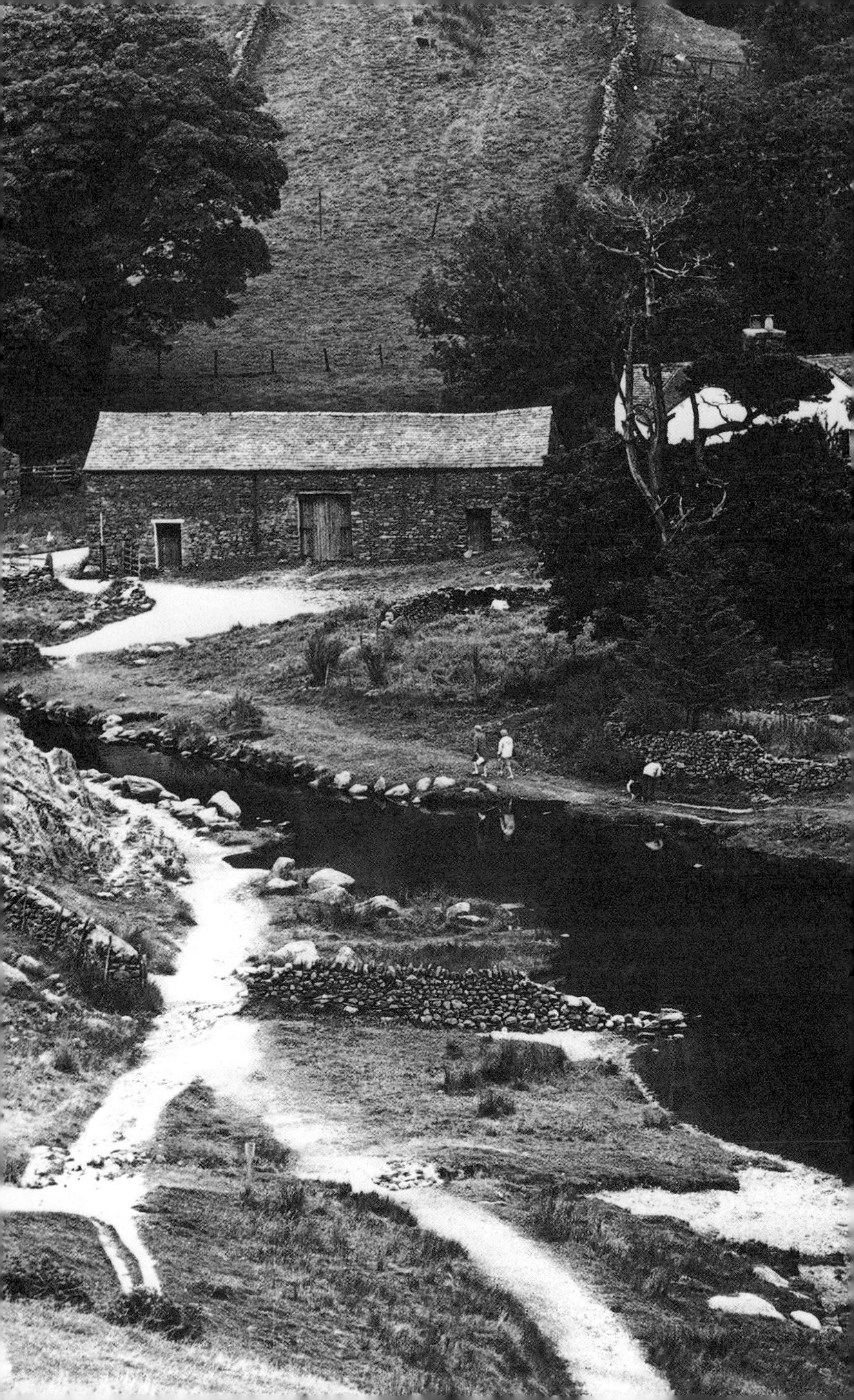

# Introducing the K1000

There are few photographic products which outlive their technological generation, and when they do, it is because they possess some exceptional quality. That quality is more often than not one of robust simplicity.

If I were asked to pick out a few products which have remained best-sellers across a span of decades rather than mere years, my list would include the Weston exposure-meter, the Saunders enlarging easel, the Vivitar 283 flashgun, the Hasselblad 500 – and the **Pentax K1000** single-lens reflex.

Like many photographers, I learned with a Pentax. For a teenager in the 1960s the **Spotmatic** was the height of sophistication, an SLR with built-in through-the-lens metering. It had a good range of shutter speeds, from 1 second to 1/1000th plus Bulb, a fast *f*1.8 lens of very high quality, and a bright eye-level pentaprism viewing screen with a simple center-needle meter coupled to the shutter speeds and working aperture. Best of all, the Pentax was a cleanly-designed camera with no sharp edges or small hard-to-use controls. The advertising slogan was 'Just Hold a Pentax' and in comparison with other makes its handling was unrivalled.

That same Pentax Spotmatic took me through from High School to working as a fully-fledged freelance professional photographer, and although I now use a very wide range of many different cameras, I still own the Pentax and one favourite old Super Takumar lens.

Today, the Pentax K1000 is unique in offering a mechanical specification similar to the model of 1965, brought up-to-date and into line to accept the entire current range of A-mount Pentax lenses. The K1000 is one of a select group of SLRs which continue to operate even if the silver-oxide cell which powers the exposure metering is exhausted. It is a mechanically-controlled camera, relying on tensioned springs to operate the instant-return mirror, aperture mechanism and focal plane shutter. All linkages between the lens and the camera body are purely mechanical, and film advance depends on the most readily-available source of energy – your right thumb!

The K1000 has the classic shutter speed range of 1/1000th to 1 second and center-needle metering in the viewfinder. Indeed, the major

*There are many subjects which manual cameras tackle as well, if not better, than automatic models. Experience may be needed, too; for this Lake District view with a 135mm f3.5 Pentax lens, Shirley Kilpatrick set the absolute minimum exposure and made a high contrast print.*

differences between the K1000 and the original Spotmatic - which was the first camera of this type from any maker - are the bayonet lens-mount, full aperture metering, and the provision of a 'hot' flash shoe to allow cordless synchronization of any electronic flash mounted on the camera. There are other refinements such as a plastic tip to make the wind-on lever more comfortable, and an improved focusing screen which may have an optical split-image rangefinder or a microprism for focusing (both types of screen have been fitted to the K1000 at different times).

The basic SLR body is available through some outlets on its own, as it is a popular second body for owners of A-series lens systems. It is normally sold with the **50mm *f*2 Pentax-A** lens.

The K1000 is one of the few cameras capable of taking a photographer from the first stages of learning to handle an SLR right through to professional work. In many circumstances it is preferable to electronic, automatic SLRs; it is certainly more functional for remote travel and wilderness photography, in school or college, as a professional second-string or backup, and for many studio jobs such as copying.

This book has been prepared as a guide to the functions and use of the K1000, still one of the most widely-purchased SLR models, and its modern sister the **P30n** (**P3n** in North America) which offers similar specifications plus both Programmed and Aperture Priority Auto exposure modes, and uses an electronic shutter with a range of 2 seconds to 1/1000, with flash synchronization at 1/100.

The P30n may lack some of the survival qualities of the K1000 and be less of a suitable choice for a month in the Sahara, but has greater appeal to those who prefer electronic displays and need a smaller, lighter camera. It also has a self-timer (delayed action), a depth-of-field preview, dedicated flash with a flash-ready indicator in the viewfinder, Memory Lock when using auto exposure, a two-way focusing screen with both microprism and split image focusing aids, and the faster **50mm *f*1.7 Pentax-A** lens fitted as standard.

You may also find the book useful if you own any of the now-discontinued variations on K-series mechanical SLRs or the P30, and the earlier small-body Pentax model **MX**, which is more or less a hybrid of the two. There have been many independent SLRs made in the past fifteen years which resemble the K1000 and use the same Pentax K-mount lens bayonet, without always achieving a similar quality in build or performance. Much of the information and advice in this book will apply to these as well, depending on the functions of the particular model involved.

To go beyond the scope of this book, using your K1000 or P30n, you have the great advantage of being able to refer to almost any good book on technique written in the past thirty years. The functions of the K1000 are the basics around which every more sophisticated SLR is built, while they exceed the capabilities of many later programmed models.

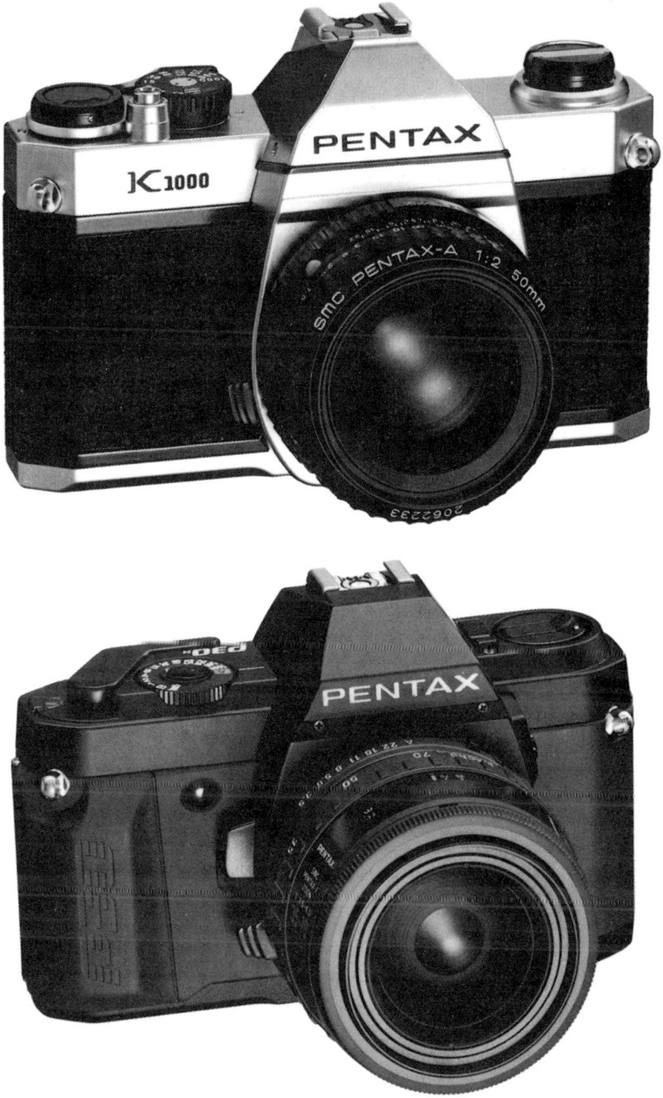


*Top : the Pentax K1000 is finished in satin matt chrome with leathercloth panels, and is a metal-bodied camera. Bottom: the P30n is much lighter, with many synthetic components, and is finished in black with rubber handling grips.*

# A little history

The K1000 is the lineal descendant of a camera which was simply called the **Asahiflex**, introduced by the Asahi Optical Co. Ltd. of Tokyo.in 1951. This was three years after the East German Zeiss factory in Dresden launched the Contax S, considered to be the first modern 35mm SLR, with its pentaprism. The Asahiflex, the first Japanese SLR, was more akin to the pre-war Kine Exakta.

Like many cameras of this date, the Asahiflex had a waist-level viewfinder. You used it rather like a Box Brownie, peering down through a magnifying lens at a small image reversed left-to-right on a groundglass screen. Any attempt to hold the camera for a portrait or vertical composition resulted in an upside-down viewing image which required a sideways squint to focus and compose. When the shutter was released, the viewing screen went totally blank, and nothing further could be seen until the film was advanced. This action 'cocked' the mirror along with the focal-plane shutter, returning it to its spring-tensioned 45° position ready to fly up the instant the shutter was released.

In 1954, Asahi introduced the world's first instant-return mirror on their model **IIB**. This basic and apparently simple innovation provides the mirror with a there-and-back action, two springs being cocked rather than one. Before the exposure, the mirror flies up; after the shutter has closed, it returns to viewing position instantly. Early models like this did not always return the mirror very reliably when held upside-down, as gravity played a part in the action - today's cameras have far more complex mechanisms which cope with any orientation.

In 1957, the company introduced a camera called the **Pentax**, the first Japanese camera with an eye-level viewing prism based on a special five-faced design, which is called a *pentaprism*. The pentaprism gave the Pentax its name, and the distinctive SLR shape with a pyramid-shaped bulge in the central top plate.

The pentaprism turns the picture right way round and right way up, regardless of how the camera is held. You are able to compose all pictures from eye-level, just as with a rangefinder camera, and use vertical or horizontal compositions. Some manufacturers kept the prism unit separate, so that it could be fitted as an add-on to the existing waist-level finder, replacing the magnifier, but Asahi made it a fixed and sealed part of the optical system from the very start.

At this stage, a lens mount with a 42mm diameter and 1mm pitch screw thread was introduced. This is still known today as the 'Pentax/Praktica' screw thread, after the two major users of the fitting. The lens provided with the camera was branded **Takumar**, Asahi's name for all their lenses up to the late 1970s, with a focal length of 55mm and maximum aperture of *f*1.8. Smaller apertures were obtained by setting

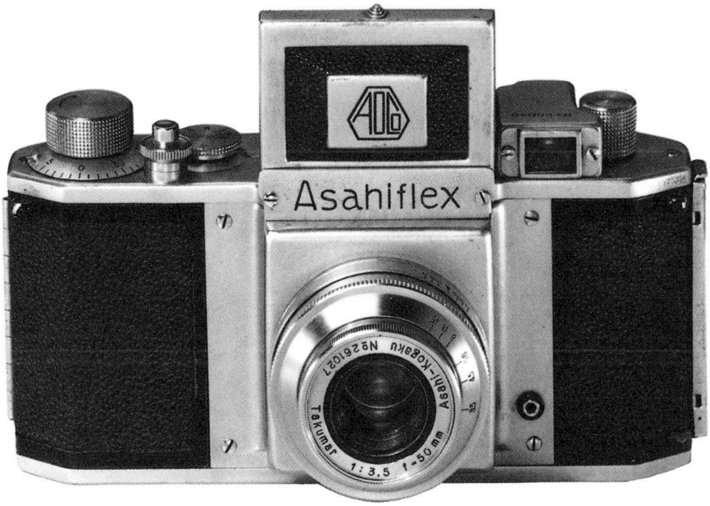


*Above: the grand-daddy of all the Pentax cameras – the original Asahiflex IIB of 1954, with its waist-level viewfinder.*

*Below – the principle of the pentaprism, an optical device which allows right-way-round viewing at eye level in comfort. This was first seen in the original Pentax of 1957.*

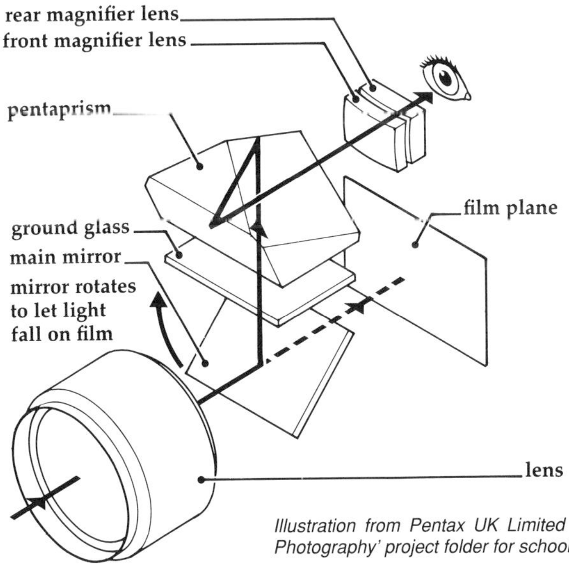


*Illustration from Pentax UK Limited 'Focus on Photography' project folder for schools*

them manually on the lens after focusing and before taking the picture.

In 1958, lenses with spring-loaded iris diaphragms (the component which reduced the light transmitted by the lens) were introduced. After each picture, the lens could be cocked by hand to its widest aperture, remaining set on the correct aperture for the picture. This made viewing and focusing much easier, right up to the instant of exposure. The lenses were called **Auto Takumar**.

Finally, in 1961 a new mechanism with a counter-sprung iris diaphragm replaced the spring-cocked type. New cameras, the Pentax S or H3 and S or H1a, had a modified 'actuator' just inside the lens mount. When the shutter was pressed, this pushed on a pin in the back of the lens and closed the aperture down to the pre-set value; after the picture was taken, the actuator simply retreated and let the spring-balanced aperture open up again.

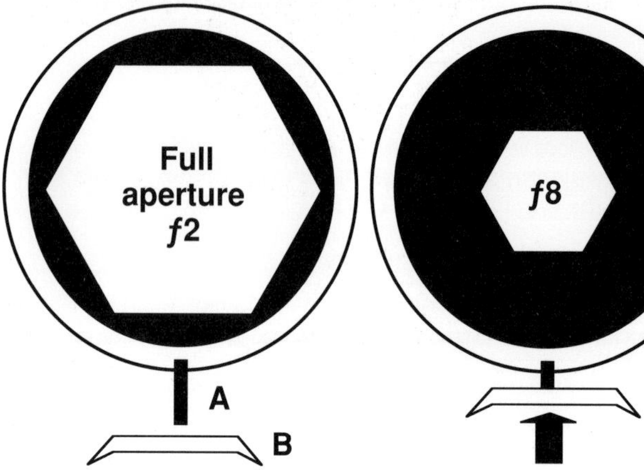


A = FAD (fully automatic diaphragm) actuator pin oin rear of lens mount. B = striker plate inside camera lens throat which operates pin prior to exposure.

*Above – how the aperture pin of a early Pentax lens worked. For viewing, the lens was at full aperture (left). This gave a bright image. When the shutter was pressed, the iris diaphragm (aperture) closed down (right) producing a dimmer image, to control the exposure. Modern lenses work the same way, but the diaphragm is sprung closed instead of sprung open. If you take the lens off the camera, the tension is released, and the aperture closes. Older lenses stayed under tension all the time, and as a result, their spring mechanisms gradually got weaker.*

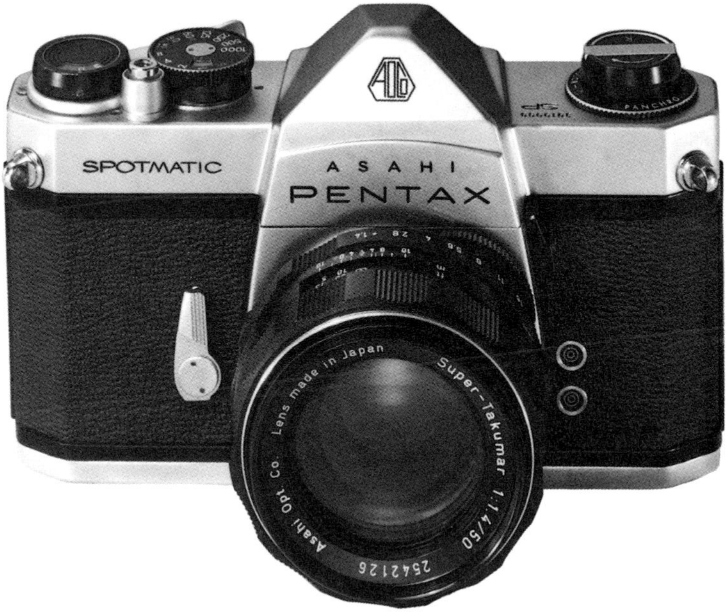



*The Pentax Spotmatic introduced through-the-lens-metering.*

## Through-the-lens metering

In 1964 the Asahi Pentax **Spotmatic** made use of this feature to provide through-the-lens metering with cadmium sulphide (CdS) measuring cells positioned inside the prism housing, on either side of the eyepiece, looking towards the focusing screen. With a circuit coupled to the shutter dial, they measured the brightness of the focusing screen in absolute terms. It did not matter what lens was fitted, or what accessories – as long as the camera was set to exactly the same state as it would be for taking the final picture, the meter could indicate the correct exposure. A small push-down switch on the side of the camera simultaneously switched the meter circuit on, and operated the actuator mechanism (stop-down preview) already described.

Because the meter system operated at working aperture, there was no need for any mechanical linkage. A needle had to be centered in a small gap, as seen through the viewfinder. This is not the same as match-needle metering, where two needles must be aligned. Match-needle metering is used when both controls of the camera (shutter and aperture) are linked to the movement of one needle, which is then aligned with a moving light-level needle by adjusting either control.

The Spotmatic also had substantially improved castings, shutter mechanism, wind-on, and optical systems when compared to older models. The mirror, for example, moved slightly backwards when it flipped up. This allowed Asahi to make a **50mm *f*1.4** lens. If this new lens was fitted to an older camera, it would be damaged because the mirror would actually hit the large glass element at the back of the lens.

The Pentax Spotmatic system had advantages and disadvantages alike. It was far simpler than the open-aperture match needle systems used by Canon and Minolta, which needed complex couplings. These couplings imposed restraints on the design of lenses. It would work with any kind of lens, including special systems for close-up work.

Stop-down metering (at working aperture) does mean that to meter, the screen must be allowed to become very dark when small apertures are used (just as we show on the previous page). Sometimes, light entering the eyepiece of the viewfinder could be sufficient to influence the reading from a very dark subject. Standing in bright sunshine and taking a photograph of a subject in shade required some care.

Despite disadvantages of slowness and relative inaccuracy, the stop-down system was retained through a second generation of Spotmatic models (the **Spotmatic II** and **500**) until the end of the 1960s, when a small modification to the screw-thread lens mount enabled full-aperture coupled metering with new lenses in the **Spotmatic F**.

With full-aperture metering came the end of the link between the stop-down preview switch and the meter circuit. Instead, an electronic switch turned the metering on as soon as the lens cap was taken off,

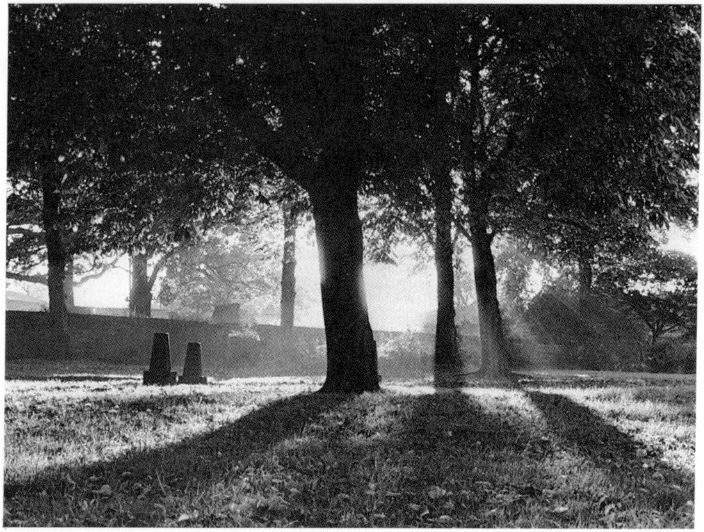

giving permanent metering while the camera was at eye-level. This was only possible because of greatly improved circuits and battery economy. Rather than change the viewfinder display to a match-needle method, Asahi kept with the familiar center-needle arrangement in which having the needle 'over' showed over-exposure, and having it 'under' showed under. An experienced user could judge exactly to what degree this applied.

For the first time, Asahi started using the familiar Pentax brand-name (originally nothing more than the name of a camera model) more widely. Lenses changed from being **SMC Takumar** – the SMC stands for Super-Multi-Coated and will be explained later – to **SMC Pentax**.

The 'F' screw thread, which had a locking stop pin and a coupling lug for the aperture control ring, was the first significant departure from the standard 'Pentax/Praktica' 42mm screw thread since the early 1950s. Many other makers used the standard thread. Asahi kept to this modified thread for their first electronic SLRs, but the superiority of bayonet mounts, which need a quick turn to lock firmly, was apparent.

Leica had changed to a bayonet mount in the mid-1950s; Nikon, Canon and Minolta had all developed their SLR ranges from rangefinder models and created enlarged variations on rangefinder bayonet themes. Only Asahi had started with an SLR from the beginning, and had based this on the Contax D German design which used the screw thread.

By the mid-1970s it was clear to them that a change to a bayonet was needed, and the **K-mount** was born.

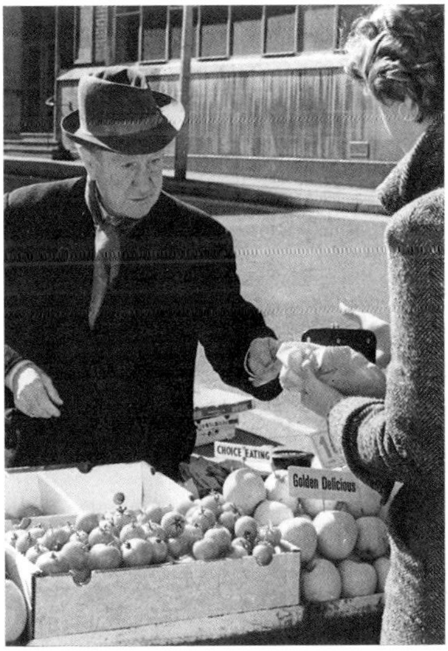


*Stop-down metering enabled photographers to take accurate readings from difficult subjects, and in many ways changed the kind of photograph which ordinary people could tackle. Without needing expertise with a hand-held meter, pictures like the scene under trees (far left) or in a busy market (left) could be taken quickly and with reasonable certainty of correct exposure, without taking the camera from your eye. New Pentaxes continue this tradition of quick, reliable exposure contol.*

## The K-Mount standard

Other manufacturers guarded their exclusive bayonet mount designs jealously. No-one apart from Canon, for example, has ever made a Canon-mount camera. Independent lens makers either copied the mounts or obtained licences to use them. As it happens, there were one or two instances of copying both Nikon and Minolta mounts, but these were short-lived.

Only the Pentax had a universal standard, shared with many other makers round the world. When Asahi announced their new bayonet mount, destined to replace the old screw thread, they took the unusual decision of making it public domain. The K-Mount was not to be exclusive – it could become, they said, the bayonet equivalent of the ubiquitous 42mm screw thread.

This is exactly what happened. The K-mount was launched with the **KX** as the replacement for the Spotmatic F, having all the features of this model including the open-aperture metering with auto switch-on and the center-needle display. A professional electronic camera, the **K2**, was introduced at a higher price and followed by the **K2DMD** which accepted a motordrive. The K1000 was a slightly simplified KX; a simpler **K500** with no 1/1000th top shutter speed, and several other 'trimmed' features, provided the lowest-cost variant.

Following the success of these models, the high specification **Pentax LX** system was introduced to compete directly with the Nikon and Canon 'F' professional ranges. This model remains in production and gives the K1000 a fine 'big brother' to look up to, making sure there is no upper limit to the versatility of the K-mount system.

Since the introduction of the K1000 in 1979 the K-mount has become the most popular bayonet, and this sturdy 35mm SLR has been in continuous production. The K-mount was developed first into the KA-mount and subsequently the current A-mount, which is used by all manual focus Pentax SLRs and incorporates electronic connections. The K1000 functions perfectly with all older K-mount lenses, but is supplied with A-mount optics.

The new A-mount standard provides interchangeability between the original K-series bodies and lenses and the latest **SF**-series autofocus cameras, plus almost all the models in between. Though the latest AF lenses are not required for use on the basic K1000, and the manual K-series lenses disable most of the auto functions of the AF bodies, they can be switched between the different camera types if necessary. There must be some regret that some independent camera makers have modified the K-mount in different ways, so that instead of one standard, there are now several K-mount variations and full compatibility is no longer guaranteed between makes. For this reason it pays to use genuine Pentax lenses when you can afford them, and only buy

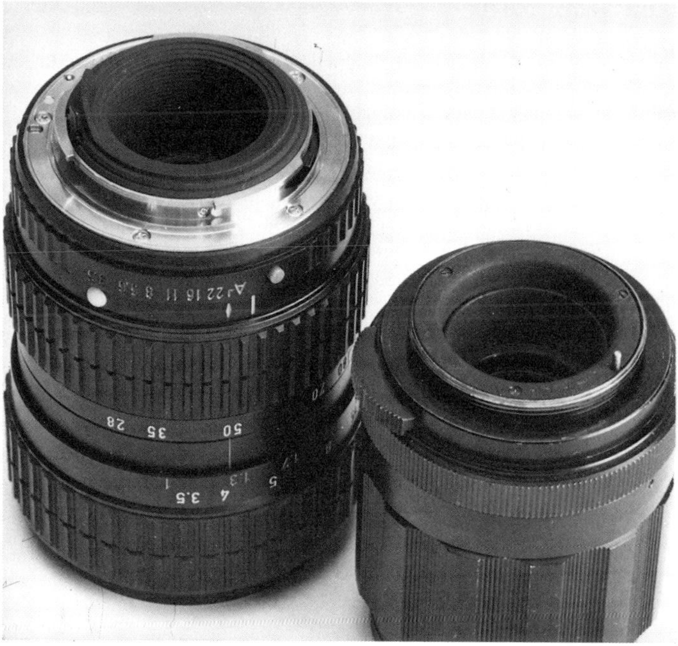

*Above: the original screw mount compared with today's version of the bayonet mount, the A-mount. The complexity and cost of the new mount is clear – but lenses today are cheaper in real terms.*

independent lenses which are specifically for the Pentax K-mount.

The Pentax name has now replaced Asahi as the name of the company itself. The cameras are no longer 'Asahi Pentax', just Pentax. For a long period in the USA and Canada the Honeywell Corporation distributed Asahi products, and even re-branded the cameras as Honeywell Pentax (prior to this, they were Tower brand under a similar arrangement). You may find old references to Honeywell models, or even Tower, but today all Pentax cameras are called Pentax even if they don't have that pentaprism! The original lens brand name, Takumar, was used in the early days of the new system to brand budget priced K-mount lenses and distinguish them from slightly higher specification Pentax named versions. Both lens types were, of course, made by Pentax and the Takumars are in every way equal in quality - they're just simpler.

## Learning more

Now you have the history of the K1000, and in the process you have gleaned a little information about such things as instant-return mirrors, pentaprisms, auto lens diaphragms, through-the-lens metering and open aperture metering. It is all too easy to assume that your camera simply has these things because that's how cameras are made – but it helps to have a perspective on the gradual introduction of all the features over the last 40 years.

However, this doesn't help you understand exactly what all these things do and how they work. You need to know this before you start using the controls creatively. In the next chapter we'll explain how the K1000 and P30n work in detail, and after that, we shall look at what you can actually do with the features and controls of the cameras.

*SLR cameras allow extremely accurate composition, focus and metering. The image on the groundglass screen shows all the tones in their correct relationship – here, the strong black shadows and silhouetted branches in the foreground could be assessed easily. For pictures like this, precise cropping and framing is vital; the spire of this New Hampshire clapboard church had to be perfectly balanced to avoid any sensation of falling over. A 24mm wide-angle was used from a close viewpoint.*

*Although it is easy to assess exposure in bright sunshine, it is virtually impossible to guess the right settings in a situation like this – a white building lit by the very last rays of the setting sun, against a clear blue sky, with heavy shadows. The Pentax metering system gives perfect results automatically. Photograph by David Kilpatrick.*

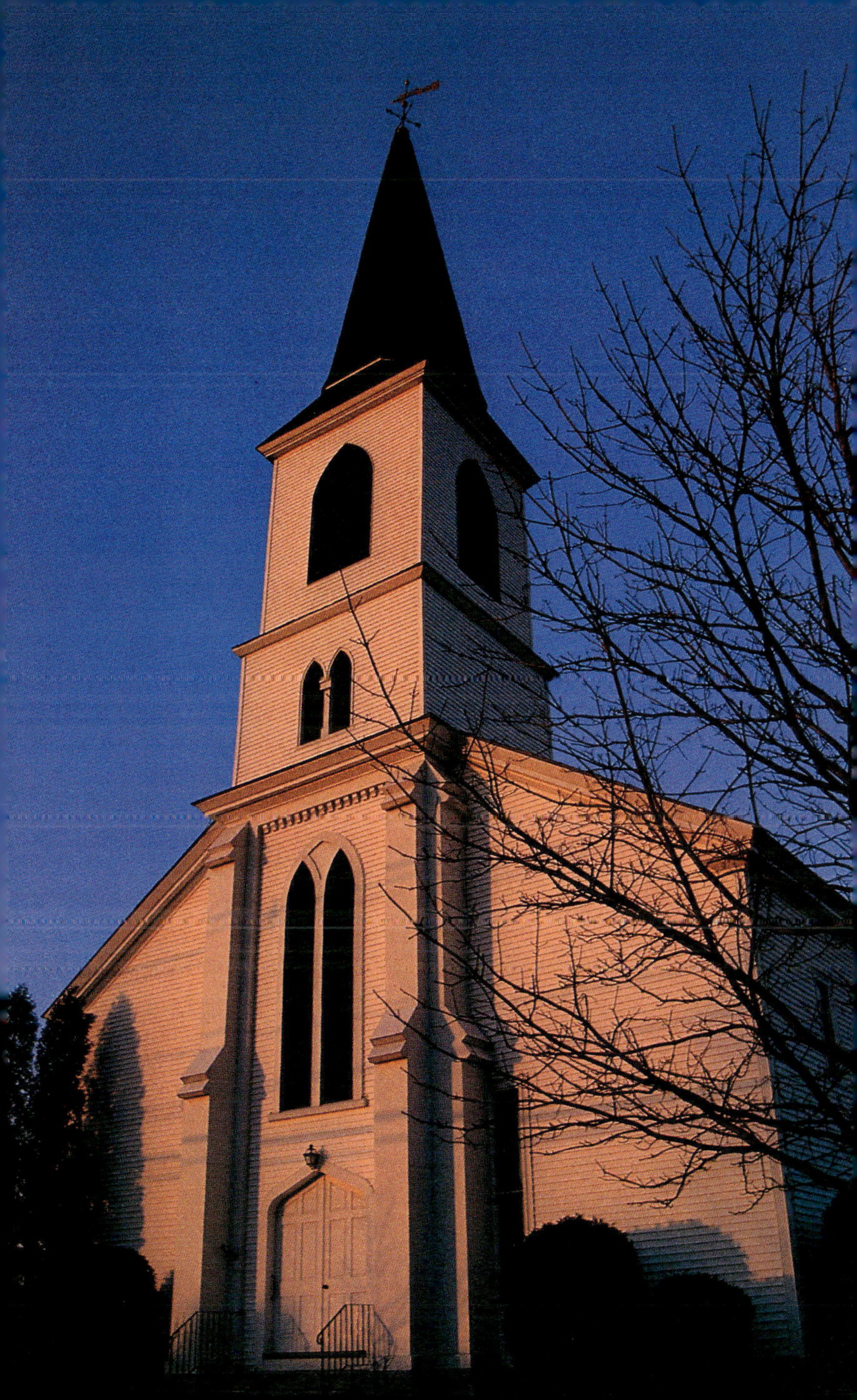

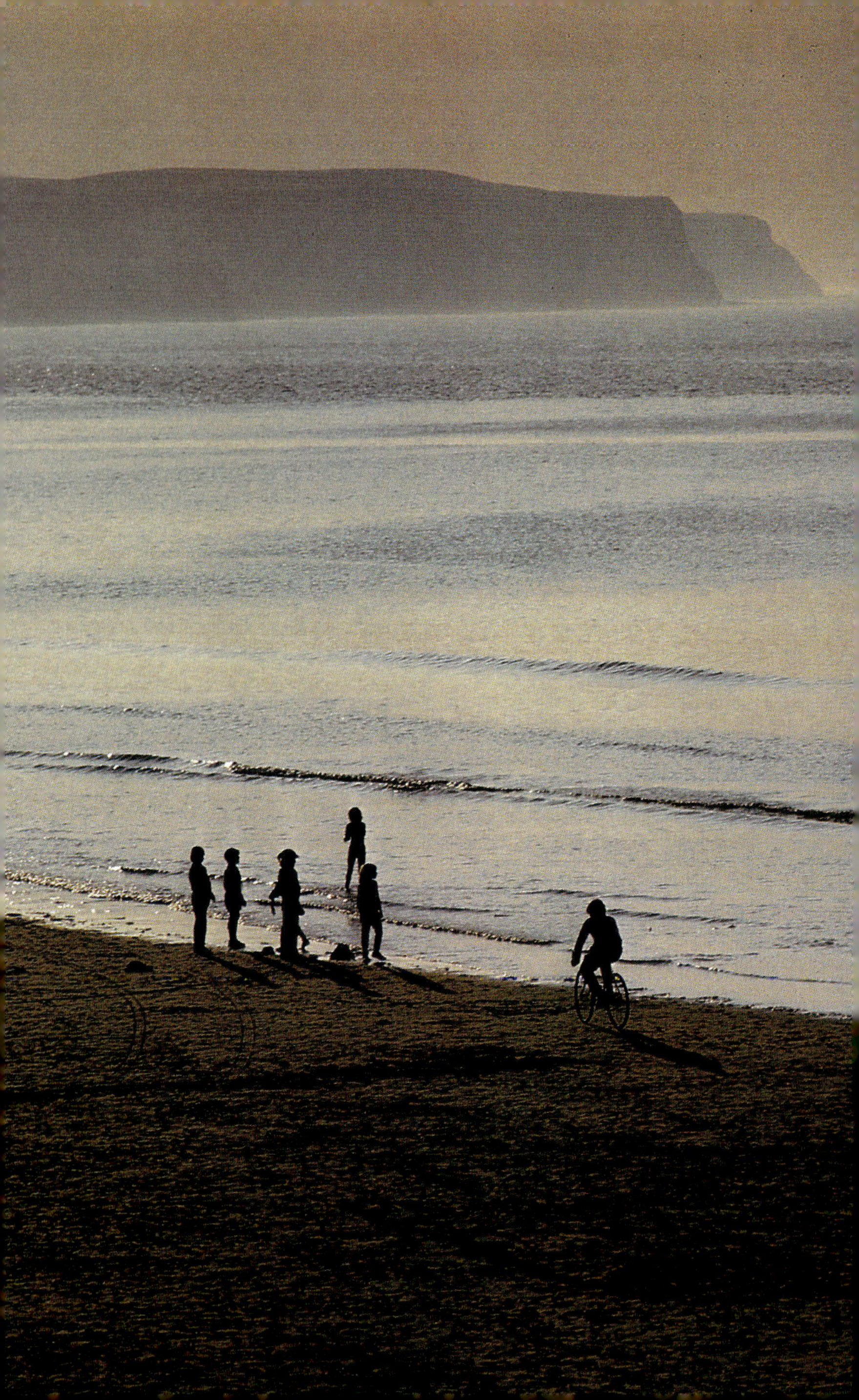

# The SLR Principle

The human eye takes in a very wide field of view, with a small central area of sharp detail. The eye's view has no sharp boundaries, and its centre of interest is wherever you happen to be looking. By moving your head and eyes you can look all round and study every part of the visible world around you.

The camera is totally different in the way that it sees the world. Although the camera's lens basically functions in the same way as the eye's lens, it does not project its image on to the surface of the inside of a sphere. If it did, the camera too would see a universal view. To be of any use for printing or projecting pictures, the camera's film has to be flat – and although cameras with circular pictures have been made before, including the very first Kodak, most people prefer rectangular prints.

The lens projects a circular image. You can test this easily, by removing a standard **50mm *f*2** lens from the camera and carefully holding it about two inches (50mm) from a sheet of white paper, inside a room, pointing out of a window. The lens should be set to '2' on the aperture scale (*f*2). You will see a circular picture of the scene outside projected clearly on to the paper, upside down. If you can use a laboratory clamp to hold both the lens and the paper perfectly parallel, you can examine this image with more care and see how objects at different distances go in and out of focus as the lens is moved.

Now draw a rectangle 1 by 1.5 inches (24 x 36mm) on the paper. You will see that this frame only covers the central part of the circular image from the lens – the sharpest and brightest area of the picture.

Ever since the first cameras were made, the problem has been to indicate to the user precisely the shape of the frame or picture format, and show the 'crop' or composition of the scene in front of the lens. Obviously, you cannot keep removing a lens and studying the projected image, and nor is it very easy to devise a system for viewing the image itself. To take the picture, a sheet of photographic film needs to be

*The eye is highly selective although it sees a wide field. From a clifftop near Whitby in north-east England, these figures were clearly visible and dominated the beach below. To secure the right scale and emphasis in a picture, however, Shirley Kilpatrick had to use a 200mm f4 SMC-Takumar lens – magnifying the image by a factor of four times linear compared to the 50mm standard lens. The final picture represents just 1/16th of a "normal" view.*

*Illustration from Pentax UK Limited 'Focus on Photography' project folder for schools*

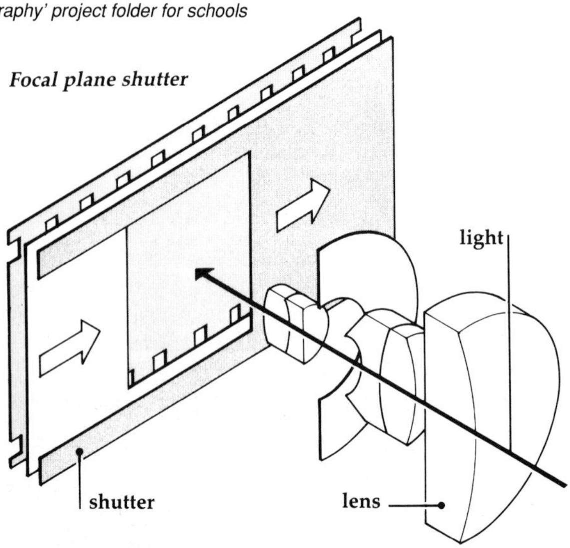


*The shutter is positioned between the lens and the film, to keep the light away until the exposure is made. The blind nearest the lens moves first (to the RIGHT of the page in this diagram) to uncover the film; the blind nearest the film follows. For short exposures, the gap between the two is very small, forming a moving slit. For exposures of 1/60th or longer (K1000) the whole area of the film is briefly uncovered.*

positioned precisely where the image is focused, and the lens needs to be blanked off to prevent the light from ruining the film. A shutter must admit the light for a fraction of a second, just enough time to expose the film.

There are many different solutions to the problem of making an accurate viewfinder. The simplest one is to assemble a small optical system, sometimes called a 'reverse telescope' because it works rather like looking down the wrong end of a telescope. A metal mask on the end of this cuts the reduced-sized view down to the shape of the picture.

Better versions of the direct or optical viewfinder use reflected (suspended) frames, superimposed by semi-silvered mirror surfaces, to show the boundary of the picture. Today there are zoom versions as well. But such viewfinders provide only a rough idea of the appearance of the final picture, and cannot be used accurately for close-ups. The viewfinder window is always a couple of inches away from the lens itself,

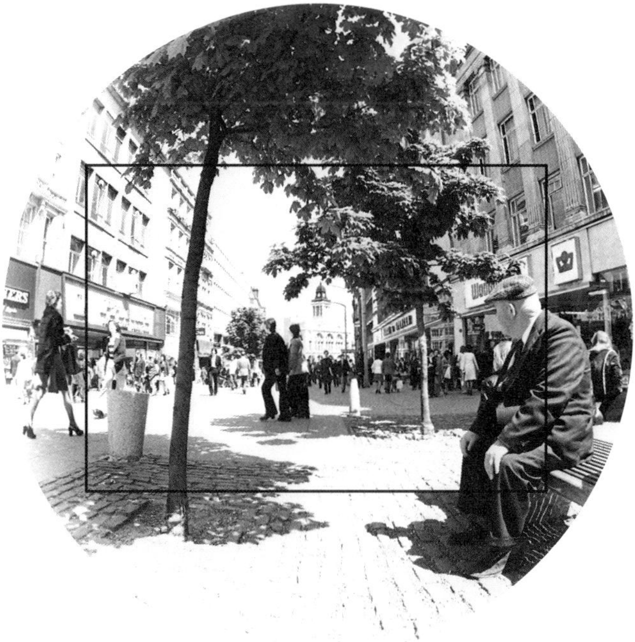

*Try holding a 50mm lens about two inches from white paper, as described on page 23. A circle of image is formed. The 35mm picture area occupies only the very centre of this coverage.*

and when the subject is closer than 4 feet you get errors in composition as a result.

The same problem applies to camera which use two lenses, mounted one above the other. The bottom lens takes the picture - the top one shows the same picture reflected upwards on to a focusing screen made of ground-glass or frosted plastic. This system, called TLR or twin-lens reflex viewing, doubles the cost and bulk of the lens because two complete assemblies are needed.

Some larger cameras do without viewfinders entirely. The film is removed, using a lightproof film holder, and the image formed by the camera lens is viewed and focused directly on a large ground-glass screen at the back of the camera. It is viewed upside-down, and a dark cloth or cloak is needed to put over the photographer's head and the camera to cut out daylight and make viewing possible. Cameras like this are only suitable for static subjects, but the viewing is totally accurate –

you see the actual image formed by the taking lens, though the lens itself.

The first photographer, William Henry Fox Talbot, also viewed the image focused by the camera lens. He did it by cutting a small hole in his wooden cameras, near the front, and inserting a rubber stopper. To view the picture, you removed the stopper and peered into the camera.

## SLR – the best solution

The Pentax camera system uses the ideal solution to the problem of getting this kind of accuracy without any of the clumsiness or slowness associated with viewing through the taking lens – or removing a stopper!

The word 'reflex' was mentioned when describing the cameras with a pair of matched lenses. The reflex aspect refers to reflection. A surface-silvered mirror is placed at 45°, angled upwards (see diagrams) between the lens and the film. You can see this mirror when you remove the lens of the K1000 or P30n, but you must never touch it. The silvering (not actually silver, but a tarnish-free metal coating) is on the surface, not behind the glass like a normal mirror. It should never be dusted, even with a brush, and the best way to remove any specks of dust is to blow jets of air using a blower (puffer) brush with the brush part removed.

The mirror diverts the image-forming rays which would otherwise go to the film, and throws the image on to a ground-glass screen in the top of the camera. In the twin-lens reflexes mentioned above, which are large cameras, this is often how you actually view the picture, like a flat TV screen inside a light-shielding hood. You look down on the composition at waist-level, or flip a magnifier into place and examine it more closely.

The optical paths involved mean the following things happen:

1: the picture appears the right way up

2: it is focused and composed exactly as the picture will be

3: it is reversed left to right

With a mirror set behind a second lens, the system is complete. But with the mirror behind the actual taking lens, no picture can be taken unless the mirror itself is removed from the light-path. It is therefore hinged at the top edge, near the film, and can be moved upwards. In the process, the mirror covers the ground-glass focusing screen entirely, sealing off any light which might get in from the top.

The Pentax uses an instant-return mirror, which Pentax invented (all SLR cameras now use them). It flips up when you press the shutter, and returns to viewing position as soon as the exposure is over. In normal daylight, all you see is a brief interruption to viewing as the whole process takes around 1/10th of a second.

The K1000 and P30n are called single-lens reflex cameras because they use this instant-return mirror behind the actual taking lens. Both

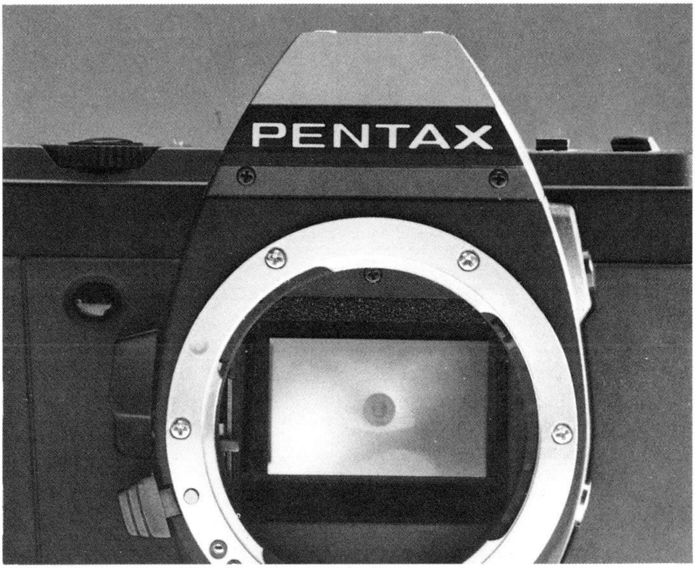


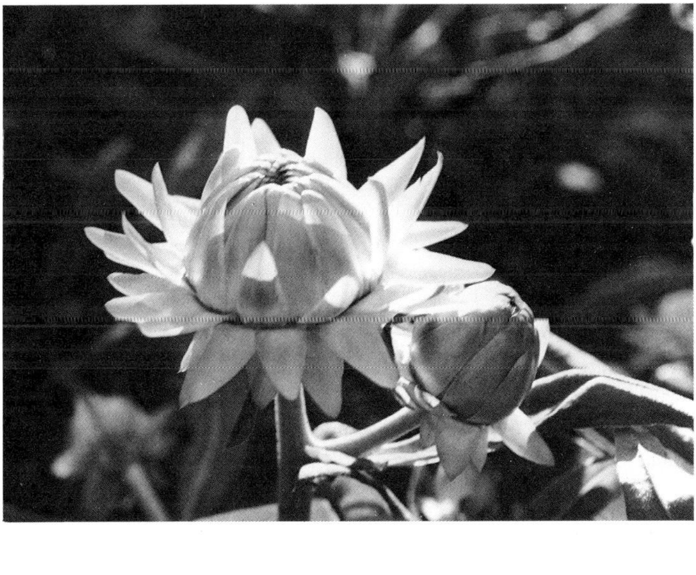

*Top: inside the Pentax, if you remove the lens, you will see this surface-silvered mirror. Never, under any circumstances, should you touch it. Bottom: single lens viewing allows perfect close-ups.*

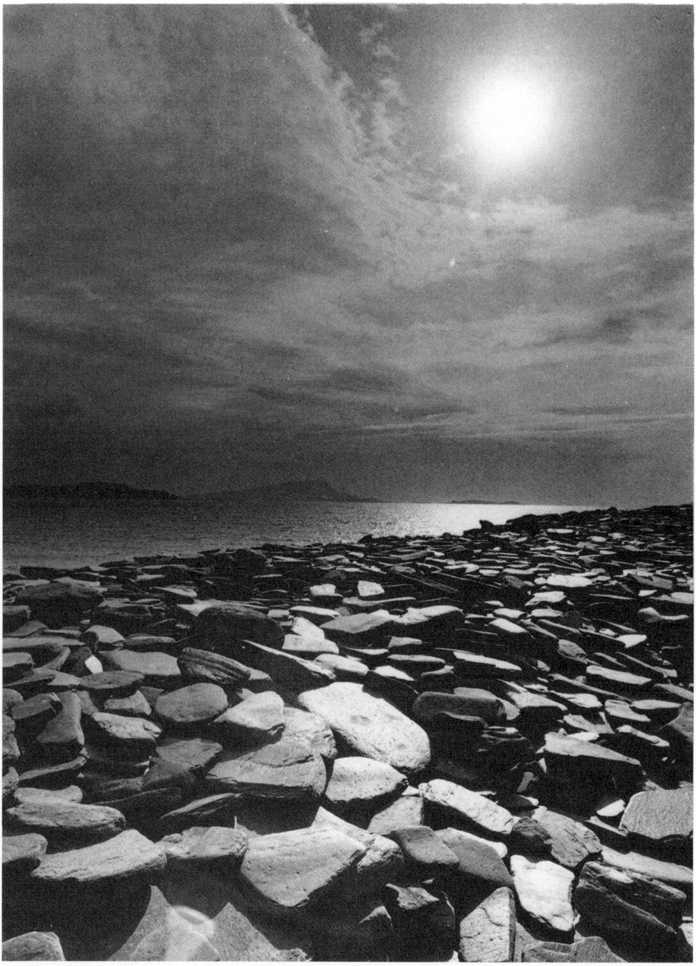

*Through-the-lens viewing has many advantages. It is possible to compose a shot like this, with the sun included fully in the picture, and judge the effect safely. The ground-glass screen of the Pentax K1000 or P30n interrupts the rays of light, and there is no risk of damaging your eyesight. With a direct-viewfinder camera (optical) it is uncomfortable to compose such a shot. You should never position the sun right in the centre of the viewfinder, and telephoto lenses (which magnify the image) are to be used with care.*

cameras have interchangeable lenses, so they are not limited to a 'single lens' in that sense.

The 35mm film frame is very small, only an inch high, and there are very few occasions when you want to view it at waist-level. The Pentax therefore uses a permanently-fixed pentaprism (see diagram on page 13) with an eyepiece magnifier. You are not aware that the eyepiece is a magnifying glass, but if you tried to look through the prism alone it would be just like peering at a 1 x 1.5 inch screen from a couple of inches away. The 'ocular' or eyepiece lens-elements are important. They provide a sharp, clear view of the focusing screen at eye-level, a little less than life-size when you use a 50mm standard lens.

Through the eye-level viewfinder of your Pentax SLR, you see precisely the same image that the film will record, with one important difference. Viewing and focusing happens with the camera lens set to admit as much light as possible - at full, or maximum, lens aperture. We will look at lens apertures and the aperture setting in the next chapter.

At this stage, all you need to know is that by viewing at full aperture the camera gives the brightest possible viewfinder image, and focusing is made easy. Look through the camera, and turn the lens focusing ring. You will see that the image in the viewfinder snaps into focus sharply.

## Focusing and eyesight

Many people buy an SLR camera without any experience of looking through viewfinders. They do not know exactly what to expect. When you look through the eyepiece, your eye should be very close to the camera, even if you wear glasses. I wear spectacles and I find I have to press them right back, with the eyepiece surround in contact with the lens. Sometimes, I have been running a course for photographers and find someone holding the camera an inch or so in front of their eye, and completely failing to view the entire picture area.

You should see, comfortably, a sharp-edged rectangle with slightly rounded corners, like viewing a television in a darkened room. If you move your eye a little, you should not see any of the edges disappear or become fuzzy.

The focusing screen of the Pentax is finely-ground in texture. You should be able to see the grainy surface of the screen when you look into the viewfinder with NO LENS on the camera (it may disappear when a lens is fitted). You should also see concentric lines, very fine rings, which are part of the optical design and help ensure brightness from corner to corner. We will remind you of this again!

In the centre of the screen of the P30n, you will see a bulls-eye arrangement with a small central circle divided into two halves, an outer circle of what looks like a honeycomb pattern, and a plain circle surrounding this. When the lens is fitted, the central circle provides a rangefinder focusing device and the honeycomb pattern (called microprisms) will shimmer when the subject is out of focus and disappear entirely when the focus is set correctly.

The Pentax K1000 is slightly simpler. There should be only one type of central focusing aid, either the split-image or the microprisms. As a rule, people with good vision find the microprism type of screen easy to use, while those with poor eyesight prefer the split-image.

If you cannot see all of these things sharply and clearly, with fine detail, you should have an eye-test. The Pentax is corrected for normal vision and a slight degree of short-sight (you will not need any correction lenses if you have up to half a dioptre of short sight). Anyone with astigmatism, long sight or more serious short sight should either wear glasses when using the camera, or obtain a prescription correction lens, which fits into the slot right inside the eyepiece. For serious astigmatism you may need two lenses, one to use for horizontal compositions and the other for vertical, though many people find it easy enough just to angle their head to view.

Perhaps you think that placing all this emphasis on eyesight, and the viewfinder, is not really necessary in a guide to the cameras. I don't think so, because I have met so many people who have never used an SLR correctly after years of owning them. They think that the slightly indefinite standard of focus they first saw is 'how the camera works'. Sometimes, they think that the circles in the centre of the viewfinder are for framing the subject, and that the viewfinder has a soft edge like one of those old 'reverse telescope' optical finders I mentioned earlier. No wonder all their pictures have a small subject right in the middle of an ocean of irrelevant detail - all they have been doing is holding the camera away from their eye, and seeing just half the focusing screen.

Now you have got the business of viewing through the camera thoroughly understood, take your Pentax for a walk without any film in. Just look through the viewfinder, composing different shots, at all kinds of distances. See how fast you can focus on moving subjects; see what the closest focusing distance actually means in terms of a flower, or a postcard, placed in front of the camera. Compare the amount of view you seem to get outdoors with the amount of your room you can manage to include. Try firing the shutter, and feel the action of the instant-return mirror. Remove the lens, if you like, with no film in - watch the mirror operate. Open the camera back, with the camera on a tripod, and take the lens off. Fire the shutter at different speeds, and see what is happening. Now try it with the lens on, and set different apertures (the 2, 2.8, 4 etc scale) on the lens.

In the next chapters we will look at the Pentax focal-plane shutter, the lens mechanisms, and through-the-lens metering.

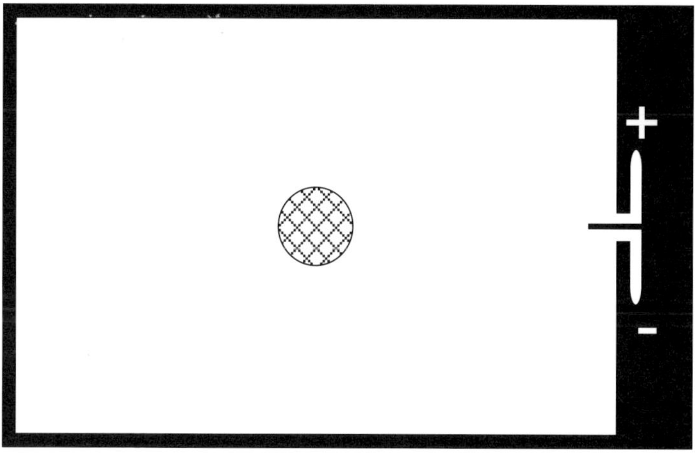

*This is what you should see through the K1000 viewfinder.*

*Below: in-focus and out-of-focus images represented as shown by the P30n viewfinder. The central split-image focusing aid will displace the image vertically, one half moving in the opposite direction to the other half. Correct focus is achieved when the details all line up. You need a subject with a firm vertical line (or horizontal if the camera is held for upright pictures) to focus on. The outer circle shows a diffused, shimmering image when the picture is unfocused, and a sharp clear one at the exact point of focus. The K1000 focusing aid works in this way only.*

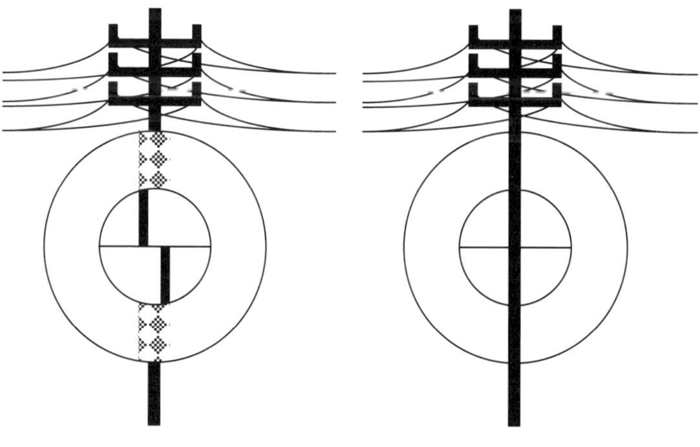

# The Camera Controls

There are only three primary settings you can adjust on any camera. These are the shutter speed (duration of exposure), lens aperture (brightness of image reaching the film) and focus (distance of plane of sharp focus from the film).

It is not difficult to master these three settings and produce a considerable variety of creative results. Although they are very simple adjustments, they are also very wide-ranging, and different combinations produce very different effects.

You may well ask why so many cameras have ten or even twenty 'modes' or 'programs' if there are only three main settings. This is because how you choose the combination of the two exposure adjustments, shutter speed and aperture, is partly determined by the focal length of the lens, the type of subject, the focused distance and the desired effect. Multi-mode and programmed cameras simply make the choices For you, according to pre-set patterns.

The Pentax K1000 and P30n are both capable of matching any of the settings which a complex multi-mode camera will produce. The only restriction is the fastest shutter speed, which is limited to 1/1000. You reach the settings on the basis of experience and judgment, instead of relying on a computer to do this for you. First of all, you need to understand exactly what the main controls of the Pentax cameras do, how they do it, and why.

## The Shutter

The heart of any 35mm SLR is the focal-plane shutter. It is called this to distinguish it from a 'leaf' or 'inter-lens' shutter. A focal plane shutter is positioned immediately in front of the film, which is always positioned at the correct point for focus, or 'focal plane'. Actually, the shutter is not in the focal plane, because the film is already there. It is often a few millimetres in front of the film. It might be more accurate if we called it a behind-the-mirror shutter!

The focal plane shutter consists of two blinds, just like roller blinds used on a window. Normally, one blind covers the film completely. To expose the film, the blind is allowed to roll up, and a second one is pulled from the opposite end to cover the film again.

For long exposures (anything longer than 1/125 of a second) the second blind is not released until the first one has completely uncovered the film. For a very short time, the film is entirely exposed to the incoming light. It is precisely this instant when a flashgun has to be fired,

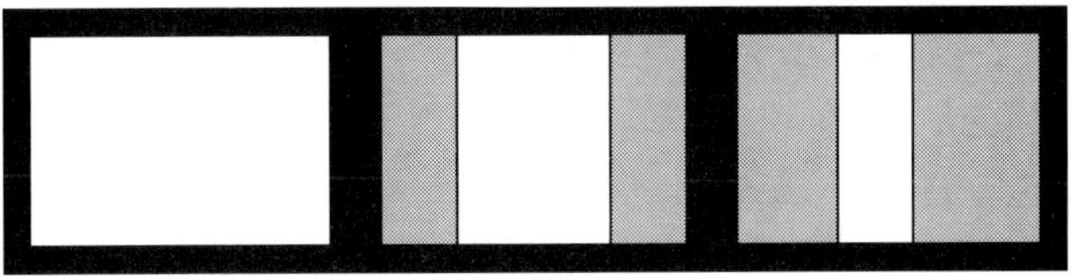

*Left – at speeds of 1/60 or more, the focal plane shutter of the K1000 exposes the entire film area at one time. Centre – the size of the "slit" when set to 1/125. Right: the slit when set to 1/250. Below: flash photographs like this must be taken with the film uncovered entirely, at 1/60 or slower (1/100 or slower on P30n).*

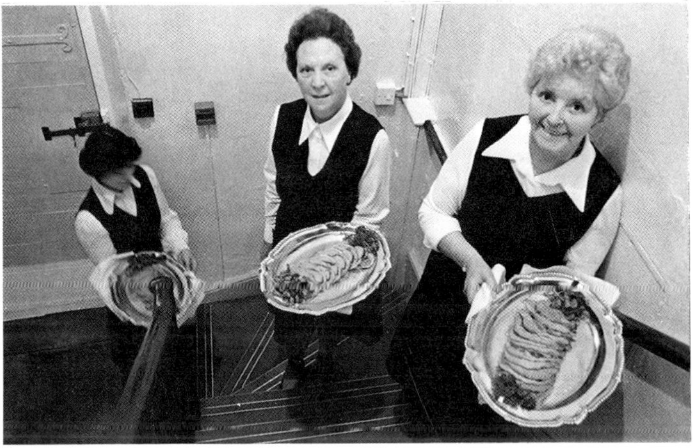

because if it was fired when the blinds were still moving, only part of the picture would be exposed. This is why the Pentax K1000 and P30n can only take flash pictures with fairly long shutter opening times. The K1000 must be used on 1/60, 1/30 or a longer time, and the P30n on 1/100, 1/60, or 1/30.or longer.

At speeds of 1/250, 1/500 and 1/1000 the second blind is released before the first one has reached the end of its travel. The result is rather like a slit scanning across the film. The speed of the blinds is precisely matched, because if one went faster than the other the slit would get narrower or wider as it travelled, and the film would be unevenly exposed.

You might ask why the slit can't just be made narrower, by releasing the second blind very soon after the first one, to get shutter speeds like 1/2000 or 1/4000. There are two reasons. First of all, the speed governing of the blinds is accurate enough for a certain width of slit, but

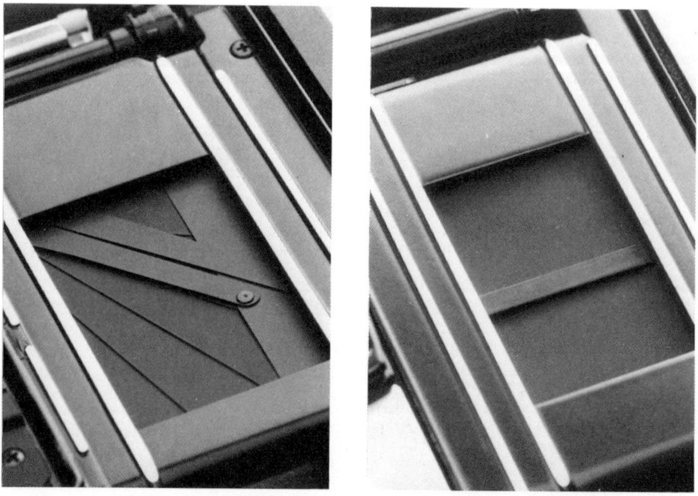

*Above: the focal plane shutters of the K1000 (left) and P30n as seen from the back, with the camera back open. The K1000 shutter has cloth blinds, while the P30n uses metal blades.*

anything narrower would require a more complex and expensive mechanism. Secondly, one blind has to be slightly in front of the other, as they have to overlap for reasons which you will see very shortly. This means that the slit is not a flat opening, but intercepts the light at two different distances (see diagram). If the slit were very narrow, the simple geometry of the set-up would mean that less light reached one end of the film than the other even if the speeds were precisely equal.

The two blinds have to overlap so that they can travel back over the film when the shutter is cocked again. When you operate the wind-on lever of the camera, you do not simply pull fresh film out of the cassette. You also tension the springs to operate the shutter, mirror and lens mechanisms. Part of the tensioning for the shutter involves returning both blinds to their start position. Still overlapping, to form a light-seal, they are pulled back to the beginning of the their travel, ready to be released again.

The blind on the Pentax K1000 is actually made of cloth, like a roller blind, but the shutter of the P30n is constructed differently. The 'shutter curtains' are made of metal, and consist of a set of flat blades or 'laminae', which overlap smoothly. These extend rather like a Japanese fan opening. This type of shutter is superior to the cloth focal plane design in many ways, though fairly easily damaged by clumsy fingers. It is called a laminar focal plane shutter.

The other difference between the two shutters is that the K1000's blinds run along the length of the film, moving from left to right as you hold the camera. The curtains of the P30n travel across the short dimension of the frame, moving vertically downwards as you hold the camera. This is why the faster 1/100th of a second flash synchronization is possible – at the same actual speed of travel, it takes only two-thirds of the time to uncover or cover the shorter side of the rectangular format.

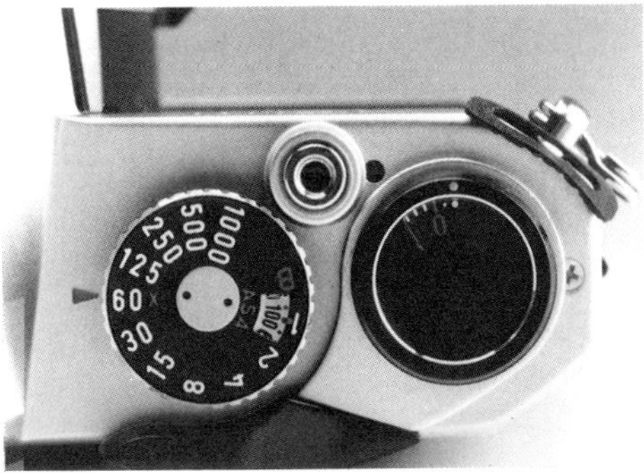


*The shutter dial of the K1000 with the range of speeds clearly visible.*

## Shutter speeds

The K1000 shutter dial is the best illustration of a series of shutter speeds. When you use electronic cameras, you cannot see all the speeds at a glance. The K1000 lets you see immediately both the shutter speed which you have set, and the other choices available. You can turn to any other speed very rapidly, with no need to step or push a control repeatedly.

The markings run from B to 1000. They all indicate fractions of a second. The first figure is 1, which is not a fraction – but of course, it is. It's 1/1 second, or a whole second. The next figure is 2, which stands for 1/2 second NOT 2 seconds. The series continues – 4, 8, 15, 30, 60, 125, 250, 1000.

In theory each speed is half the last one, but if that were really true, the shutter dial would look different. It would read 1, 2, 4, 8, 16, 32, 64, 128, 256, 512, 1024. If you're familiar with computers you will recognise that sequence! However, photographic exposure is not such a very precise thing; films and shutter speeds only have to be within 20% accuracy. The very first Asahiflex cameras had speeds on an old scale which went 1, 2, 5, 10, 25, 50, 100, 200 which was too inaccurate. The modern scale is as close as you need to get to perfect spacing between the shutter speeds.

You can see that each step is double or half, depending on the direction, of the adjacent speeds. The 'B' setting stands for Bulb or Brief

Time exposure, and when you use it the shutter will remain open as long as you keep the shutter release pressed down. You can time speeds of 2 seconds and longer using a watch with reasonable accuracy.

The dial has 11 settings, or ten steps each of which doubles or halves the exposure from either extreme. The control given by such a wide range is exactly as the settings themselves indicate – a speed of 1/1000 of a second will cope with light 1,000 times brighter than a speed of 1 second and give the same exposure. This is an enormous difference, like moving from brilliant sunshine into a heavily curtained room. The P30n has an extra step, 2 seconds.

If film and exposure needs to be accurate to about 20%, you probably wonder how such big steps can cope. What if you need half as much exposure again, and not double? What if the light-level changes by 40%? Many new programmed SLRs have intermediate steps between the shutter speeds, but you cannot set the K1000 dial between the marked click-stopped positions. To handle finer adjustments of exposure you need the other main control, the lens aperture.

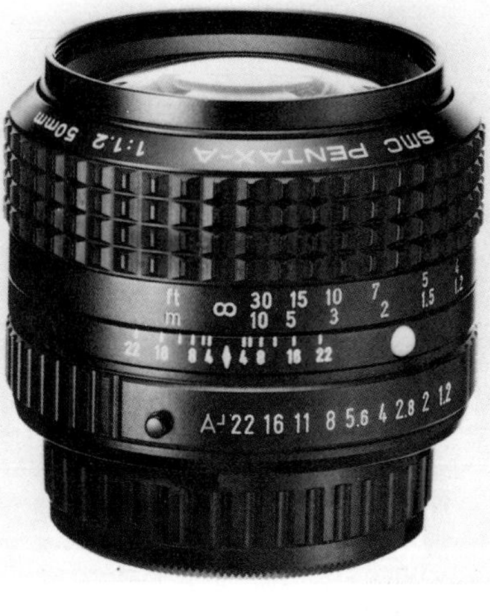


*The aperture ring of the fast 50mm f1.2 lens is the bottom-most control in this photograph.*

## Apertures

Each A-mount lens you buy has its own aperture control ring, or *f*-stop scale. This is not part of the camera body, and it cannot be controlled by the camera. Different lenses have different scales, but they are all based on the same series of numbers. To start with you need to understand the numbers and what they mean.

Shutter speeds are simple to understand. It is easy to see that if you open the shutter for twice as long, twice as much light will be admitted.

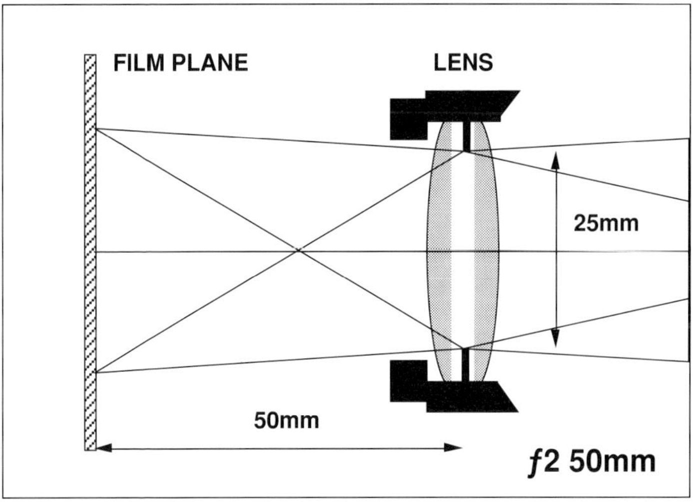


*A 50mm standard lens is actually 50mm away from the film when focused on infinity. The f2 lens has a diameter of 25mm – which divides two times (f2) into the focal length of 50mm.*

The aperture is a little harder to understand, but it helps to remember that the SIZE of the numbers has the same effect as it does on the shutter speed scale – larger numbers REDUCE the exposure by admitting LESS light.

The lens aperture is rather like the size of a hose pipe, if you think of the light being water and the shutter an on/off faucet. If you have a fire hose four inches in diameter, it's easy to understand that it will let through four times as much water as a pipe two inches in diameter, and eight times as much as an ordinary one-inch hose. If you double the diameter, you increase the cross sectional area by four times, and it is the area which determines the rate of flow.

Lens apertures are worked out on areas as well. If you focus a lens on infinity, it will be the same distance from the film as its own focal length. A 50mm lens will be 50mm from the film, a 100mm lens will be 100mm away, and so on. Camera lenses are complex optical groups and they are specially designed to get round this – your zoom lens bayonets on to the camera just like a standard lens or wide angle. But behind all the optical tricks the theory holds good. The zoom lens behaves as if it really WAS somewhere between 70 and 210mm away from the film!

If you produced a lens with the same diameter opening as the focal length, which would be an expensive exercise, it would have a maximum aperture of 1. The aperture number would 1, or *f*1. Sometimes this is

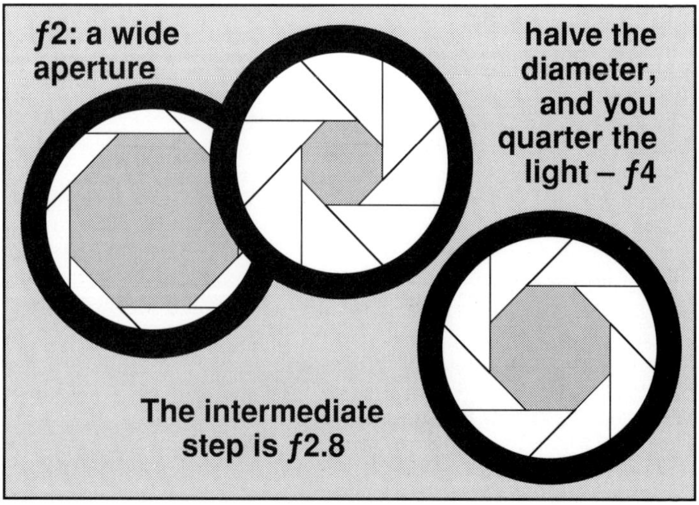


*The unusual numbers on the aperture ring are caused by the f-stop being worked out on the basis of the area involved.*

written F1 or f/1. It stands for the ratio of the focal length of a lens to the diameter of its opening. So, if the lens has a maximum aperture of *f*2, i.e. 2:1, and a focal length of 50mm like the standard lens for the K1000 and P30n, you can work out that the lens opening is actually 25mm in diameter. We will use the simplest way of writing *f*-stops:

***f*2**, ***f*2.8**, ***f*4** and so on.

The unusual numbers of the aperture scale are caused by the need for accurate steps to match the shutter scale. To double the area of a circle, you must increase its diameter by approximately 1.4 times (strictly 1.4142, which is the square root of 2).

The scale runs:

*f*1, *f*1.4, *f*2, *f*2.8, *f*4, *f*5.6, *f*8, *f*11, *f*16, *f*22, *f*32 and *f*64

Your 50mm Pentax lens probably goes from *f*2 to *f*22; some lenses start at *f*1.4 or *f*1.7, and some end at *f*16 instead of *f*22.

The *f*1.7 figure is, of course, missing from our scale. This is because a lens does not have to be an exact fraction of its focal length in diameter. You will find lenses with odd maximum apertures like *f*4.8 or *f*3.2. However, the next step down on the aperture ring will always be an exact figure from the standard scale, so that if you buy a lens which starts at *f*3.5 the next step will be *f*4, although this is not a complete step. Genuine Pentax lenses, however, do not always include the next *f*-stop if it is very close to the maximum aperture. An *f*1.7 standard lens will have a scale which runs *f*1.7, *f*2.8, *f*4 and so on.

# Half stop steps

As you turn the aperture ring, you will notice that there are unmarked click-stops between each of the marked figures. These are, in fact, half-stop settings. They can be used to fine-tune exposure in half steps, overcoming the problem with the large steps on the shutter speed dial. Without the half-stops, there would be times when you had to decide whether to have the metering needle high or low, and could not get it exactly centered.

These settings do have values - indeed, they are often the values you find on lenses with odd maximum apertures. The click between *f*2.8 and *f*4 is more or less equal to *f*3.5 (in fact it's *f*3.2) and that between *f*4 and *f*5.6 is *f*4.5.

No-one ever uses these figures, because some of them run into two decimal places and they are not needed. Instead, photographers call the half-stops '*f* eight to eleven' for the step between *f*8 and *f*11, or sometime '*f* eight and a half', which is technically unspeakable but easily understood! They are written like this:

*f*8-11, *f*16-22

This may be clumsier than saying *f*9.5 or *f*19, but it is so widespread in popular use that even professional lecturers now use the terms to describe the intermediate settings.

Some exposure meters use an LCD display with decimal places. This has resulted in a new way of describing the intermediate *f*-stops. Instead of saying '*f*8 and a half' photographers now say '*f*8 point five'. They do NOT mean *f*8.5, which is something different.

When using your Pentax, just remember that the half-stop positions exist and are there to be used. I suggest you call them by the double-barrelled way of describing them – *f*8 to 11, and so on. That is how it looks when you set the ring between *f*8 and *f*11, and unlike the other ways of describing these settings, it can't be misunderstood.

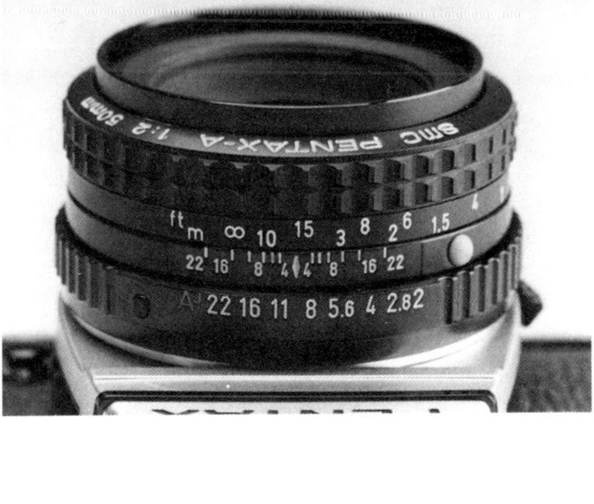


*This Pentax lens has been set to the half-stop between 8 and 11 – which we call, for convenience, f8-11 (f 8 to 11).*

## Light and *f*-stops

The relationship between light and the lens aperture is direct. If you take a picture with the lens set to *f*4, changing the aperture to *f*5.6 will cut the light by exactly half. A further stop down to *f*8 will cut it by half again, and so on.

To reduce the light, in bright conditions or with flash at a close distance, you need to STOP DOWN or CLOSE the aperture. This is also termed using a SMALLER aperture. In fact, the number on the scale will be larger, not smaller. The aperture setting *f*16 is only one-eighth of the size of *f*2. If you think of the *f*-stops as representing one-half and one-sixteenth you get the right impression, but fractions are already used for shutter speeds, so this is never actually done.

To increase the light, you need to OPEN UP or use a WIDER aperture. No-one ever says 'stop up'. Lenses which have wider maximum apertures are termed FAST lenses, but the term 'slow' is not often used. Someone might tell you that you need a faster lens than your 70-210mm zoom for indoor action sports photography. They would mean a lens with a wider maximum aperture to transmit more light.

Each marked step on the aperture scale matches a step on the shutter speed scale. You will find, by looking at the metering display while aiming at an area of constant brightness, that if you change the two scales you can achieve identical exposures with a wide range of combinations.

For example:

**1/125 at *f*11** is the same as
**1/30 at *f*22** or
**1/500 at *f*5.6**

All Pentax lenses have the aperture scale running in the same direction. This is necessary to couple the lens properly to the camera's meter system. After a while, you will get used to knowing exactly which way to turn the ring to alter the exposure display, or to match a change made by turning the shutter speed dial. At first you will probably turn it the wrong way some of the time. Some older lenses made to fit the K-mount via an adaptor have scales which work the wrong way round. They are not very good mechanically, because of the gearing used, and you lose the confidence of having all your lenses handle in the same way.

*Top right: 1/30 at f22 is the right exposure for a sunny day with medium speed film.*
*Bottom right: so is 1/500 at f5.6. Can you spot any differences between these two pictures? All will be revealed later!*

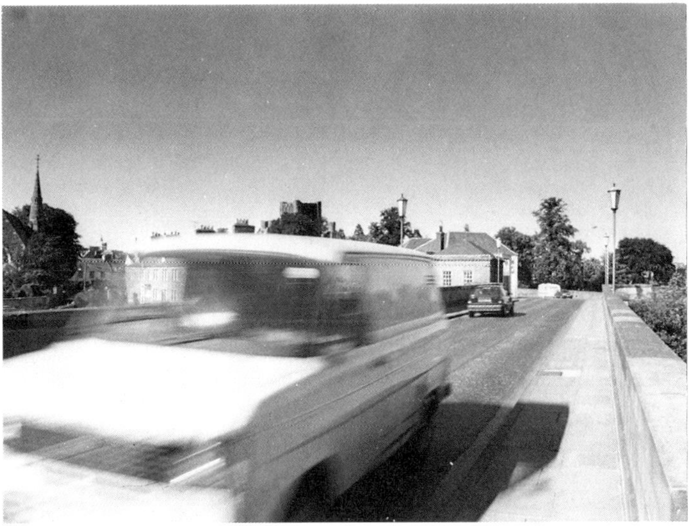

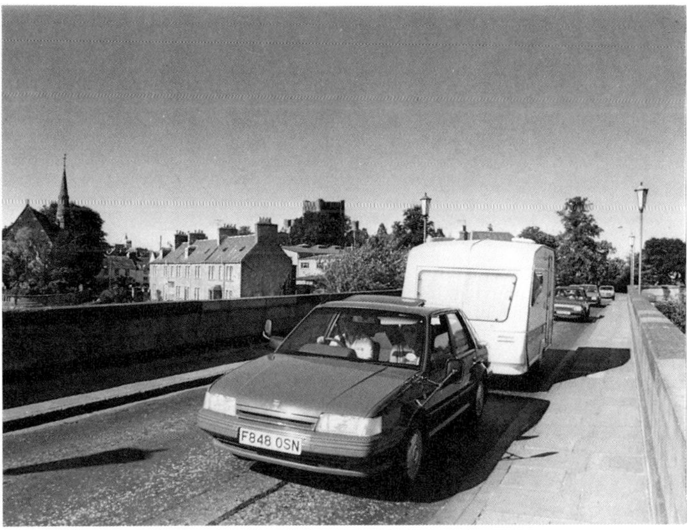
F848 OSN

# Light control

Now let's look at the effect of both controls, as you find them on a Pentax K1000 fitted with the standard 50mm *f*2 lens. The shutter speeds have ten doubling steps, as you have already learned, which will cope with light changes of 1000 times. The aperture scale has the following markings:

***f*2, *f*4, *f*5.6, *f*8, *f*11, *f*16, *f*22**

This allows six steps of adjustment from your starting-point at either end of the scale. The smallest aperture lets through 1/64th of the light of the widest aperture. You still have this whole range of control available even when you reach the end of the shutter speed scale. You can change the exposure from 1 second at *f*2 right down to 1/1000 at *f*22.

This gives you a total combined range between the two exposure controls of 1: 64,000. This is a remarkable range, for such simple controls. The camera, without any accessories, can cope with lighting conditions ranging from moonlight (which would require a typical exposure of 1 second at *f*2) to the most brilliant sunshine possible - in fact, there is nowhere on earth where the light is bright enough to need 1/1000 at *f*22 with normal film.

The K1000 will handle from a glimmer of light to conditions sixty-four thousand times as bright and the P30n to 128,000 times. You probably didn't see your camera quite this way before, or even realise that such a range was possible. For the sake of comparison, a typical fixed-focus (so-called 'focus free') pocketable 35mm camera will often have just one single setting, and no adjustments whatsoever.

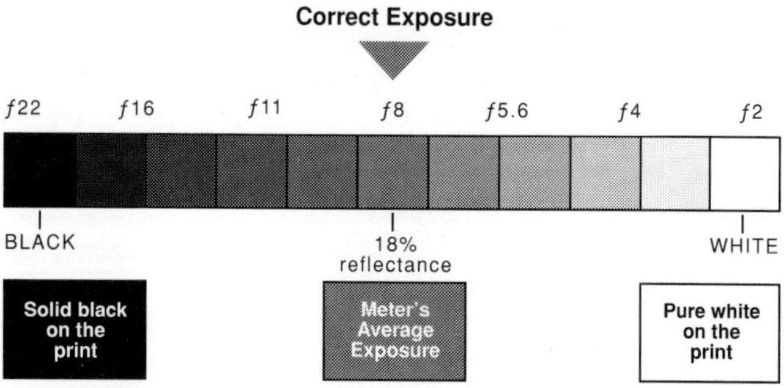


*Above: the f-stop scale alone can change a picture from correct exposure (f8 in this example) to solid black all over (f22) or a plain white print (f2). Accurate exposure is therefore very important. Right: a picture with a full scale of tones exposed using the K1000's meter which takes the average of the scene as a whole.*

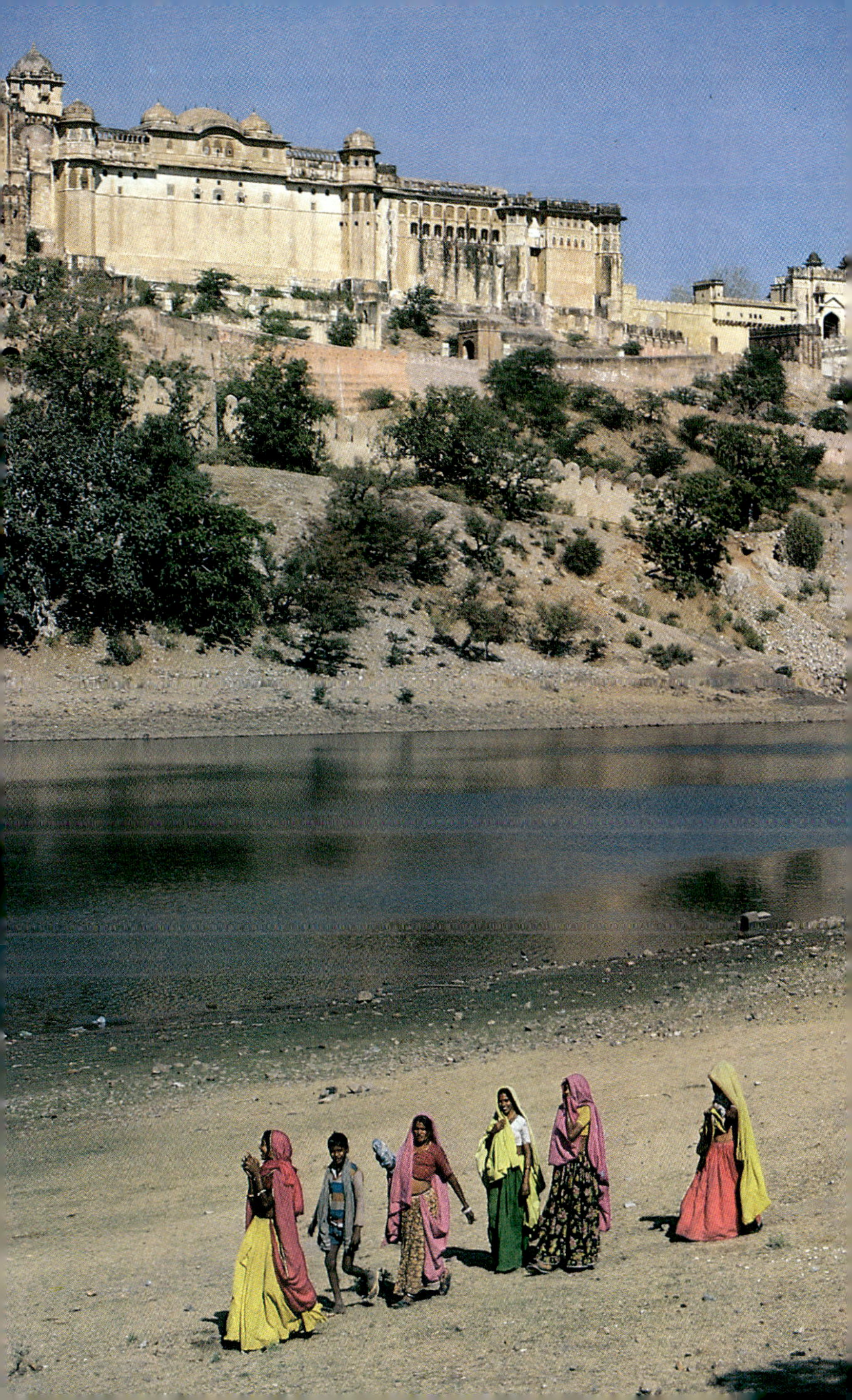

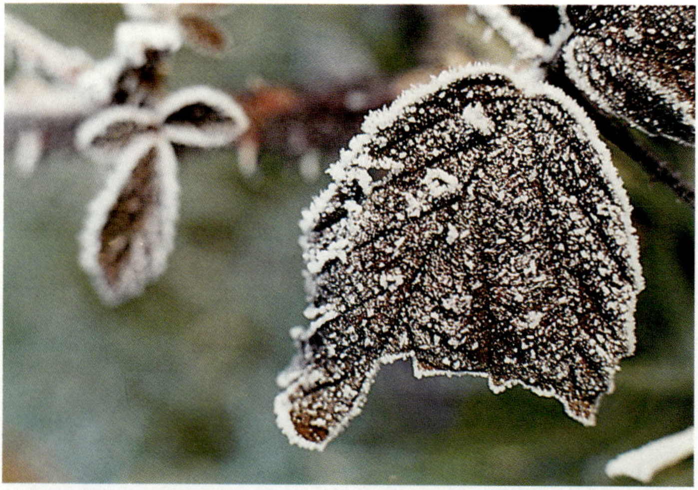

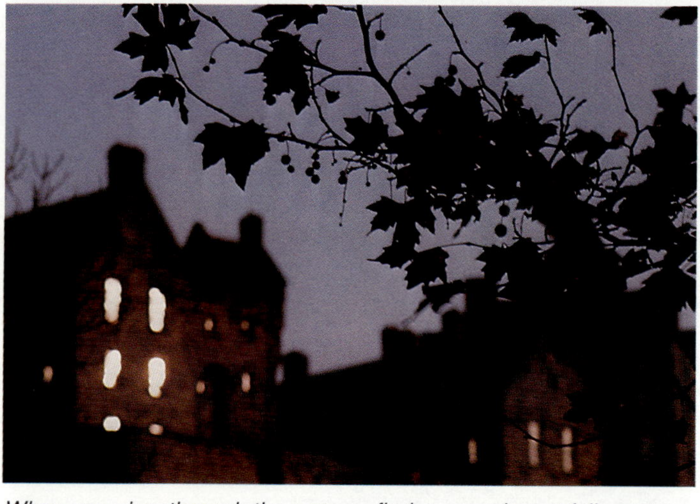

*When you view through the camera finder, you view at full aperture. There is very little depth to the sharp focus zone. You can use this to produce attractively blurred backgrounds – just take the picture at an ƒ-stop close to the maximum (e.g. ƒ2.8). Top: winter leaf, 35mm SMC-Takumar, ƒ4. Bottom: Edinburgh Castle, 300mm at ƒ5.6, focused on plane tree in foreground – a coloured filter was used to obtain the sky tone. Photographs by David Kilpatrick.*

# How the aperture operates

You will have noticed that there is no visible change through the viewfinder when you alter the *f*-stop. With no film in the camera, wind on and set 1 second exposure. Set the lens to *f*8. Hold the camera facing you, and look into the front of the lens. Now press the shutter. You will see that during the 1 second exposure, a set of metal blades forms a smaller ring in the lens. This is the aperture mechanism working.

Now remove the lens, and you will see a small lever on the back which can be moved very easily. Taking care not to touch the glass element at the back of the lens, place the lens face down on a clean surface. Set the *f*-stop to *f*16. Gently move the lever, and you will see the blades operate. Try different *f*-stops. If you set *f*16, the blades can form a small aperture, but if you set *f*4 it does not matter how far you move the lever, they always form a larger hole.

Inside the bayonet mount throat of the K1000 or P30n body is a small actuator which mates with the lever. When the mirror goes up before the exposure is made, this actuator moves the lever on the lens to close down the aperture. You will also find a coupling between a lug on the lens and a ring inside the lens-throat. This conveys the information to the camera about which particular *f*-stop is set, and how it relates to the maximum aperture of the lens. This enables the metering circuits to function accurately regardless of what lens is fitted.

The P30n has a depth-of-field preview mechanism. Operate this, and the lens will close down to whatever working *f*-stop you have set. You can then see the effect of this on the focusing screen.

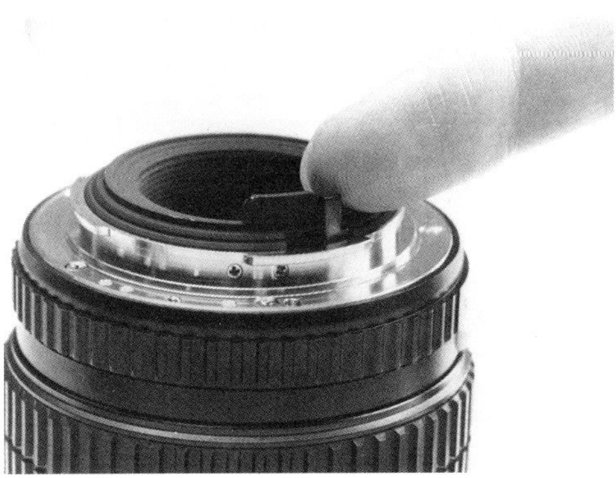

*The aperture operating lever on the A-mount; try moving it gently, with the lens removed.*

# Focusing

There is one remaining primary control on your camera's lens, the focusing ring. As you have seen, the only control actually on the camera body is the shutter speed dial. Like the aperture setting, the focusing is done by the lens itself.

The focusing ring is positioned further away from the camera body than the aperture ring, as it does not have to be connected to the body mechanically. It is usually a broad collar with rubber ribbing so that it can be gripped firmly between finger and thumb, and rotated easily. The movement is not slack, or stiff; it should be very smooth, with no grittiness or slop.

Pentax-made lenses all focus in the same direction. To focus on closer distances, you always turn the lens to same way. This is not the case with some independent makes, and you should try to keep all your lenses compatible, as it speeds up the way you use the camera.

In the last chapter, I suggested that you try composing pictures without taking them, just looking through the camera and learning to understand the focusing screen. Your lens has a scale with both feet and

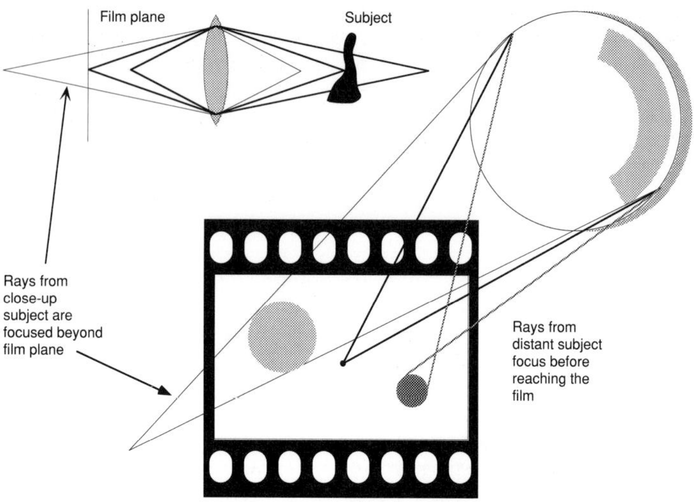


*Above: the lens forms a cone of light, with a sharp apex. This is the point of focus. If the lens is positioned the wrong distance from the film, the cone will form large circles or blobs of light instead of sharp points – these make up a blurred image. These diagrams show how objects both too far and too near produce blur.*

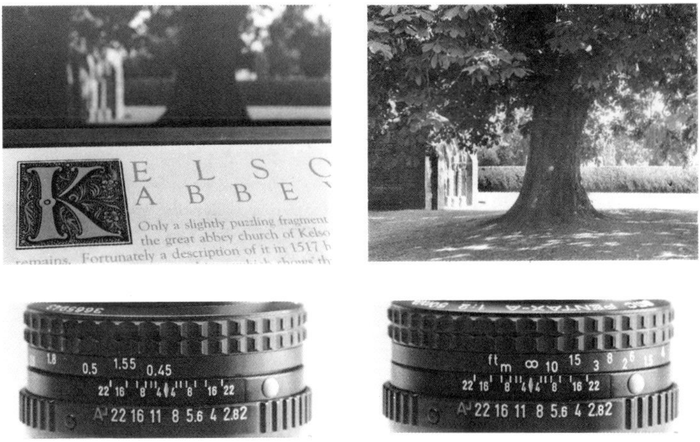

*Left: focusing the 50mm lens on its closest distance of 45cm.*
*Right: focusing on infinity.*

metres marked, and a single symbol – ∞ – at one end. This ∞ mark is the scientific symbol for infinity, or any distance which can be considered too far to make any difference to the focusing adjustment. You should not need to use the distance scales to set the focus you adjust the lens while looking through the viewfinder. The scales are there to help you when using flash, and to allow you to control the amount of the picture which appears to be sharp (see below).

With your 50mm *f*2 lens, infinity is anything beyond 30 feet. For landscape views with no foreground detail, you can simply move the lens to this focus position.

The close-focus limit depends on the lens. On the 50mm *f*2, it is 45cm or 18". The faster 50mm *f*1.4 lens does not focus as close, but the special Macro 50mm will focus to about 25cm and produces a picture on the film which is half life-size. All these distances are measured not from the front of the lens, but from the focal plane at the back of the camera, where the film is located. As the camera and lens are a few inches thick, the 18" close focus setting seems even closer than it is.

There are no click-stops on the focus scale. Unlike the other two scales, focus needs to be finely adjustable with no margin for error. In good lighting, you need not be so precise, for reasons which are explained shortly.

Focusing errors are unlikely because you can see through the viewfinder, but you should be careful when using the camera on a tripod and changing lenses. Always remember to check through the viewfinder and focus the lens you have just fitted.

# The Depth of Field scale

On the lens, you will see some of the figures from the aperture ring repeated on either side of the diamond-shaped 'focusing index' which marks the set distance on the focusing scale.

The smallest aperture (*f*16) is furthest away from the index, and it is repeated on either side. There are two other markings, for *f*8 and *f*4, getting progressively closer to the central index.

This is the Depth of Field scale, and it is there to help you judge the final effect of focus and aperture combined. When you view through the lens, it is at full aperture. A very small shift in the focus setting is enough to put the subject distinctly out of focus. Backgrounds to close-ups look very blurred, or blended into a smooth tone.

Such limited 'depth of field' is a result of using a wide aperture. It helps when focusing, but if every picture was taken like this, backgrounds would be unrecognizable. At smaller apertures such as *f*8 or *f*16 detail in front of and behind the subject focused on becomes progressively sharper.

You can read this off on the Depth of Field Scale of the lens. Simply see what far and near distances are shown against the markings which correspond with the *f*-stop you are using. This will be the limit of sharp focus for a typical print (if you make very large prints, unsharpness will be emphasized, and the scale does not hold true any more).

There is no sudden cut-off, and even within the depth of field shown there is a progressive loss of sharpness. It is purely a guide to the expected results.

You can use this scale, in conjunction with SLR focusing on the viewing screen, to set intermediate distances and small apertures which permit you to include a foreground and background subject in equally sharp focus. First focus on the foreground subject, and note the distance; then focus on the most distant element you want to be sharp, and note the distance. Now adjust the focusing ring until the diamond index is exactly midway between these two distances.

If they fall beyond the limits of the smallest aperture shown on the depth of field scale, you cannot have both distances sharp simultaneously. You may have to move back a little from the foreground subject. If they fall within any of the *f*-number pairs shown on the scale, use a tripod if necessary for a long exposure and use the appropriate *f*-stop (or a smaller one).

The best way to understand depth of field is by studying the diagrams and photographic examples. When using the P30n with the popular 35-70mm zoom, often sold in place of the 50mm, the depth-of-field preview mechanism must be used to judge the effect visually, as the lens has no markings.

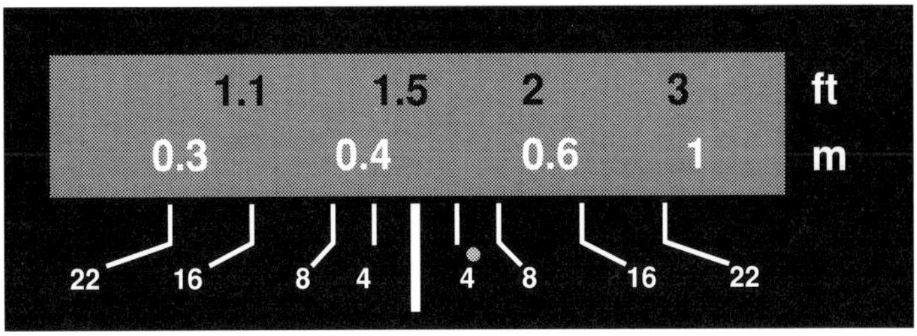


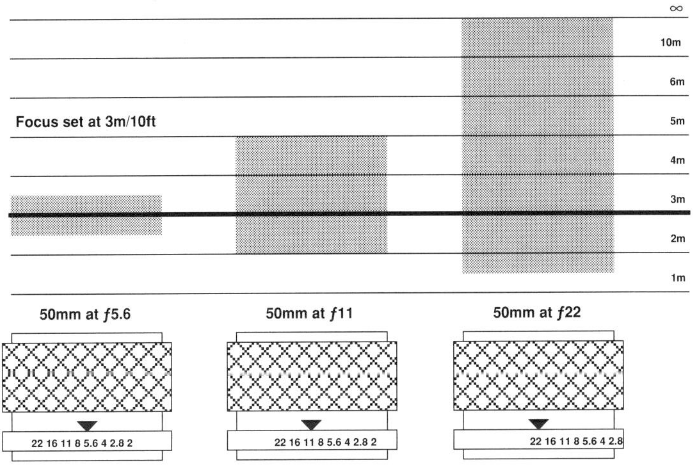


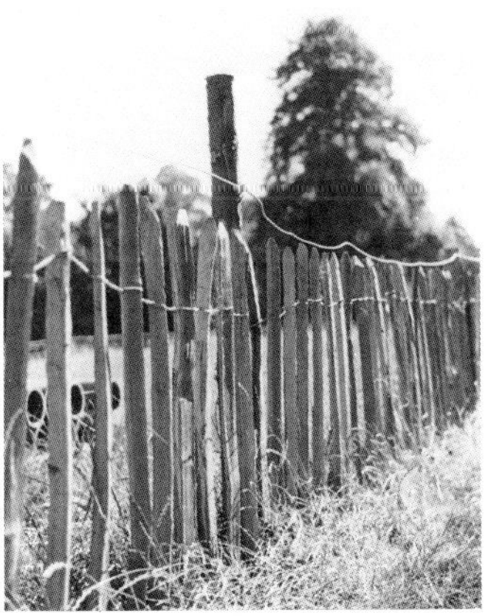

*50mm at ƒ5.6 focused on 3m*

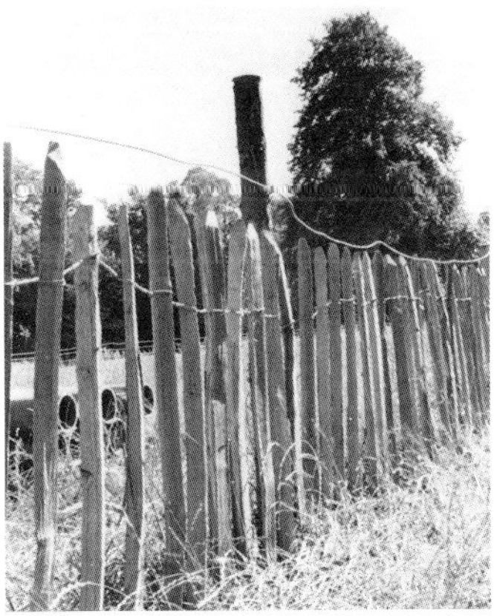

*50mm at ƒ22 focused on 3m*

# Exposure Metering

The heart of any Pentax SLR is the built-in through-the-lens (TTL) exposure metering system. Although the K1000 will function perfectly well without using the meter, it is hard for anyone except an experienced photographer to judge what settings should be used. The P30n has more automatic functions which depend on the meter, although it too can be used manually.

The exposure meter measures the level of light. Like the Pentax's own shutter speed and aperture controls, it has to be able to cope with a great range. If you use a normal speed of film the metering can take readings at almost any shutter speed, but if you change to a slow (relatively low sensitivity) or fast (high sensitivity) film there will be some cut-off of the range at one end or the other.

Your choice of film speeds and types makes the meter essential. If there was only one kind of film, it might be enough to have those symbols for sunny, cloudy or rain. The Pentax models are designed to take many different kinds of film, and some films are a hundred times more sensitive to light than others. So a symbol scale or a fixed exposure would be out of the question.

Compact 35mm cameras may have no more than two film speed settings. These are 100, which stands for ISO 100/21°, and 400, which stands for ISO 400/27°. The K1000 can use films between ISO 20 and 3200, and the P30n between 25 and 1600.

These film speeds are rather like shutter speeds; the high numbers indicate a faster film. If you want to use fast shutter speeds, then you also need a fast film. As a guide, a film with about the same numerical speed as the shutter speed you intend to use is a good choice. With ISO 1000 film it is easy to use 1/1000th of a second in most conditions, even bright sunshine. If you use an ISO 3200 film, you cannot use the K1000 in sunshine. To do so would require a shutter speed of 1/4000th.

The range of film speeds for the K1000 corresponds closely to the films you can actually buy. It would be difficult to get a film faster than 3200 or slower than 20.

There is one big difference between the K1000 and the P30n. The film speed for the K1000 is set by the user, and has to be changed every time a different type of film is loaded. The camera has no other way of knowing what kind of film is being used; if you set ISO 400 on the film-speed scale, but really have an ISO 100 film in the camera, you will get ruined pictures. On the other hand, setting the speed manually means you can use any type of film, even one which you load yourself into re-usable plastic cassettes from a long roll of "bulk" 35mm film. You can change the way the film is exposed if you do your own processing.

The P30n is opposite to this in every way. You cannot set the film speed manually – it's impossible. The cassette chamber has electrical contacts which can read off the film speed from the DX-coding on the cassette. Each time you load a new film, the camera reads the film speed, and sets it automatically. You cannot accidentally leave it set incorrectly. But if you load a cassette which does not have DX-coding, the camera cannot tell what film speed is being used, so it reverts to the average – ISO 100, the most common film speed around.

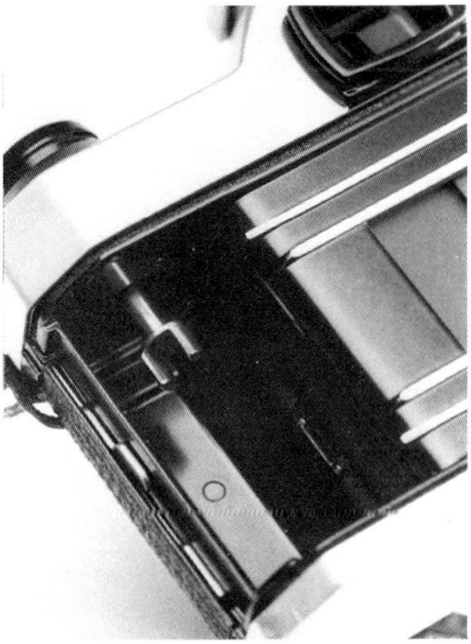

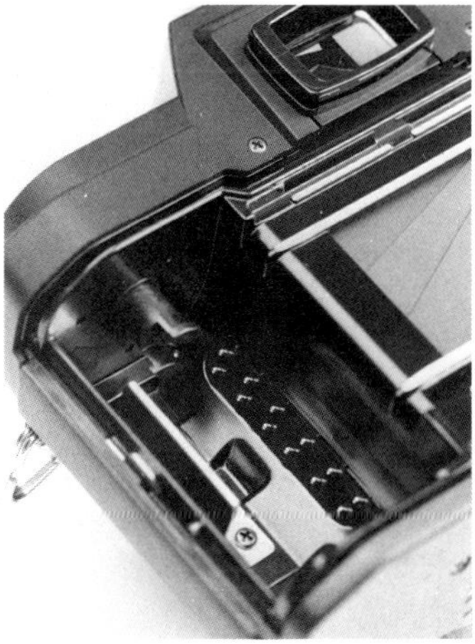

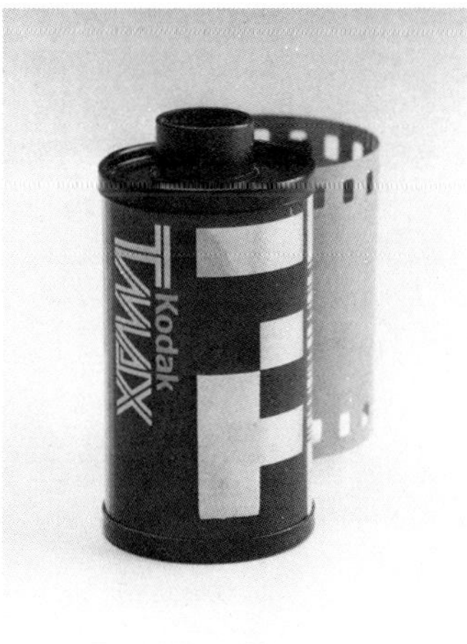


*Above: the K1000 cassette chamber, left, is totally plain. It does NOT have contacts to read the ISO film speed directly from the cassette. Right, the P30n cassette chamber has contacts – there is no need for any manual film speed setting, and none is provided.*

*Left: the bare metal areas on the 35mm cassette are an electrical circuit-maker which codes the film speed directly into DX-equipped cameras like the P30n.*

## What is film speed?

Photographic film consists of microscopic crystals of silver salts suspended in a gelatin layer. The silver salts, which are light-sensitive, are prepared in the dark. After a very short exposure to light, they can be chemically treated to produce a silver image which is proportional to the amount of light reaching the individual grains at the time of exposure.

Some films have very large, flat grains which are very receptive to light. These are fast films, which you would use for low light, night-time shots, floodlit sports, theatre and similar shots. When enlarged to form a print, the grains are easily visible to the eye – they are fairly coarse, and this affects the sharpness of the picture. In the case of colour pictures, the grains are responsible for forming the clouds of coloured dye which make up the image. Fast films form larger clouds of dye, giving an image made up of visible dots in the three colours magenta, cyan and yellow.

Obviously the best image quality will be given by a film with very small crystals of silver salts, forming equally small grains of silver or dye clouds. For many reasons, smaller crystals are less sensitive to light, despite big advances in improving this. So slow films, which are less sensitive to light, may be finer-grained and sharper, but you can't use them for action shots unless the light is very good.

In between the two extremes – which are around ISO 25 and around ISO 1600 – there are medium-speed films which are fairly sensitive to light, for all normal photography, but give a fine enough picture grain for a print to show no visible sign of the structure of the image.

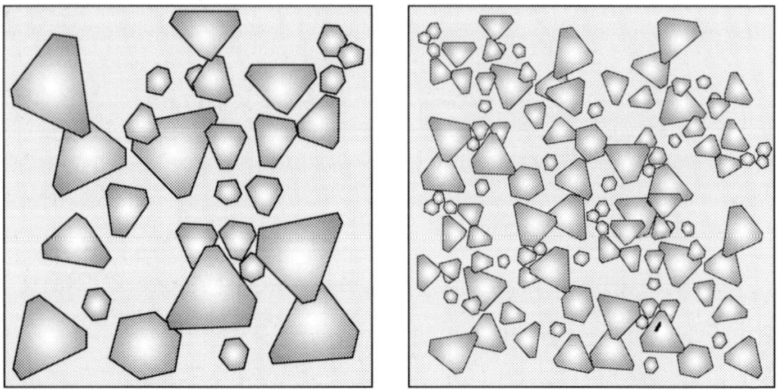

*Above: a fast (high speed, more sensitive) film will have much larger grains forming the image than a slow film. As a result, the picture looks coarser, with a visible grain structure. Slow films are capable of better sharpness because of the smaller grains used.*

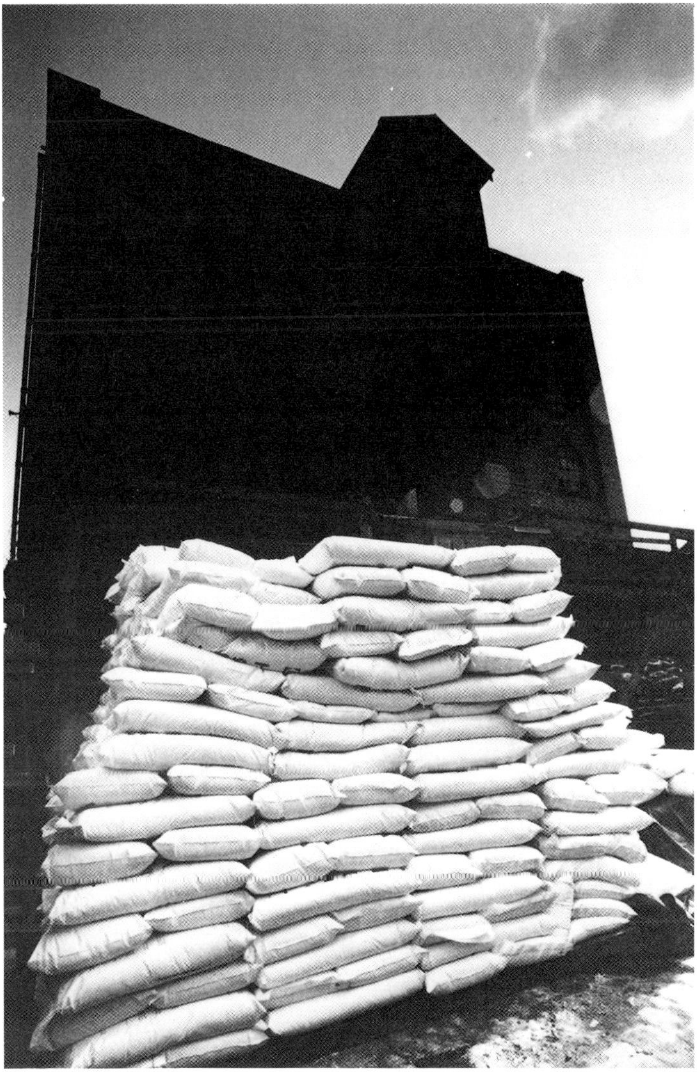

*You can use the grain of fast films for deliberate effects by enlarging a small section of the negative. This works best in black and white, if you have your own darkroom. Manufacturers try to make grain as fine as possible.*

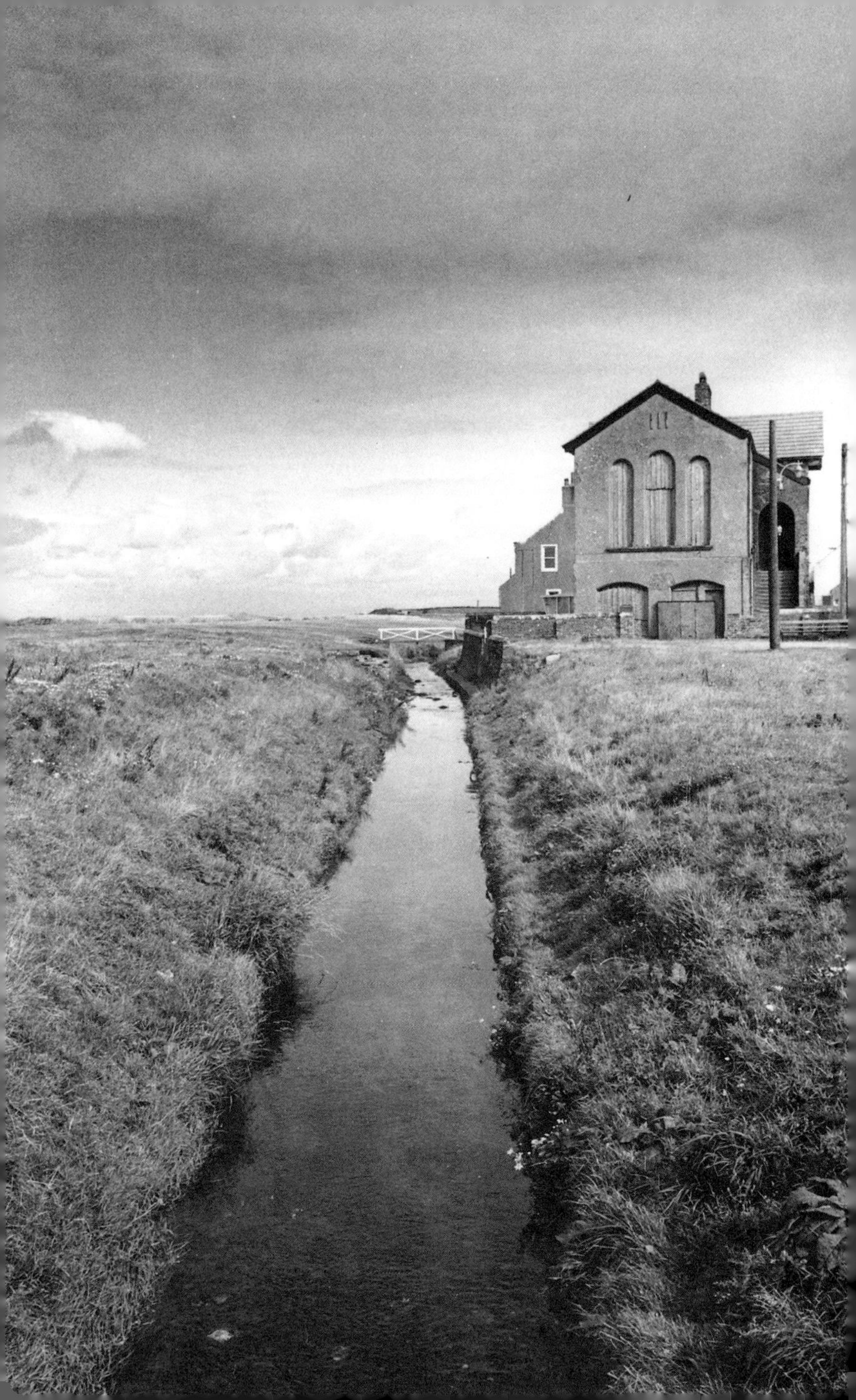

Medium-speed films are from ISO 100 to ISO 200, and these are the films you will use most of the time. Naturally, film speed does not go in huge jumps. You can buy a fast colour print film of ISO 400, which is enough for action shots in daylight or easy shooting on dull winter days, and the grain will be acceptable. You can buy a slide film of ISO 64, and have such a high image-quality that it is indistinguishable from a slower film except by an expert, but almost as fast as a normal ISO 100 material.

Each year, films are improved. A 100-speed film today has grain as fine as a 50-speed film of ten years ago. All films are sharper, have better colours, and are more reliable. This is going to continue. The Pentax cameras will simply use new films as easily as older ones. There has not been any new film launched in the last few years which exceeded the range of the K1000's settings. If this ever does happen, the film will be very special and intended for photography at night!

When it comes to buying film, you only really need to know about two film speeds. For everyday photography, in good light out of doors, buy ISO 100 film. For evening, sports and action, really dull days, interiors, existing light pictures in shopping malls or in theatres, pictures by window light indoors at home – for all these things, buy ISO 400 film. It does not matter whether you use black and white, colour print or colour slide film. The choice of speeds is the same.

## How the meter works

Inside your Pentax SLR there is a photo-electric measuring device. It controls a display according to the amount of light reaching its sensor cell, and electrical input from the camera's own controls.

This metering circuit is calibrated at the factory to match an international standard. If you measure the amount of light from the sun or sky, then measure the amount reflected back (and not absorbed) by a whole range of different typical scenes, the average turns out to be about 10%. A snow scene reflects about 90%, and a portrait against a light background about 20%. But most streets, fields, mountain scenes, buildings and so on reflect just 10%. These are averages for Japan, Europe and northern America. If you happen to live in Arizona, Egypt or Iceland your local conditions will be different.

Pentax cameras are therefore calibrated on the assumption that

*Fine-grained films are the right choice for static, highly-detailed subjects where you can use a tripod and take great care with focusing and composition. For bright outdoor scenes, they can be used without such care, but medium-speed films are often better. Photographed with a 24mm lens and orange filter on the coast of the Solway Firth by Shirley Kilpatrick.*

about 10% of the illumination falling on a subject is reflected from it. This produces accurate exposure 80% of the time, and small enough errors to give good prints or slides on all but the most difficult subjects. Some camera makers still use an old standard, 18% reflectance. This is OK for photographic exposure meters which just measure a small part of the subject, but it can lead to washed-out results with slide film. Pentax SLRs are slightly less generous than some makes, and produce richer colours on slide films.

On the K1000, the metering display could not be simpler. It is a zero-point system; you adjust one or both of the shutter speed and aperture controls until the needle is precisely centred in a gate. It does not matter whether the correct exposure is 1/1000th at *f*16 or 1/30th at *f*2.8 – the object is to get the needle in the middle of the gap. If there is too much light (over-exposure) the needle will be ABOVE the gap, if there is too little (under-exposure) the needle will be BELOW. It is very logical.

The P30n is slightly more complicated because it does more. It has two automatic exposure modes as well as manual metering. These will be explained later on. Unlike the K1000, the P30n displays a range of shutter speeds using illuminated figures in the viewfinder. When the camera is used with auto exposure, the setting selected by the camera itself is displayed. When you use manual metering, the shutter speed set on the speed dial is illuminated, and one of the figures above or below this will be rapidly flashing. If you adjust the lens aperture, the position on the scale of the flashing shutter speed alters; if you adjust the shutter speed dial, the constantly-lit one moves.

Correct exposure is achieved when the two coincide, leaving just one constantly-illuminated shutter speed displayed – no additional flashing speed. This system is just as easy to use as the K1000, and provides rather more information, but you may need to study how it works a little more closely.

There is one very important thing about the K1000 which many people forget. The meter has no external switch – it is on all the time that there is enough light entering the lens to take a photograph. If you leave the lens cap off, the meter will drain the battery as long as there is light. Closing the case-front (ever-ready case) or putting the camera in a closed bag will switch the meter off just as well as putting the lens-cap

*Right: the P30n shows exactly how far out your exposure is by indicating the difference between the correct shutter speed and the speed you have set. On automatic exposure, just the speed selected by the camera is displayed. Other displays include P = Programmed Mode, M = metered Manual, flash symbol for flash ready indication, Blinking "1000" for over-exposure (P or A), blinking "1" for underexposure (P or A), blinking shutter speed = Memory Lock in use (one speed only displayed).*

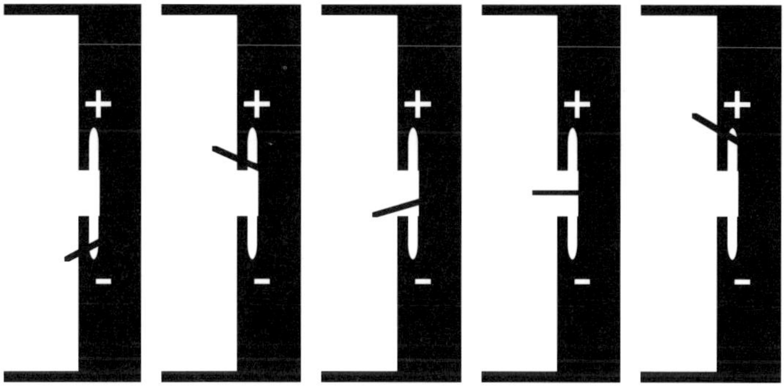


*Above: the metering needle of the K1000 conveys a considerable amount of information. With no battery or in too dim light for metering, the needle is at rest (far left). With the lens cap off, it will rise to give a meter reading. You can tell the relative exposure from the needle position – if it is just into the black area, there is a one-stop error (second to left indicates one stop of overexposure). If it is just within the gap, there is a half stop error (centre diagram shows half stop under). Correct metering and exposure is shown by an exactly centered needle. Battery check is obtained by setting the camera's filmspeed dial to ISO 100 and the shutter speed to "B" (technically, out of the metering range). The needle should rise to the maximum possible UP position (right). If it does not, replace the 1.5v silver oxide battery.*

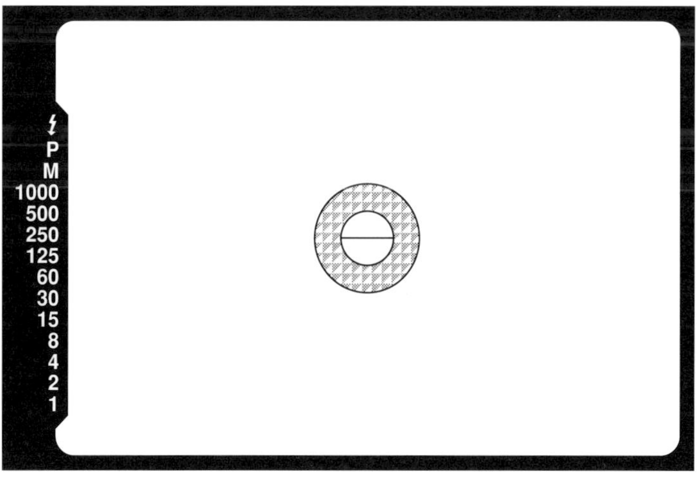

on. But you should not simply leave the K1000 out with the lens cap off for weeks at a time.

The P30n meter only operates when you press lightly on the shutter release, and the entire camera circuit can be switched off at the main switch. Even when this switch is on, there is very little drain on the battery. Both cameras use the same type of battery; the reason the P30n uses two cells instead of one is because the illuminated read-out in the viewfinder, and the electronic timing of the shutter, require more power.

## How to meter

There is no need to worry about aiming the meter at small areas of the average scene. Most of the time, if you frame up a shot and centre the needle on the K1000 you will get perfectly exposed pictures. With the P30n, just set the lens to "A" and the camera will do everything for you – once again with perfect results.

There are two or three cases which produce incorrect exposure – we will look in more detail at minor adjustments later. Major errors are produced by very bright or plain white sky areas when you aim the camera upwards. For example, if you are sitting down and aim upwards to take a portrait of someone standing beside you, the meter will tend to produce a silhouette. The same happens when you photograph an aircraft or a balloon against a white sky, or try to take a study of a single tree on a skyline against an overcast sky.

A similar error is produced by a scene consisting of snow, or very white sand and sea. A white-painted wall occupying all of the shot apart from a figure standing against does the same – it tells the camera to reduce the exposure. The result in all these cases is a dirty grey image.

The solution to this – all the examples are actually a single basic problem – is to meter selectively. Aim the camera at a medium-toned area, perhaps your own knees, or a friend standing near you, so that at least 75% of the frame is filled with mid-toned details. Use this selective reading (press the Memory Lock on the P30n) to get the correct exposure for the scene in general.

We will explain how to fine-tune meter readings and use the Memory Lock later on. The under-exposure caused by the instances mentioned here is so serious and so common that it is worth mentioning right away. If this is the only time you ever correct or adjust the exposure, it will be worth it – you will get snow scenes, seascapes, and pictures of airborne subjects which come out well instead of being complete failures.

*Two cases where you must find an AVERAGE target to meter from, and not rely on the camera – snow scenes, and seaside scenes. Both are popular subjects which often end up coming out very badly because of wrong exposure.*

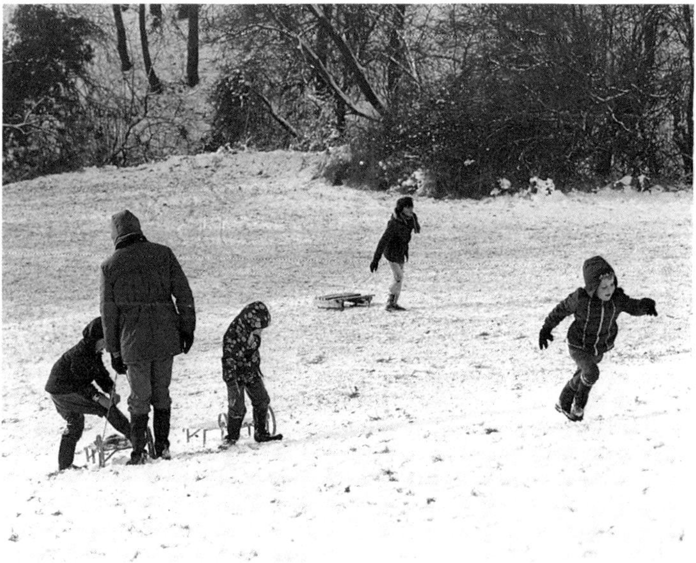

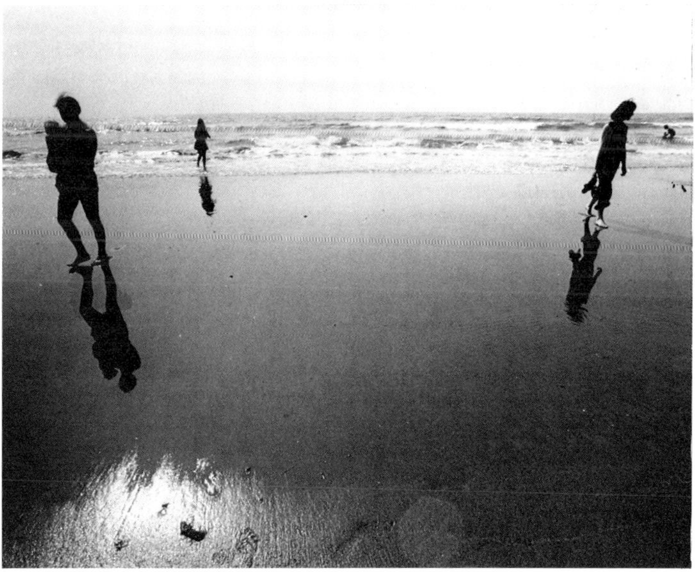

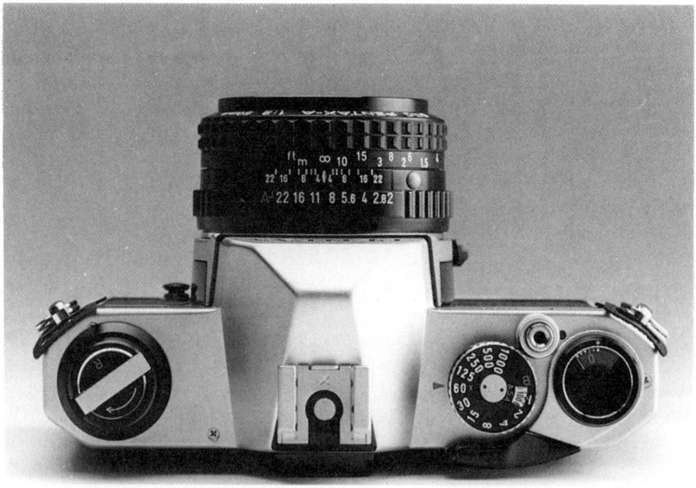

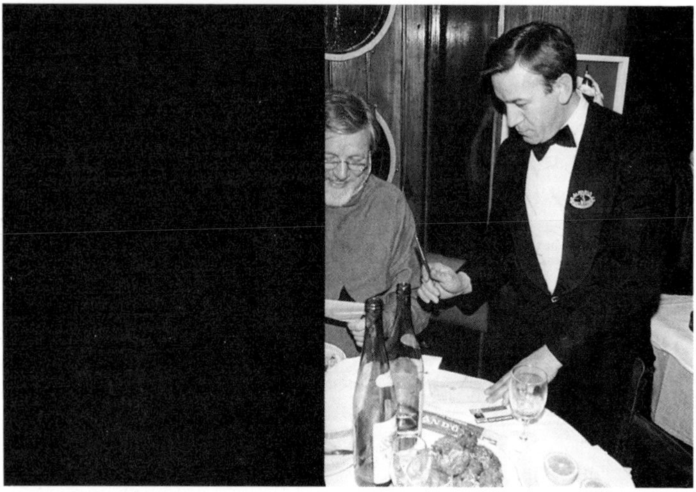

*Top – the top plate of the Pentax K1000 as viewed from above. The left and right ends are shown here as described in the text.*

*Bottom – if you try to take a flash picture at a speed faster than 1/60, part of the picture will be cut off by the shutter blind. This is the result of making a flash exposure at 1/125,*

# The K1000

*This chapter is for owners of the K1000. If you have a P30n, still read this section first, because it explains how to hold and view through the camera, and these things are the same for both models.*

The Pentax K1000 is unique because it is mechanical – no other popular system has a camera like this still in production. Pick it up. It is heavy, but very solid, and fits the hands well. Cradle the camera between your hands, one at each end; then try holding it with one hand cupped under the centre, so that your finger and thumb can operate the aperture and focusing rings of the lens (and the zoom ring, if you have a zoom). Try both horizontal and vertical compositions. You may prefer to have your right hand at the top of the camera, or at the bottom, for vertical shots. It helps to use the same hold every time.

Press the camera firmly against your nose and forehead, with your eye centered behind the viewfinder eyepiece. You should be able to see a rectangular screen with slightly rounded corners, and a cut-out at the right hand side (horizontal) with a black meter needle swinging or static near this aperture. If the edges of the picture area look soft or fuzzy, or you have to move your eye from side to side to see the meter cut-out, you have the camera too far away from your eye.

Even if you wear spectacles, you need the camera CLOSE to your eye and CENTERED accurately. Otherwise, the focusing device in the centre of the screen will not be easy to use. If you cannot see the graininess of the screen, the concentric rings in a fine pattern, and the central circle of slightly shimmering detail (on some cameras, a split-image with two clear semi-circles and offset image detail) – if you can't see all this clearly then your eyesight correction is wrong. You must be able to see this to use the camera properly. Eyesight correction lenses are available.

I wear spectacles and I press the camera viewfinder eyepiece right against my glasses. I push my specs back against my eyebrow and cheek. It is the only way I can be sure of viewing properly through an SLR like the K1000.

Correction lenses for the K1000 slide into the outer grooves of the viewfinder eyepiece, and are easily removed and changed (some cameras have lenses which slot semi-permanently into the eyepiece itself). You can also slide in a rubber eyecup, which can help protect glasses from scratching, but is more use when used against a naked eye, to seal light out entirely and ensure accurate centering.

## Winding and firing

Most of the camera's controls are visible from the top. At either end of the body, there are triangular split-rings to attach the strap, which comes loose inside the camera packaging. There are leatherette gaiters behind the rings. Do not remove these; they stop the strap from rubbing the chrome plating of the camera. Fit the strap before using the camera, and always put it round your neck. It may be comfortable to sling the camera over a shoulder, but it is easy to let it fall or knock against things.

On the top plate you will see a cluster of controls at one end, the right-hand end when holding the camera normally. Nearest this end is the wind-on lever, which has a window set in it marked with dots and 0. This scale is the exposure or frame counter. When you load a film, it does not move until you wind the lever. Then it moves one dot for each complete frame. There are two dots before 0, because you must wind the lever twice after loading the film in order to reach the first frame. This ensures you do not take pictures on film which has been fogged (exposed) by the light when you loaded it.

The wind-on lever first moves out a small amount, then reaches a point of greater resistance. The first movement is called stand-off. When you wind the lever fully, it will go through 160° before reaching a point where it stops firmly. When you let go, a spring returns the lever to the 10° stand-off, leaving it jutting out enough for your thumb to pick it up easily for the next shot. The stand-off helps when you take pictures of action.

You cannot wind the lever twice; try it. The resistance is too great. It is impossible to advance the film and leave a blank. You have to fire the shutter before you can wind on again. Just between the wind-on lever frame counter window and the shutter release (the button nearest the front of the camera) there is a small circular window on the top plate. This is a very useful Pentax feature – still rarely copied – to show wind-on status.

When the window is black, you can wind on – but if you encounter resistance when the window is black, it means that you have definitely reached the end of the film. You might think you have wound on, because the lever will not move, but you can't fire the shutter. Just check the small window. If it is red, then you have wound on, and the shutter can be fired. Whichever the case, never force the wind-on lever.

## The shutter speed dial

The shutter speed dial is the largest control in this cluster. It is marked from 1 to 1000 with a "B" next to the figure 1. There is also a small window marked "ASA". This is a throwback – today, we refer to filmspeeds as ISO, not ASA, but they are just the same. ASA is the film

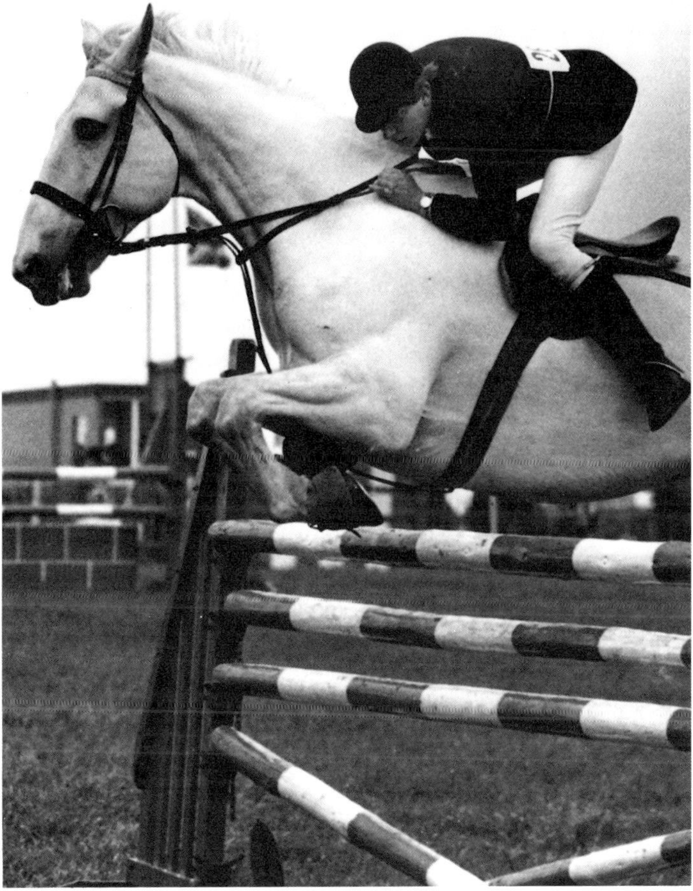

*The K1000 does not use a motordrive of any kind – each frame must be wound on by hand before you can fire again. With careful timing, action pictures present no problems, but you only get one chance – so pick sports which present repeated opportunities. Photograph by Shirley Kilpatrick.*

speed setting, and you can change the figure shown in the window by lifting the outer rim of the shutter speed dial firmly between opposed finger and thumb, rotating to a new position while watching the figures and dots on the scale, and dropping it into place.

The shutter speeds are:

| | |
|---|---|
| 1 | 1 second |
| 2 | 1/2 second |
| 4 | 1/4 second |
| 8 | 1/8 second |
| 15 | 1/15 second – closest to half of 1/8 |
| 30 | 1/30 second |
| 60 | 1/60 second |
| 125 | 1/125 second – closest to half of 1/60 |
| 250 | 1/250 second |
| 500 | 1/500 second |
| 1000 | 1/1000 second |

You will notice that there are two points where the sequence does not go to a perfect half of the speed before. This is necessary, to make a smooth range between 1 and 1/1000, and the discrepancies are so small that they do not matter. The actual speeds are accurate within about 20%, often better. If they are within 20%, the camera will work perfectly.

The "B" setting beyond 1 stands for Brief Time or Bulb exposure. On this setting, the shutter opens when you press the release, and stays open until you let go. You can give any time of exposure you like, and with a special locking cable release (an attachment which screws into the shutter release) you can clamp the shutter open and leave the camera unattended, for exposures like 30 seconds or even 30 minutes.

You will see a small X against the 60 setting. This is to show you that you MUST set 1/60 when using flash. The flash-shoe is on top of the camera's prism housing, just above the eyepiece, and there is an X marked on this to remind you. If you have used a camera where the flash sets the shutter speed for you, be careful! The K1000 does not work like this. You must remember to set everything yourself when you fit flash. You can actually use any speed SLOWER than 1/60 – such as 1/30, 1/15 or 1 second. Most of the time, it matters that you set 1/60 and no other speed for flash.

This marking is also a good guide to choice of shutter speeds. If the speed is equal to or shorter than the X speed – 60, 125, 250, 500 or 1000 – then it is OK to hold the camera by hand. If it is longer – 30, 15, 8, 4, 2 or 1 – then you should use a tripod. With care, you can hand-hold 1/30

*Even in bright sunshine, woodland scenes may call for shutter speeds around 1/30 as so much light is stopped by the trees.*

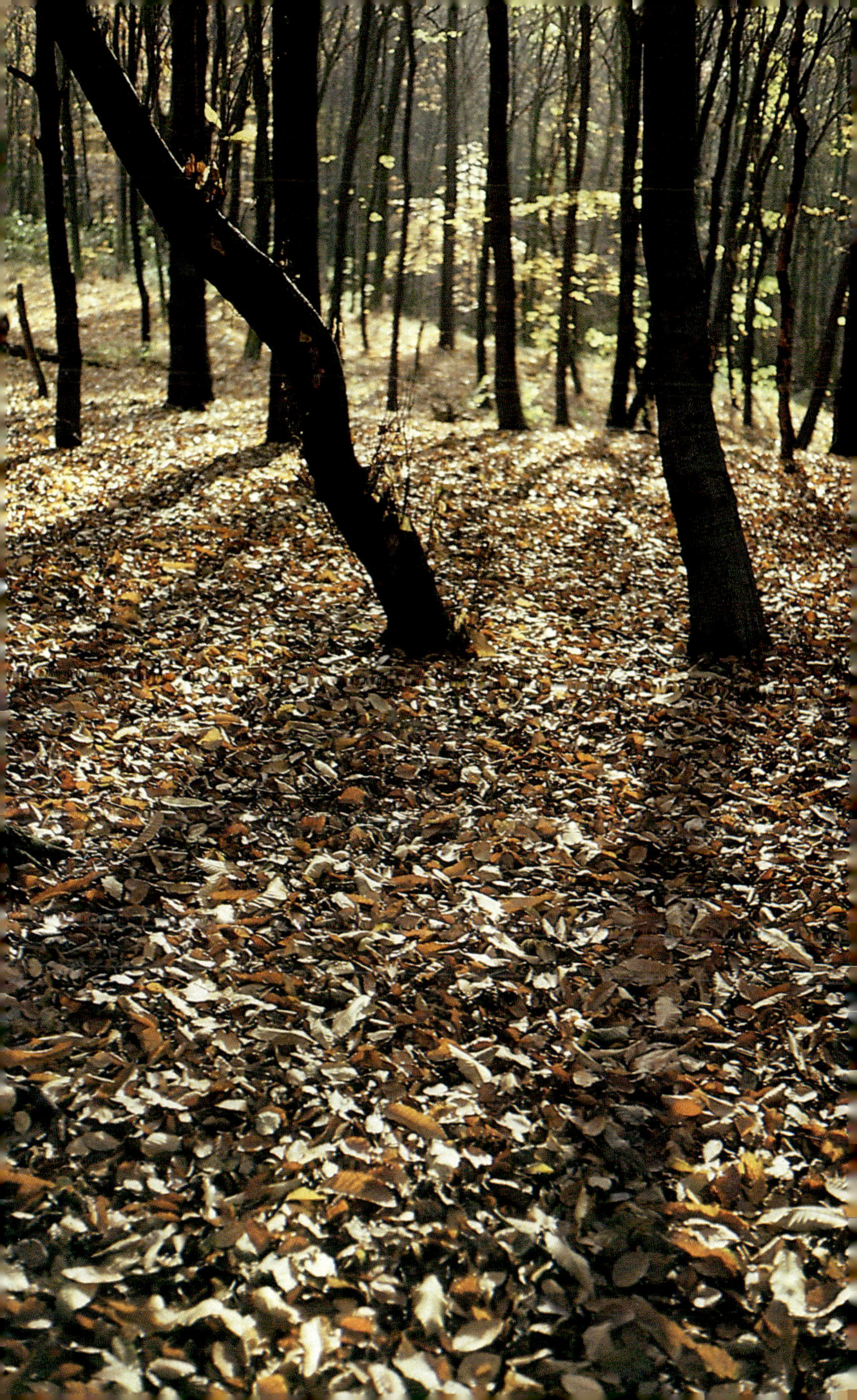

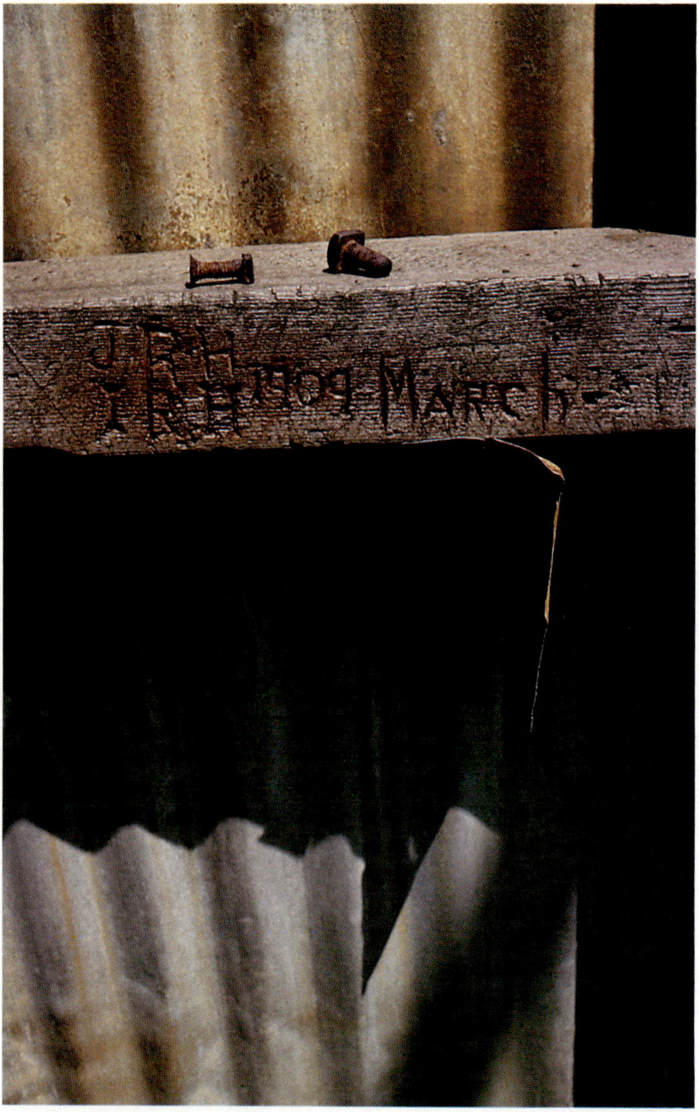


*Choose a slow film like Kodachrome 25 for close-ups which rely on being able to see the fine detail of the subject. Found in a derelict lead mine in the Welsh hills – photograph by David Kilpatrick.*

but it is not a good idea, especially with zoom lenses. We will look at shutter speeds in more detail later but for the moment, just remember to keep the speed above the X mark if you want to hand-hold the K1000.

## Film speed setting

The ASA setting in the centre of the shutter dial goes from 20 to 3200. When you get the camera, set it to 100. If you use an unusual film like Ektar 25 (setting 25) or Fujicolor 1600 (setting 1600) be sure to re-set the dial to 100 when you take the film out. Your next film may be something different, perhaps not 100. But 100 is the average speed of films – it is called "medium speed". The chances are you will load a 100-speed film. If you leave the ASA set to something like 25 or 1600, and then forget to re-set it, you would ruin all your results totally even with a 100-speed film. You are more likely to remember to re-set it when you load an unusual film, anyway, so the chances of accidentally leaving it on 100 when you have just loaded a special Konicacolor SRv-3200 (the fastest the camera will take) are slim.

Get into the habit of ALWAYS leaving the ASA set to 100 when the camera is empty. One day you will be very glad you did!

The markings on the ASA scale go in logical intervals – 50, 100, 200, 400 and so on. In between each figure are two marks. These stand for the in-between speeds. The scale goes like this:

20<br>32<br>40<br>50<br>64<br>80<br>100<br>125<br>160<br>200<br>250<br>320<br>400<br>500<br>640<br>800<br>1000<br>1250<br>1600<br>2000<br>2500<br>3200

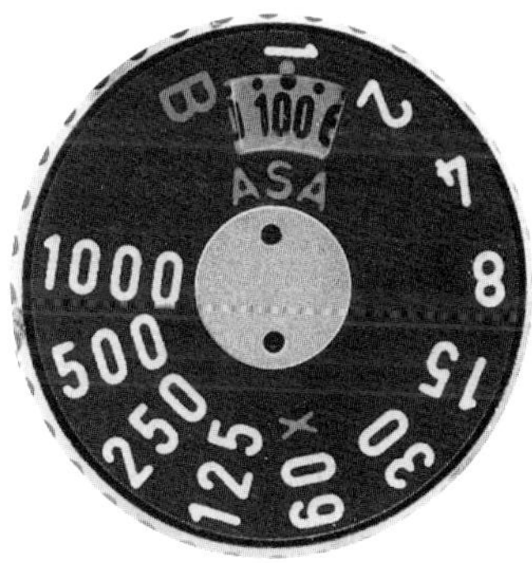


*The shutter speed dial houses the ISO (ASA) film speed setting window. The intermediate speeds (see table, left) are represented by dots.*

Refer to this table if you are unsure which setting to use for a film like Kodachrome 64. It is the first dot after 50, not the second, which would be used for a film with a speed of ISO 80/20°. The ISO speeds you see on the film box may have this oblique slash and a second figure with degrees after it. Ignore this. It is always the figure immediately after the ISO marking which counts. So a film labelled "ISO 200/24°" would be set to the 200 marking on the ASA scale – NOT to ASA 25, which would result in a serious exposure error.

## The shutter release

Although it may not seem to need much explanation, the shutter release is an important control. There is no need to keep your finger on it all the time; the metering is switched on by removing the lens-cap, and you should only place your finger on the release when you intend to shoot. Some Pentax models have a lock on the shutter release, but not the K1000. It is a good idea to leave the camera fired, rather than putting it in a holdall ready-wound, as anything falling against the release may fire the shutter and waste a frame of film.

The correct way to fire the shutter is to press gently until resistance is felt. Any further pressure will immediately trip the shutter, and you need to squeeze very gently. Never jab the release down suddenly. You can buy a large flat pad which screws on to the top of the release to act as a soft shutter, which some people find improves their technique.

The screw thread is a Compur socket for a cable release. You use this when the camera is on a tripod, copying stand or with close-up attachments, to prevent vibration when the shutter is fired. A more detailed look at the cable release is given in the P30n chapter following, as this camera has a special separate socket for a release.

## Flash connections

The flash hot-shoe, we have already seen, is above the eyepiece. How to fit a flashgun is self-explanatory. It is worth mentioning that although there is a central contact in the shoe, this is isolated when no flashgun is fitted. No damage can be done by water, or a metal object shorting across the centre and edge. There is no current present and the circuit is cut off totally from the second flash connection.

This second connection is on the front left side of the camera, near the bottom. It is a coaxial **PC socket**, or standard flash terminal. It is used to connect flashguns without a central "shoe" contact, flashguns which are used off the camera on brackets, and professional studio mains flash units. You should never plug a separate flashgun into the coaxial socket when a camera-top flashgun is already attached to the hot-shoe. This risks damage to both the flashguns and the camera.

# Loading and unloading

On the left hand top plate end is the rewind and back opening knob, combined. If you grasp the circular knob and lift firmly, against resistance, the back latch will undo and the hinged camera back will open; don't do this with a film in!

To load the camera, pull the knob up, resting the K1000 lens-down. I usually sit down, and have the lens between my knees, providing a firm platform for the camera when the back opens. Place the cassette in the chamber, with the knob still lifted – see the photographs for how to position the cassette. Push the knob back down, with rotation if necessary to locate the cassette spindle.

Now draw enough of the film leader out to slot into the take-up spool at the other end. Be very careful not to poke the cloth shutter-blinds, which can be seen clearly. The film goes round the take-up spool in the REVERSE of the winding from the cassette – see the diagram. Do not try to make it go the other way! Turn the take-up spool to tighten the film and locate the sprocket holes on the toothed wheels of the film winding mechanism. With the back still open, operate the wind-on lever half-way, to see that all is working (you may need to fire the shutter first). Now close the back, and wind on twice to reach frame one.

If you flip over the small crank lever on the rewind knob, and turn in the direction marked, you will start to rewind the film. Very soon you will not be able to turn any more, as you have just tightened the film on the cassette spool. Now when you next wind the lever, you will see the rewind knob rotate. This shows that the film is advancing properly. Any time you feel unsure that you have film in the camera, or that you have correctly attached it to the take-up spool, just tension the film with the rewind, and watch when you wind on again. If it does not turn within a couple of frames, something is probably wrong.

When you reach the final frame of the film, the camera will let you know you are there by preventing any further wind-on. There is no need to stop at 24 or 36 – you may get an extra frame. Now turn the camera over, and you will see a small button on the baseplate. This has a dot on it. Press the button in firmly, and hold it in while you wind a couple of turns in the direction of the arrow (clockwise) on the rewind lever/knob.

If you encounter resistance, stop, and press the button in again. This button releases the mechanism to allow free back-winding of the film. It must be drawn all the way back into its cassette to be sent for processing. You can take your finger or thumb off the button once you are sure that rewinding is under way, and as you wind, you will see the button rotate (the small dot shows you this). At the end of the film, you will feel a click as the film pulls out of the take-up spool slot, and very shortly afterwards, the button will stop turning. If you now open the back, the cassette will still have an inch or so of film sticking out – this is useful when you process your own, or want to rewind and later reload a partly-used film. Normally, just wind a few more turns and the film will be taken right back into the cassette, safe from accidental reloading, and ready to be sent for processing.

When you open the camera back, the film counter resets automatically. You do not need to zero it. If you momentarily open the back by mistake with a film in, half-way through, it will NOT ruin the entire film. You will lose the exposure you have just taken, and probably two or three more. Unless the accidental opening is in bright light, or for more than a brief instant and only slightly open, no more damage will be done. Close the back immediately, and wind on two frames to reach unaffected film.

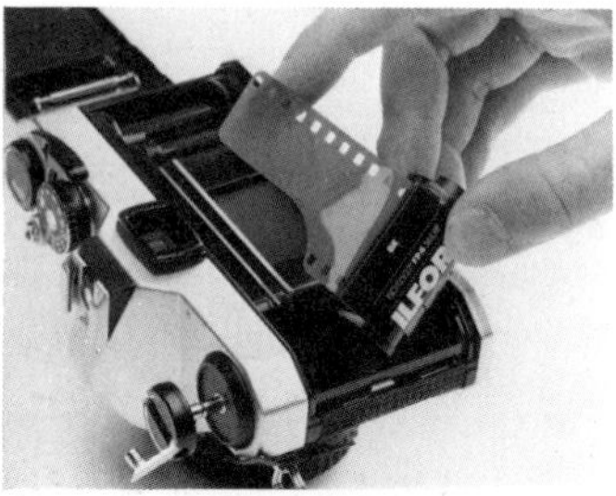


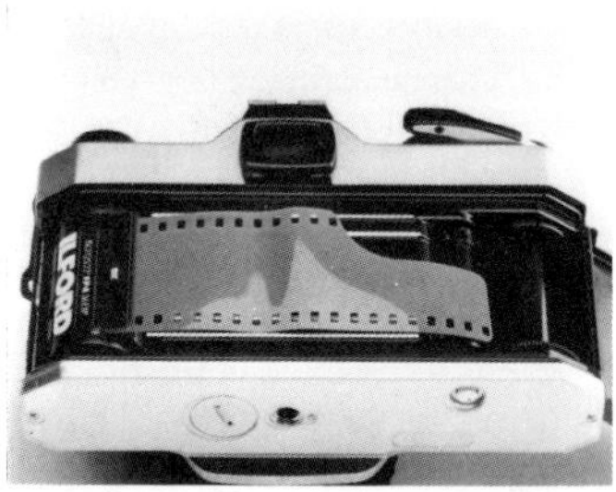


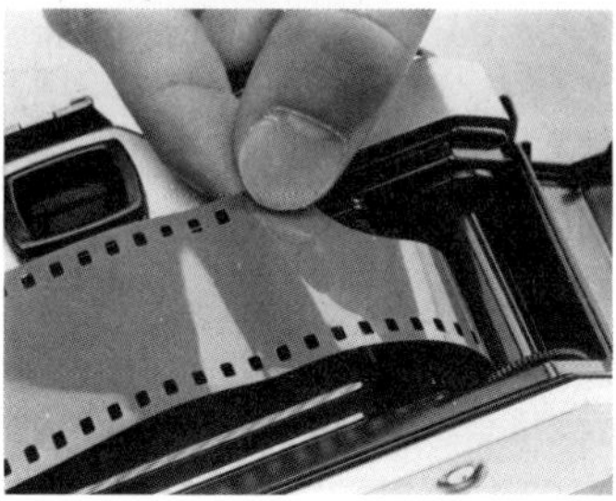

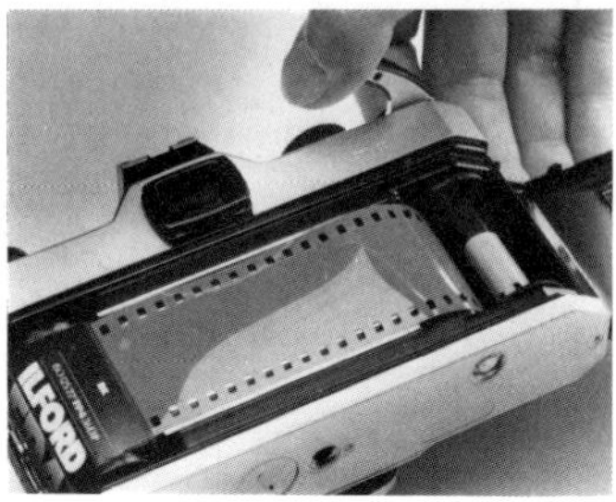


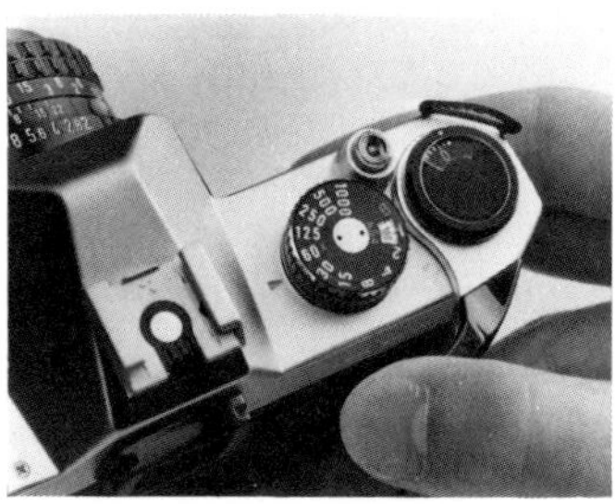

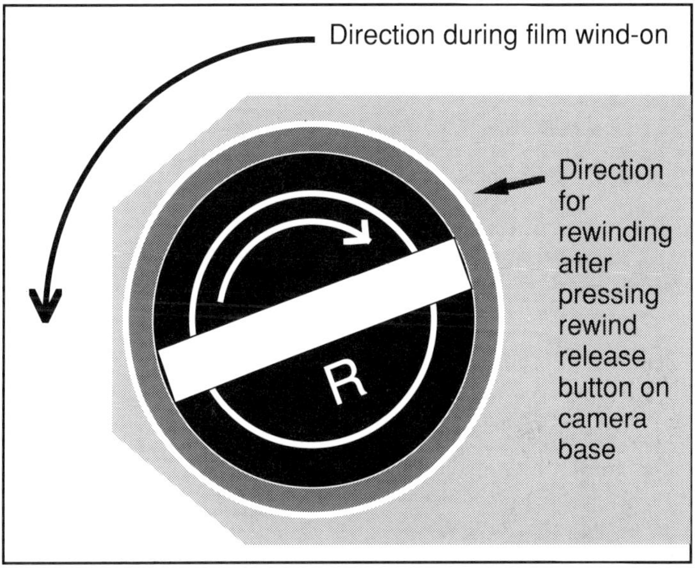


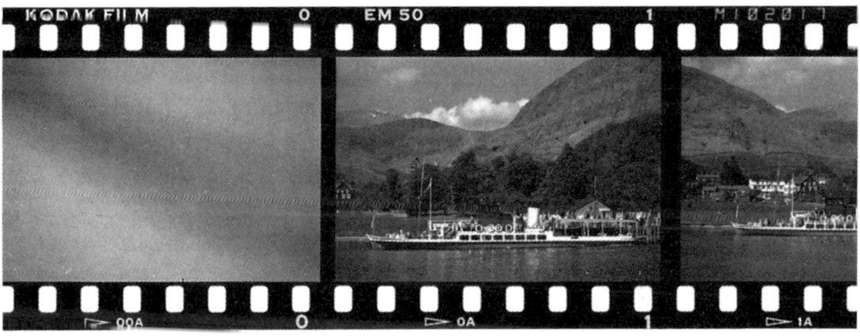


*Top: the arrow on the rewind knob indicates the direction you MUST turn when winding the film back. During use, you should see this knob turning the other way each time you wind on.*

*Above: the first three frames of a film – the maker puts numbers such as OO or OA before 1, as you are intended to wind on a couple of times to reach Frame 1, avoiding any risk of fogged pictures.*

*Left: the sequence of loading the Pentax K1000 with a fresh roll of film.*

## Other features

The K1000 baseplate has two further features – the tripod bush, and battery compartment. The battery cover unscrews using a small coin, and you simply drop a type LR44 (S-76) 1.5v silver oxide cell into position, plus sign upwards, and screw the cover back on. The tripod bush is threaded with a 1/4" Whitworth screw – the standard for amateur tripods. You may find some tripods which have a 3/8" thread and do not fit; an adaptor is available.

Be very careful with old tripods. Some have long screws. You should not screw anything longer than 1/4" into the camera – otherwise, you may damage the K1000. Never over-tighten. The baseplate has a plastic coversheet when you buy the camera. Leave it on – it will do no harm, and protects the chrome for a year or two.

On the camera mirror-box right hand side there is the lens release button. This enables you to remove the lens, and fit new lenses as required. You grasp the lens firmly round its barrel, press the button fully towards the camera body, and while keeping the button pressed in, turn the entire lens anti-clockwise. After one-third of a turn, it will bayonet out, and may be placed on a level surface on its front. Fit a rear lens cover immediately. Now fit a new lens, or fit a body cap to the camera – NEVER leave the K1000 without a lens fitted.

## Lens handling

You will soon get to change lenses single-handedly. At first, use your eyes. When you fit a new lens, line up the red focus/aperture index with the dot on the camera mount, and it will go home easily. There is also a large white dot on the lens, made of plastic. This is for working in the dark, or without looking. Do NOT line this up with the dot on the body mount – just line it up with the lens-release button. To secure the lens, twist it clockwise until it clicks home.

After you fit any Pentax lens to the K1000 do this:
**CHECK THE APERTURE SETTING**

Current Pentax-A lenses have an "**A**" setting beyond the smallest aperture (smallest = *f*16 or *f*22 on most lenses). This is **NOT** for use on the K1000. If you set the lens to this, you will get wrong exposures all the time. Make sure that if the lens was set to A before fitting, you press the small button near the A marking and move to one of the regular *f*-stop markings. I suggest you always set the lens to *f*8 – then if you forget to adjust it for any reason, the chances of a serious error in exposure are minimized.

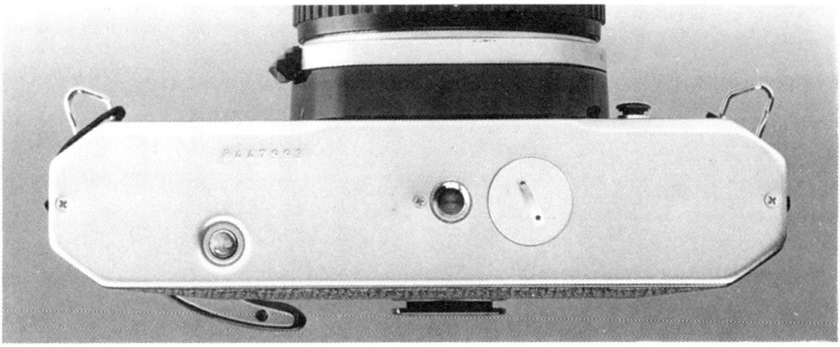

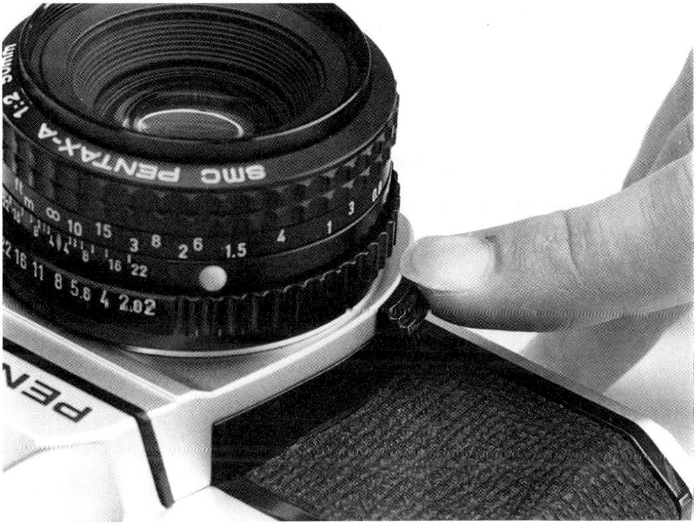


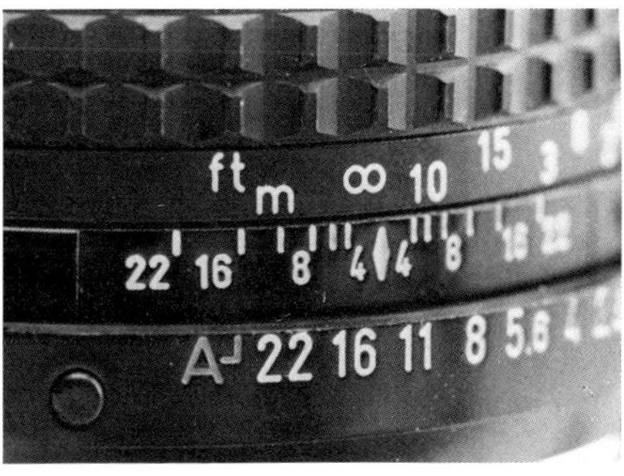


*Top: the baseplate of the K1000 with tripod bush, rewind button and battery compartment cover.*

*Above: the lens release button.*
*Left: make sure the lens is NOT set to "A" if marked.*

# Care of the camera

Now you have taken a full guided tour of the K1000, you are ready to put it away. Do this:

Take a final picture, or release the shutter – it helps if the shutter is not left cocked.

Put the lens cap on.

If the camera is to be stored for a few months, remove the silver oxide battery and pack the kit away in its original box with the silica gel drying bag still there.

To clean your K1000, use a soft cloth such as the Pentax lens cleaning cloth. I use new lens-cloths to clean the viewfinder eyepiece, and I only touch the lens if something serious happens, like a fingerprint by mistake – then you should clean it off quickly. Otherwise, any dust is blown off without even touching the glass using a blower with a tube. I never use the aerosol blowers because sometimes they send a jet of frozen propellant on to the lens and seriously mark the coating.

After your soft lens cloth has been used for a few months, to clean the eyepiece or wipe filters, it may be time to replace it. Don't throw it away. Keep it to clean the chrome of the camera body. Use a cotton bud to clean between the shutter release, speed dial and wind-on lever and to clean the ISO window, hot shoe and the very edges of the eyepiece. I wrap my cameras in old lens cloths when I put them in my camera case. It helps keep them free from dust and knocks, and takes no extra space.

*If you keep your camera and lenses clean – especially the lenses – your pictures will be sharp and retain detail in both highlights and shadows. A fingerprint or grease-mark on the lens front surface can seriously degrade the contrast and sharpness of all the pictures you take until it is cleaned off. This can have a serious effect on into-the-light studies like this 24mm close-up: photograph by David Kilpatrick.*

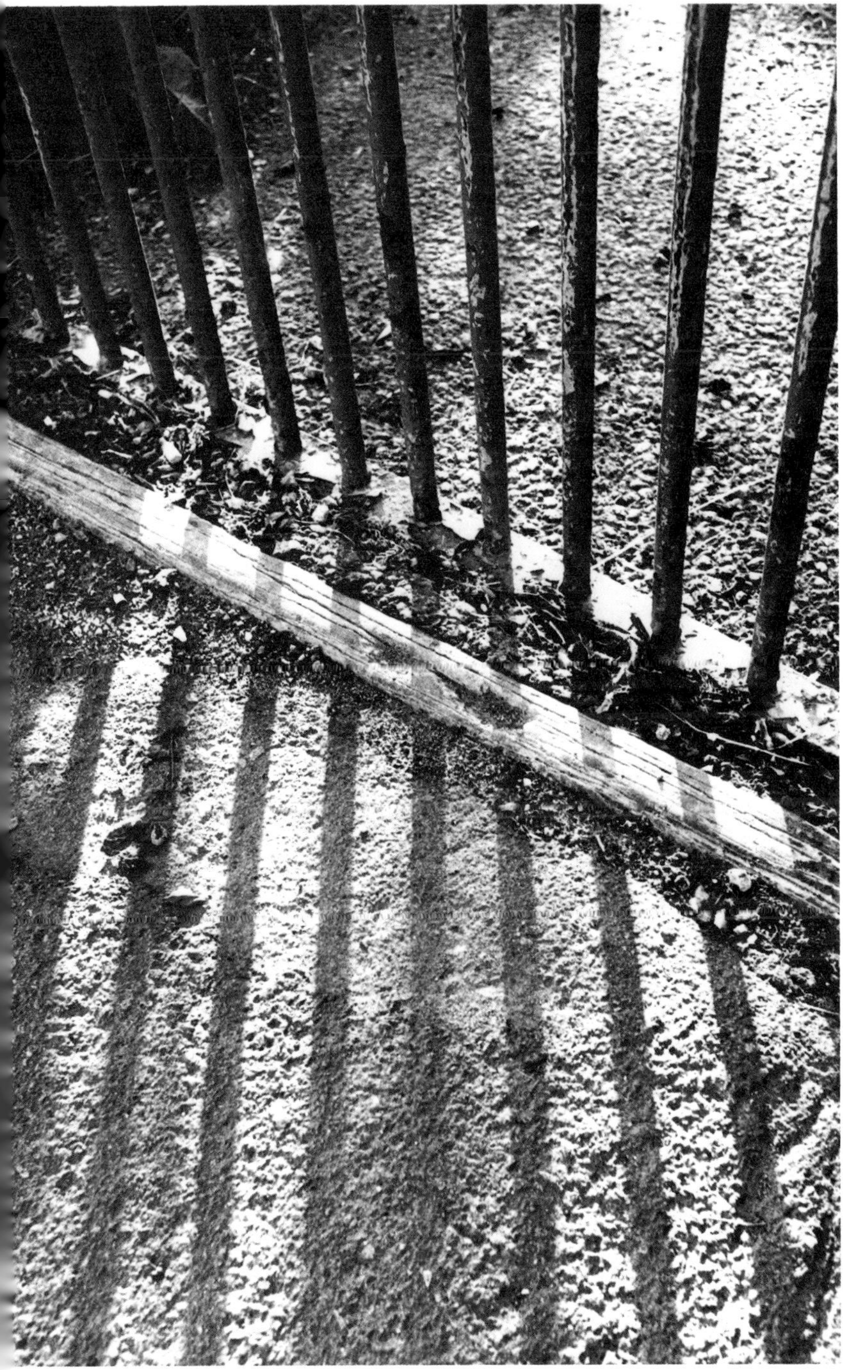

# The P30N/P3N and P30T

*This chapter is for owners of the P30n, or P3n as it is known in North America. You should have read the chapter on the K1000 first, because many of the basic controls are similar. The camera has additional features as well as one or two omissions, and is built using different materials.*

The first thing you will notice about the P30n is that this is a small and very light camera, which fits the hand better because it has a non-slip matt finish and a rubber grip at the right-hand end. This grip does not house batteries; it is just there to make the camera easier to hold securely. The camera is finished in black, and made of synthetic materials (plastics) around a solid alloy central casting. It is this casting which bears the weight of the lens, the mirror mechanism, and the shutter.

The P30n has been designed to keep most of the controls flush to the body profile, especially on the top plate. You may not spot the shutter release button at first – it is a flat central pad in the middle of the shutter speed and Mode dial. It is electronic, not mechanical, and this makes it very sensitive and light in use.

If we look at the top plate of the P30n, the wind-on lever, frame counter window and shutter dial once again form a cluster in much the same arrangement as the K1000. There is no wind-on indicator, and the speed dial has no lift-and-turn collar for ISO film speed setting. The lever wind has a much bigger stand-off angle than most cameras – before you start to wind, it pulls out a full 35°, with plenty of space for you to leave the camera at eye-level yet wind on quickly, repeatedly, for action shots.

The actual stroke is a short and crisp 130° action, and it is fairly firm. The variation in resistance as you wind on is caused by the effort needed to cock the spring-loaded metal shutter.

The frame counter starts at 0, and there is no position for S or 1. Instead, it is marked with even frames as numbers (0, 2, 4, 6, 8 and so on) with dots for the odd frames between. The numbers 12, 20, 24 and 36 correspond to the most popular loadings of 35mm film.

The shutter speed dial is electronic, and this means that it does not have to be gripped between finger and thumb to turn. A thin knurled rim projects slightly to the front, leaving the rest of the dial flush with the camera top. This rim can be turned easily with the forefinger you normally use to release the shutter, moving your finger forward from the central shutter release pad to change the setting. As the speeds are displayed in the viewfinder, you do not need to take the camera away from your eye to use this shutter speed dial. Combined with the rapid

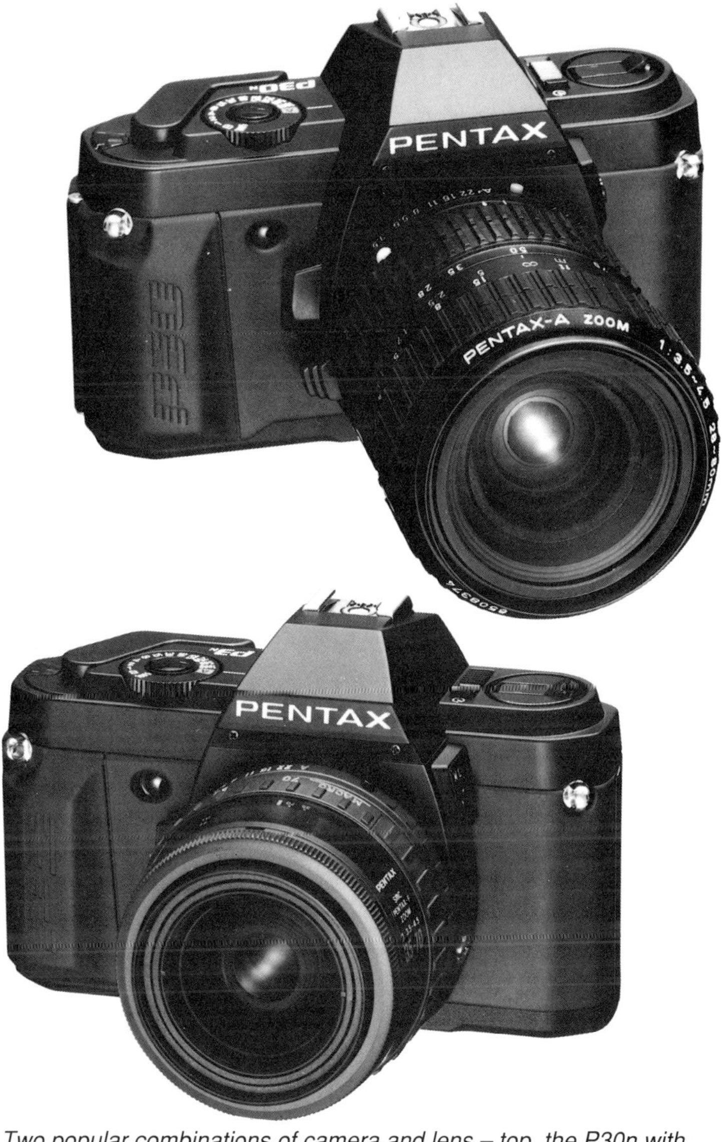


*Two popular combinations of camera and lens – top, the P30n with the 28-80mm Pentax-A zoom, and bottom, with the SMC Pentax-F 35-70mm zoom. This compact lens is part of the autofocus range but is fully functional on the P30n, and is often supplied in place of the 50mm ƒ2 standard lens.*

wind-on lever, this makes the camera particularly good for action photography.

The shutter speed scale of the P30n is identical to the K1000, but has two extra positions. Beyond the 1000 setting, there is a green box marked with an "A". This stands for Automatic, and is used for three different operating modes – Programmed Exposure, Aperture Priority Auto Exposure, and Programmed Flash. Beyond the B setting there is a separate speed marked 100 with a small lightning symbol next to it. This is a special separate flash speed, the highest speed which will work with flash. It is 1/100th of a second on the P30n because the focal plane shutter moves vertically, and uncovers the film across its 24mm dimension, instead of moving horizontally and uncovering the frame across its 36mm length.

The shutter also moves a little faster, physically, to achieve flash (X) synchronization at 1/100. In practice, you can also use the 60 and 30 settings on the main shutter speed range. If you use the 1/125 setting, one edge of the frame may be cut off by about 1mm. The special 1/100 setting is provided to ensure full uncovering of the film when the flash fires. On some electronic cameras, this speed is mechanical, and along with "B" provides a fail-safe if the batteries run down. The P30n is totally dependent on batteries, and the 1/100 and B are both electronically controlled. There is no mechanical setting, and the Auto speeds are limited to the same as the manual range – 1 second to 1/1000.

## Switched on and off

If you have started to explore the P30n, you may find the camera is "dead". First of all, look at the on-off switch. This is the other side of the pentaprism top, and consists of a slider. There are three positions – off, on and self-timer. This last position provides the camera with an electronic delayed action shutter release. Nothing will happen when you press the shutter, because the P30n has now switched to using a 10-second delay. You will see a small red LED (diode) on the camera front below the shutter dial rim. This flashes when the self-timer is operating.

You cannot set the P30n to self-timer without depressing the small button next to the self-timer symbol mark, and sliding the main switch forward over this. Only if someone else has used the camera and left it in this state might the self-timer be accidentally set – or if you press the button and push the switch forward in the process of getting the know the camera.

With the switch off, the whole camera is dead. It does not just control the metering. It powers the shutter as well. Without batteries, the P30n cannot be used. So, after checking that the camera is ON at the switch, if nothing further happens you should make sure you have batteries loaded.

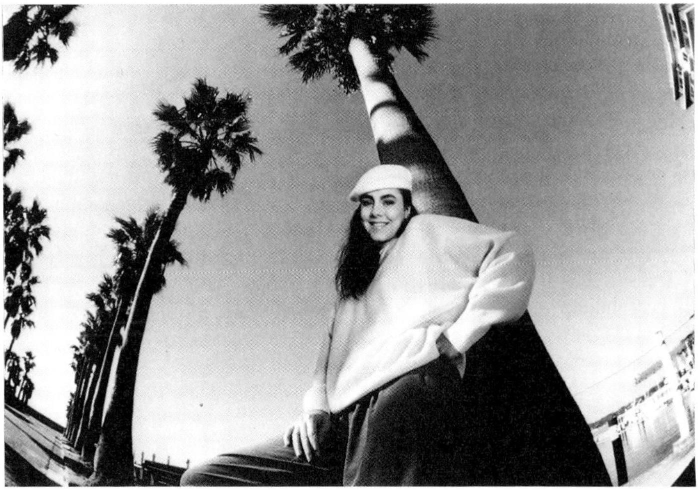

*Above: this example taken using the Pentax 16mm fish-eye lens could easily be followed using a small table tripod and the camera's self timer. As the lens covers 180°, it is hard to avoid including yourself in the picture.*

*Below: the P30n's programmed exposure makes it ideal for action photography. Photograph by Peter Lester.*

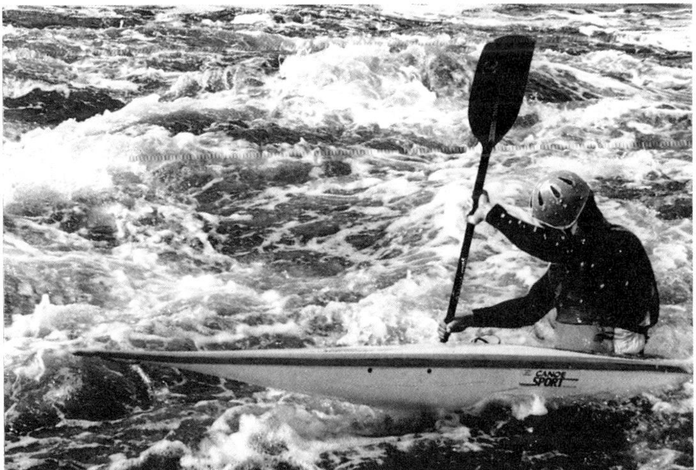

Turn the camera to look at the baseplate. There is the usual tripod socket, a rewind button, and a battery compartment cover which opens at a push. This cover is rather flimsy, but with care it should last for ever. At least it cannot come off and get lost. The camera needs TWO LR44 (S-76) silver oxide or compatible (NOT LITHIUM) batteries. The baseplate also carries the camera serial number, which is needed if you insure your equipment, or return it under guarantee for service.

The is no clear diagram on the compartment to indicate which way round the batteries go – they drop in with the + sign topmost, and are retained by a spring which prevents them from dropping out during loading . The lid completes the circuit with a spring contact on its inner face. If the betteries were a tighter fit, it would be very difficult to remove them. The only danger is that when dropping the first button cell into the compartment, it may flip over and end up the wrong way round, and then be hidden by the second cell which shows the + sign in the correct position. Be careful, and do not handle the cell with your bare fingers. Use a tissue or pop it straight through the back of its packaging into the compartment – most batteries come in packs with pre-cut slots to allow you to push the cell through in this way. Be sure to close the plastic cover firmly (this is another slightly weak point of the design).

What if the camera still does not work? Look through the viewfinder and slightly press the shutter button. A shutter speed (it does not matter which one) should light up. If there is no display, the batteries may be dead or installed face-to-face. This is the battery check procedure. When a set of batteries begins to run down, the shutter speed will flash at 1 second intervals, easily distinguished from the rapid flashing of the display when using manual metering (see later section).

If you forget to switch the camera off, it will not drain the circuit. The metering is only switched on when you press the shutter lightly (first pressure) and remains active for ten seconds if you remove your finger. After this, the circuit shuts itself off.

## Handling the P30N/P3N and P30T

Now that you know where to switch on and where the shutter release is hidden, try viewing through the P30n and taking some exposure readings. With no film in the camera, the P30n will still make dummy exposures, unlike some AF SLRs which will not meter or allow you to fire the shutter without having a film in place.

The camera sets itself to ISO 100 with no film in. If you go outdoors on a sunny day, and set the lens to *f*11, the viewfinder should display a shutter speed between 1/60 and 1/250 when the shutter dial is set to "A". This is the kind of exposure you expect in sunshine. Keeping your finger lightly on the shutter release, aim the camera at different areas of the ground, the sky and parts of your surroundings. You will see the

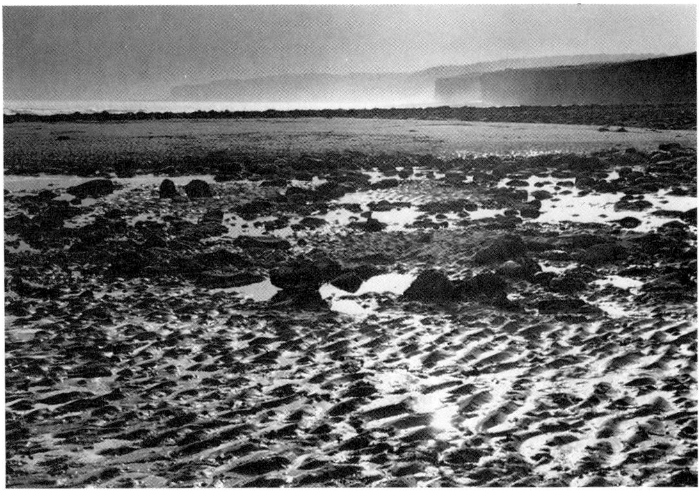

*Automatic exposure metering lets you catch sudden changes in light – however difficult the conditions may be to judge for yourself. Above, a beach on the coast of South Wales was so bright that it was almost impossible to look into the distance without sunglasses. Programmed exposure copes well, giving a dramatic result. Below, rapidly changing light over Derwentwater in the English Lake District called for fast shooting, but the moody image also needed a reduction in exposure by switching to manual.*

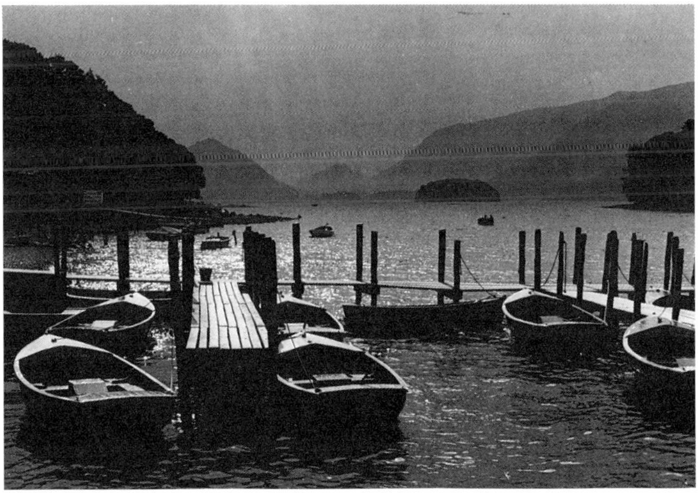

shutter speed display change. Try releasing the shutter a few times, and learn how much pressure you can put on the button for metering, and how much is needed to fire the shutter itself.

When you first unpack your P30n, the viewfinder eyepiece is covered with a plastic cap. This is NOT just a protective cap from the factory! It has a use, as we will see later. Keep if safely; you do not need to put it on the camera all the time, and if you carry it round everywhere it may get lost. So store it away with the camera packaging, but remember that you possess this small accessory.

The P30n viewfinder is superior to the K1000. It features a bright fresnel field, with a dual focusing aid in the centre. A split-image rangefinder device is surrounded by a microprism, giving the best overall performance with a wide range of lenses and suiting people with varying eyesight conditions.

## Loading

The P30n is a modern camera, and film loading is much improved. The back opens by lifting the rewind knob fully, in the normal way. You will notice immediately that there are several stainless steel rollers and spring guides fitted to the camera and to the hinged back.

Inside the cassette chamber, a spring grips the cassette once you have dropped it into place, and prevents it from falling out by accident. It also pushes the metal cassette against the set of contact-pins which read off the DX-coding to set the film speed. Pull the film leader out and across the guide rails – note that the shutter consists of very thin metal blades, which are just as fragile as the cloth blinds of earlier cameras.

The leader should be pulled out just as far as the bright red mark below the take-up spool on the lower left-hand end of the camera's interior. If now pushed to lie flat, the film should fit exactly on to the sprockets (gear teeth) of the winding-on spindle, and also on to some sprockets which are present on the take-up spool itself. This is unusual.

The film is wrapped in the same direction as its natural curl – looking from above, it goes anti-clockwise round the spool. There is no slot to push the leader in to, as the spool and its small teeth grip the film naturally. Tension the film a little by partly winding the wind-on lever; you will see it start to take up on the spool. Now close the camera back.

As you do this, rollers and spring tensioners help keep the film flat and wrapped on to the take-up mechanism. Once the back is closed, complete the stroke of the wind-on lever and fire the shutter once. Now gently REWIND the rewind knob crank until you feel the tension taken up in the film cassette. Wind on with the lever again, and if all is well you will see the rewind knob rotating anti-clockwise. If it does not do this after a few shots, you may suspect that the film has not been loaded properly.

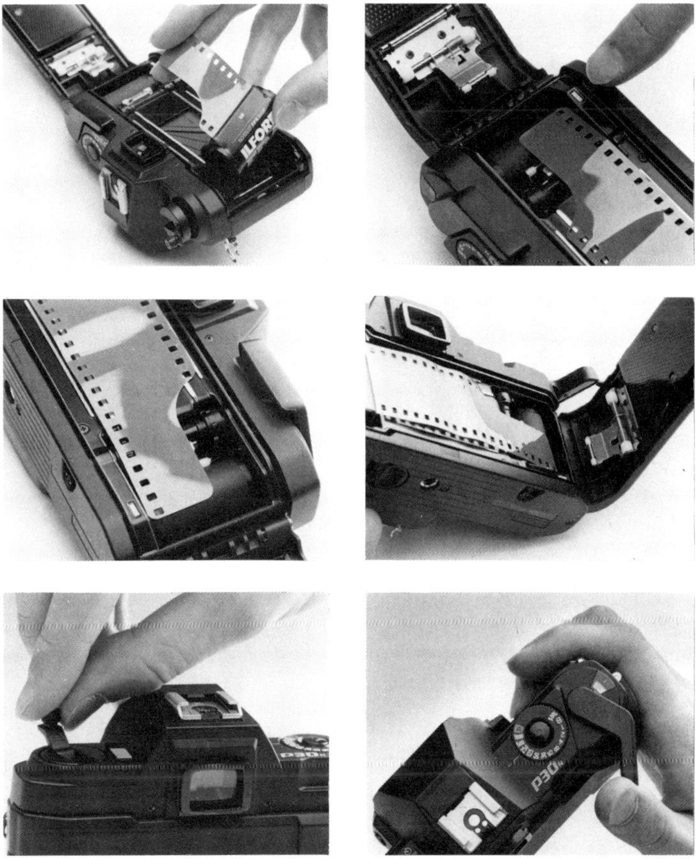

*Loading the P30n: the leader is engaged on short sprocket teeth on the take-up spool, and wraps round in the same direction as the natural curl of the film. When loading, check that the film has engaged properly by taking up the slack before closing the back.*

The take-up spool is comparatively large in diameter and has a slightly rough or tacky surface in addition to the sprockets on the bottom edge. This surface grips the film. A further roller under spring tension holds the film from the left hand side. It is important that you do not use

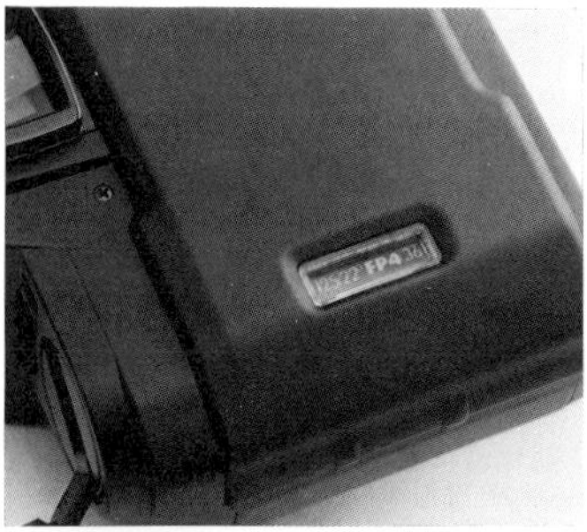

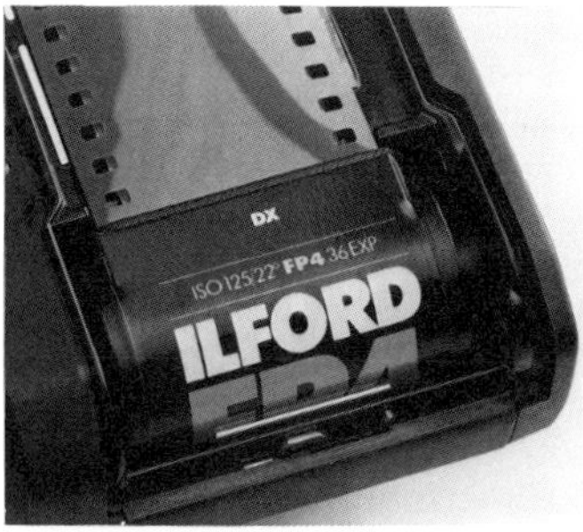


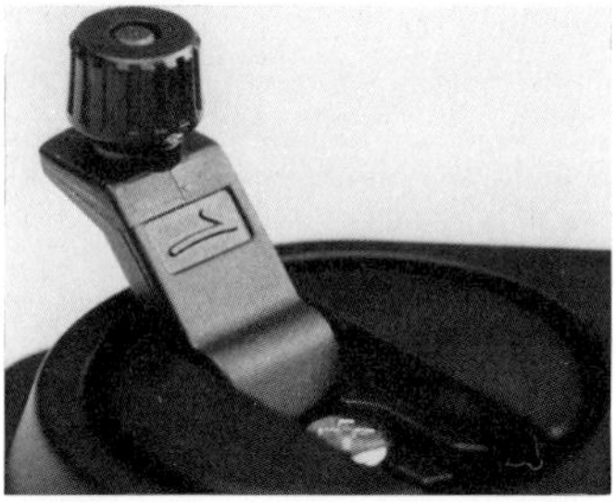

*Top left: the film type viewing window in the camera back. Top right: the cassette markings are positioned to coincide with this window. Cassettes without these markings may NOT be DX coded. Above left: the rewind direction is shown by this discreet arrow.*

*Below: as the P30n has no separate ISO setting, the window tells you what film type you have already loaded. You would not want to take a sunny landscape (below) on a fast grainy film.*

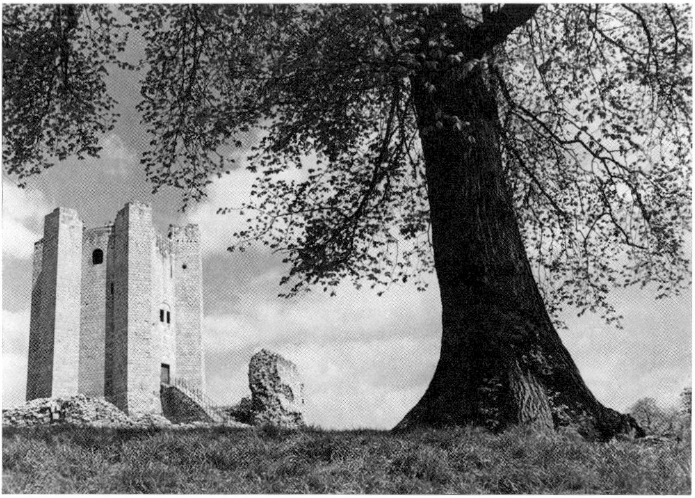

more than a normal 36-exposure film with the P30n, as the maximum capacity of the take-up spool is strictly limited. If you load you own film into re-loadable cassettes, never allow a few extra exposures "for good measure".

The rewind knob under the camera is marked with an embossed "R" and rotates during film transport. This serves no useful purpose, as the button will rotate even with no film present, and rotates if the film is accidentally torn or broken. In fact, there is nothing which prevents it from rotating apart from pushing it in to rewind, and when you do this it does not rotate in the reverse direction to show that the film is winding back correctly. The precise reason for making the rotation of the button visible is something of a mystery.

The back, once closed, has a small clear window at the left-hand end. With a foam light seal to prevent any fogging, this small window is positioned to display the film cassette's special markings. Through the window, you can see if the camera is loaded, and check both the type of film and how many exposures are on it. This is useful, as it is no good knowing you have taken 22 exposures if you don't know whether the film loaded is a 36 or 24 exposure.

## Unloading

When the end of the film is reached, the usual warnings apply – you can't wind on to shoot any more, and you should not force the lever. Turn the camera over to press the rewind button on the baseplate, keeping it depressed fully while you start rewinding using the crank handle on the rewind knob and turning clockwise. There are no markings on the outside of the rewind knob, but if you look very hard you will see a small reminder arrow embossed on the inside of the crank handle after you flip this up. After a couple of turns, you can release the rewind button. Now rewind smoothly and evenly – never too quickly – until you hear the film click free of the take-up spool.

Complete rewinding (back into the cassette) takes a couple of turns after the film leaves the take-up spool. If you want to leave the film leader sticking out of the cassette, you must stop as soon as the film clicks off. The rewind button underneath does NOT give any indication of when this happens and you must use judgement.

Open the camera back by lifting the rewind knob by its outer rim, not by the rewind lever itself. The cassette is easily removed, but the spring keeps it in place when the camera is positioned vertically on a tripod, reducing the possibility that the cassette will fall out. I have had this happen with other cameras, and on one occasion the cassette burst open, ruining the film. The overall design of the P30n film track, cassette chamber and take-up mechanism is first-class and highly reliable.

## Additional controls

The P30n has the lens release button in the same place as the K1000, but the lens mount is different. The K1000 uses the K-mount to its original standard. The P30n uses the A-mount, which accepts all K-series lenses and all F-series lenses (autofocus) as well as the recommended A-series lenses. Both A and F lenses give access to the full range of functions including Programmed Auto Flash, and have electrical contacts which match those on the P30n body mount. K-series lenses have no electrical contacts, and work in Aperture Priority Auto Exposure and Metered Manual modes only. Flash is restricted to automatic setting of the shutter speed to 1/100 by dedicated flashguns – all exposure control must be done manually on the lens whether or not you are using the auto-exposure functions of the flash itself.

Just above the lens release, there is a large push-in lever, slightly concave to fit your fingertip. This is a stop-down preview or depth-of-field preview control, and is an additional feature not present on the K1000 (although it was necessary, and present, on the very first TTL metering Pentax SLRs, and is fitted to many K-mount lenses as a function of the lens independent of the camera body).

The stop-down preview closes the lens from the maximum aperture, used for viewing and focusing, to the aperture which you have set on the

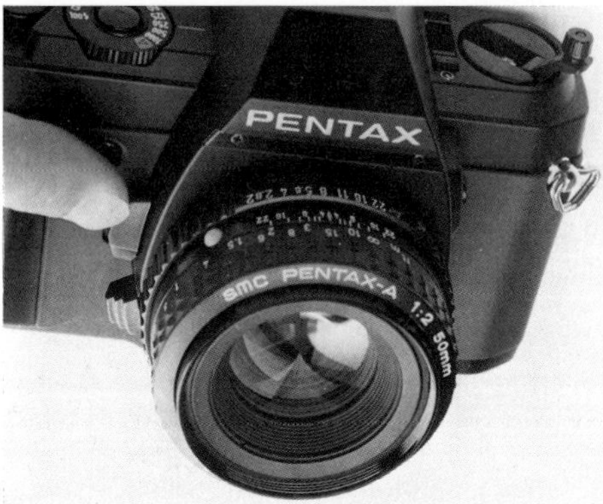


*The stop-down preview lever is above the lens release button.*

*Right: a wide-angle lens is ideal for landscapes. This picture was taken with a 20mm Pentax lens and shows the author at Seil, in Western Scotland. It was photographed into the light, without exposure correction or Memory Lock, by Shirley Kilpatrick. Overleaf, left: using a 50mm lens, Shirley shot this scene at the same location, with the light to ensure colour saturation.*

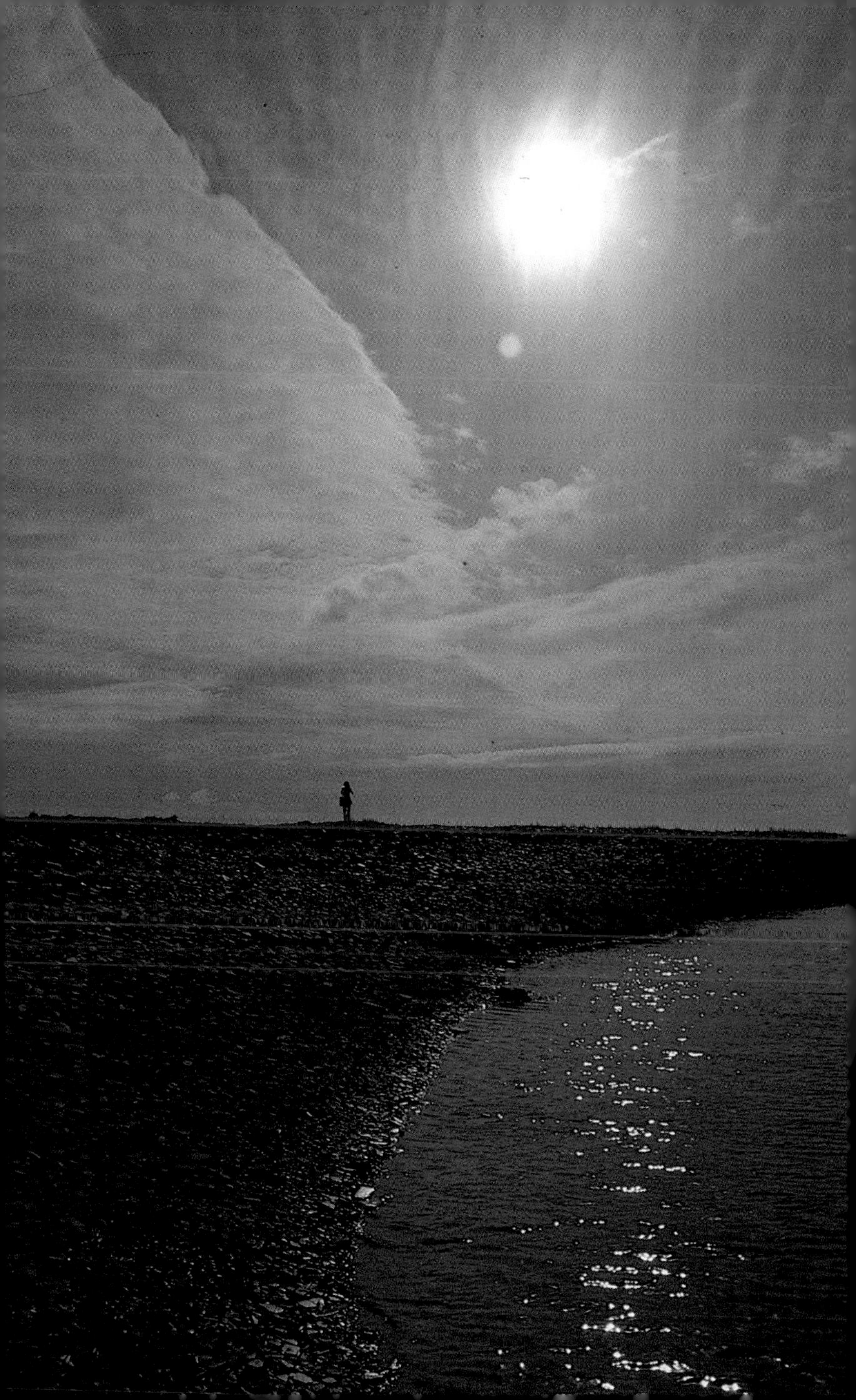

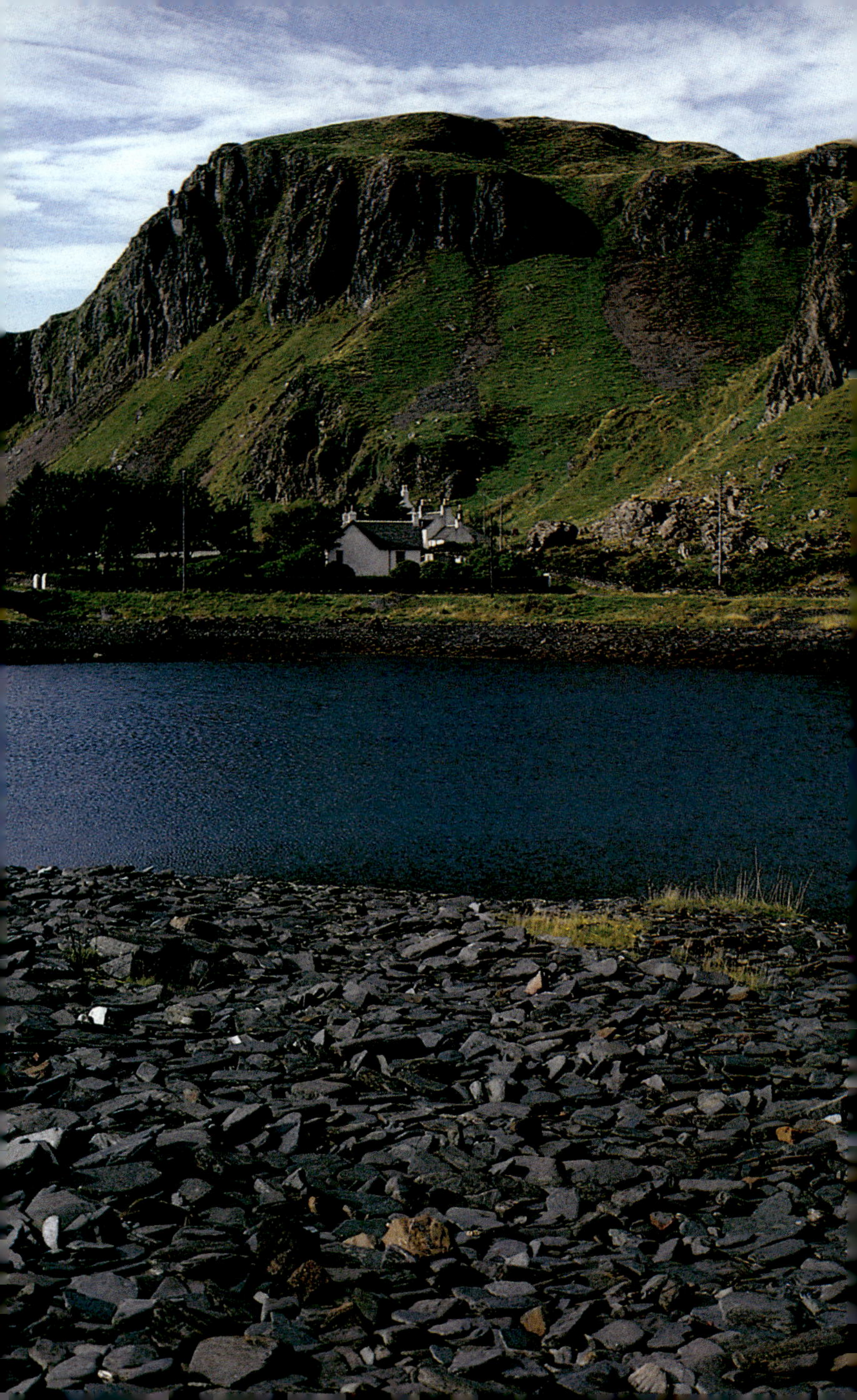

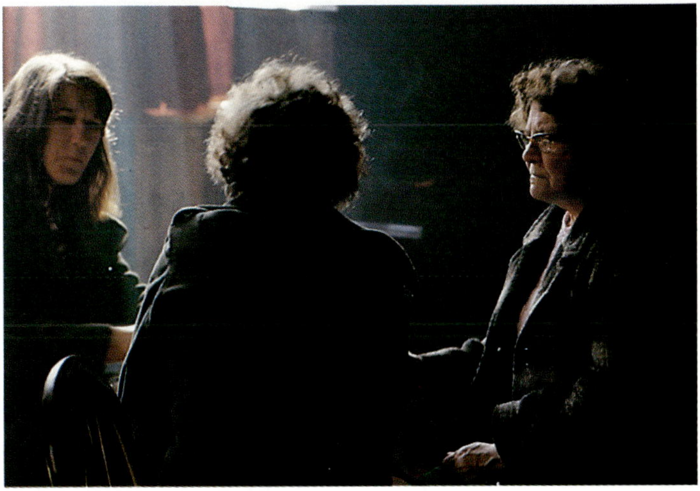

*Above: automatic exposure helps you take candid photographs, quickly and without being noticed, in situations like this – a smoky pub in Yorkshire. Photograph by David Kilpatrick.*

*Below: the stop-down preview of the P30n lets you judge depth of field effects precisely. Photograph by Shirley Kilpatrick, 50mm ƒ1.4 Pentax lens used at ƒ8.*

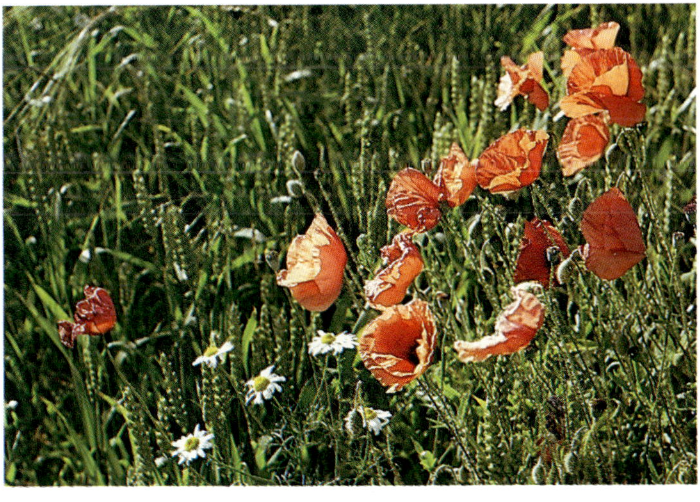

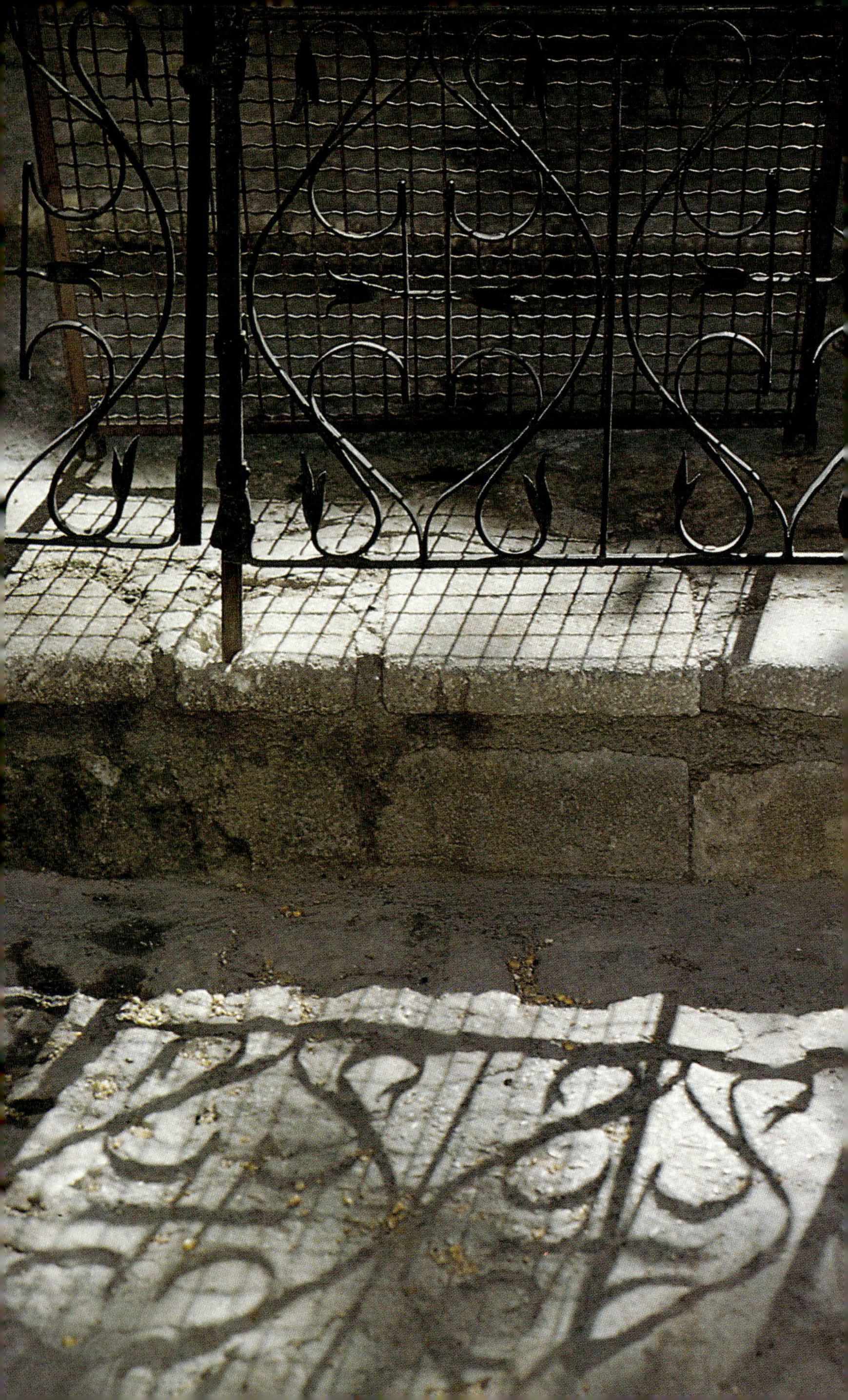

lens scale. If you have set *f*8, pressing the lever will close the lens to *f*8. The viewing screen will darken considerably, and you will see that objects in the foreground and background which were blurred become appreciably sharper. If you set *f*22, and try the stop-down preview, the sharpness will extend over a considerable range, although it is very hard to judge the effect as the screen becomes so dark.

The preview must not be used when the lens is set to "A", because it will always close the lens to minimum aperture, regardless of what setting the camera has determined to be correct. It must be released to return to full aperture before you take the picture in any automatic mode, or the exposure will be incorrect; in Metered Manual mode, any metering must be done without pressing the preview.

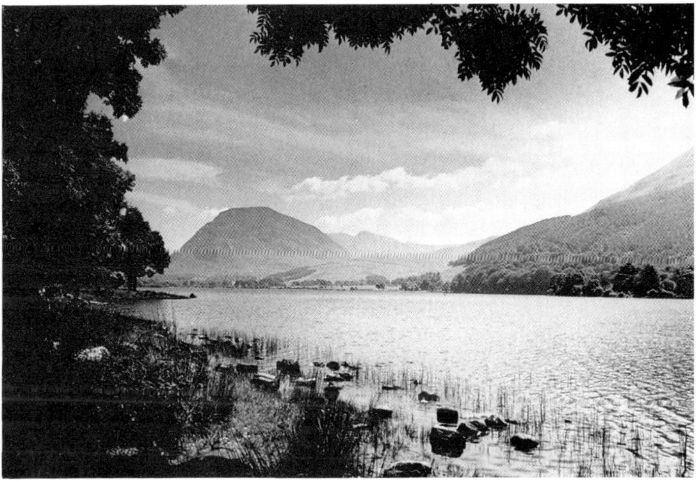

*Above: don't forget the depth of field scale just because you have a depth-of-field preview! In cases like this, it is easy to set the aperture on a 28mm lens to provide adequate sharpness from one metre to infinity. The preview is more valuable for close-ups where the quality of the focused images changes substantially according to distance.*

*Left: using the stop-down preview to fine-tune the aperture can give a wrong impression of the result with a subject like this. Because the screen darkens, the feeling of light and brightness is lost. It is important to study your subject directly, by eye, as well as through the viewfinder. Shadows in Les Baux, France, by David Kilpatrick.*

There are two controls on the opposite side of the lens mount. The upper one is a button marked "M L". This stands for Memory Lock, and when pressed it will hold the current exposure setting. M L is used when conditions call for a selective exposure reading, such as aiming the camera down to cut out a very bright sky. You aim at your "metering target" (an average area of scene, without any strong dark or light tones and lit in the same general way as the important parts of the scene to be photographed), press the shutter release lightly to take a reading, then press the M L button with one finger of your left hand. This is a one-touch button – there is NO NEED TO HOLD IT IN.

A time delay retains this memorized setting for about 10 seconds, even if you have taken your finger off the shutter release entirely. If you return your finger to the shutter release and take first pressure once again, the memory will not be interrupted, but remains fixed for as long as you keep your finger lightly on the shutter release. This enables you to lock an exposure and wait for an event such as a passing car in a motor-sport event. Each time you remove your finger from the shutter, the Memory Lock allows you ten seconds to resume. If you leave the shutter for more than 10 seconds, you lose the memorized setting, and must take another reading.

M L is cancelled when you shoot, even if you keep your finger on the release during winding-on. The exposure returns to a direct reading. If you want to shoot sequences with a selective or adjusted exposure, M L is not a good solution; you are better off switching to Metered Manual mode.

Below the M L button is a small threaded socket. This accepts a standard taper-threaded Compur-type cable release. A cable release is a flexible cord with a mechanical shutter release action – an inner cable runs in the outer sheath, and a plunger at the end lets you release the shutter without touching the camera. The flexibility of the cable means that no vibration is transmitted. The cable release is used when the camera is on a tripod. You can also fit a pistol-grip (of independent make) which has a trigger and cable to fit this socket; some types of close-up accessory equipment also use cables to synchronize the lens and body actuation, and once again this socket is used.

Be sure to buy a Pentax cable release if you can. This socket is not precisely the same as the one in the centre of the K1000's shutter button, and needs a slightly more accurate form of cable. Some cable releases may have too long a plunger travel, and risk damage to the camera.

*Top right: the Memory Lock button and Cable Release socket are positioned on the left hand side of the lens mount (looking from above). Bottom right: the Cable Release facility is useful for a night-time shot like this – Pentax 28mm lens, tripod, 20 seconds on B, Tri-X ISO 400 film, ƒ8.*

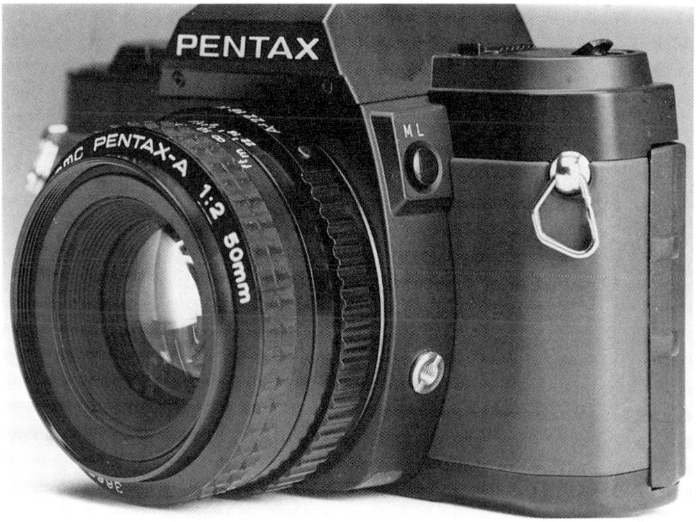
PENTAX
M L
smc PENTAX-A 1:2 50mm

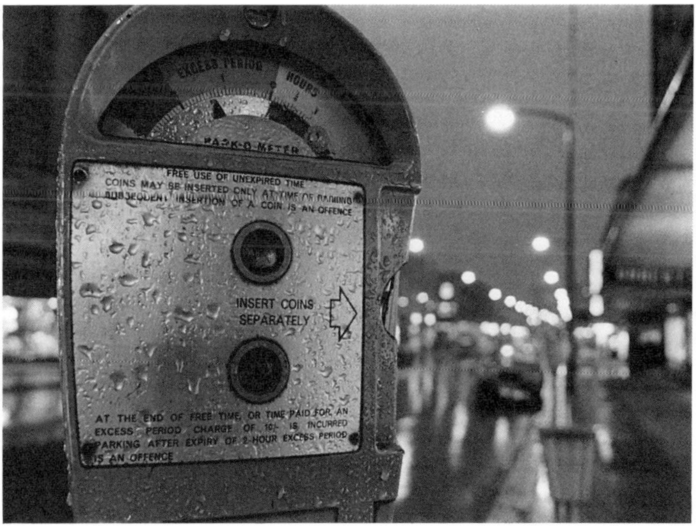
EXCESS PERIOD
HOURS
FREE USE OF UNEXPIRED TIME
COINS MAY BE INSERTED ONLY AT TIME OF
INSERTION OF A COIN IS AN OFFENCE
INSERT COINS
SEPARATELY
AT THE END OF FREE TIME, OR TIME PAID FOR, AN
EXCESS PERIOD CHARGE OF 10/- IS INCURRED
PARKING AFTER EXPIRY OF 2-HOUR EXCESS PERIOD
IS AN OFFENCE

# About Exposure Modes

## Modes with the K1000

The K1000 is a camera which has just one exposure mode. It is manual, which means that both the shutter and aperture must be set by the user. Although the camera has a built-in exposure meter coupled to the two controls, it cannot set either of them on its own. The photographer must turn the shutter dial or the aperture ring to centre the needle.

Using the K1000 is straightforward. As the meter is always switched on when the lens-cap is removed, you need only check the position of the needle to see if the exposure needs adjustment. In general terms, users of colour negative or black and white film will find it safer to let the needle ride a little high; colour slide users can afford to let it drop slightly to the low side.

If the needle is outside the cut-out, it should be re-centered by adjusting either the shutter speed or aperture – or both.

## Shutter priority

You can use the K1000 in shutter priority mode by setting the shutter speed you require, and leaving this fixed. This is your decision, not a function of the camera. You give the shutter speed priority when you determine the settings.

At a sports event, for example, you may decide that 1/500 of a second is necessary to stop action. All your pictures will need to be at 1/500. So you set 500 on the shutter dial, and for every change of exposure you adjust the lens aperture ring and never touch the shutter dial again. Only if the light falls so low that the full aperture of the lens leaves the needle UNDER the gap should you then switch to 1/250, and then 1/125, and so on down. The likelihood of light being so bright that you are forced to use 1/1000 is remote.

This is the normal way to use the K1000. You would usually set 1/125 or 1/250 on a bright day, dropping to 1/60 on a dull overcast day, though it would be better to use a faster film (ISO 400) and keep to 1/125 if possible. The lens aperture will vary between *f*5.6 (subjects in open shade under trees or in the shadow of buildings) and *f*16 (bright open landscape such as a beach scene). It is much easier to adjust the lens aperture, because it falls to your left hand and can be done before or after focusing – the controls are adjacent. Your right hand in the meantime will be poised over the shutter release. Changing the shutter speed is less convenient and not easily done at eye-level.

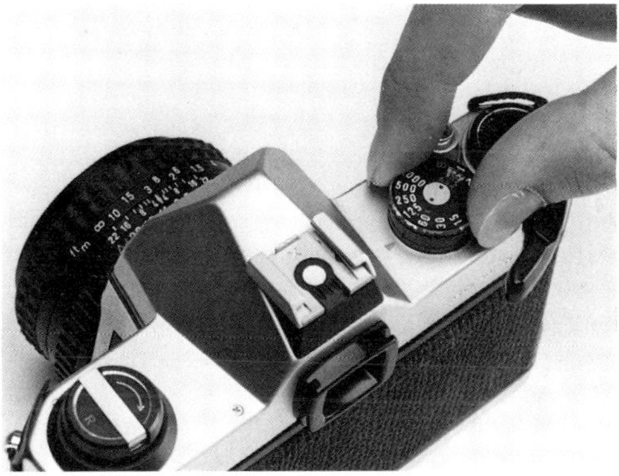

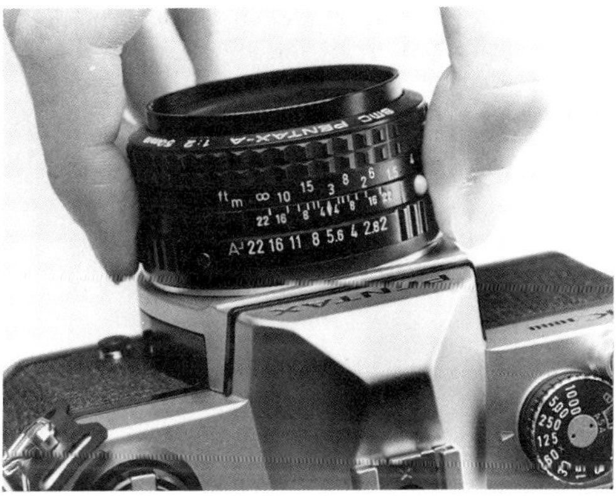

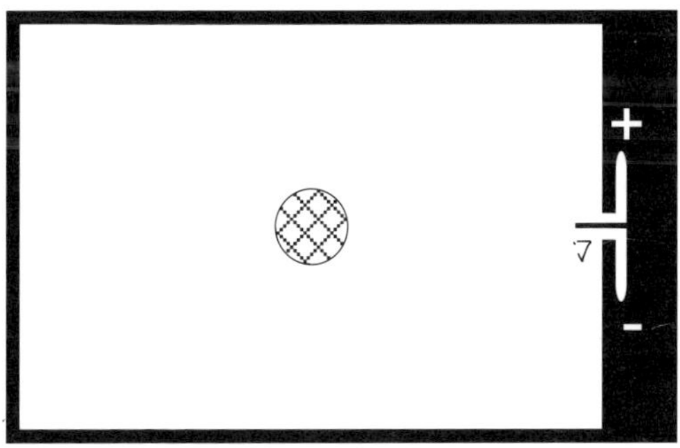

*Using the K1000 for shuttor priority manual metering: first, set your chosen shutter speed.*

*Then examine the viewfinder metering display to see the position of the needle. Adjust the aperture ring on the lens (centre) until the needle is more or less exactly centered (bottom).*

## Aperture priority

The opposite way of working involves setting the lens to an aperture like *f*8, and then changing the shutter speed to center the needle. There are very few conditions where this method is necessary. They include tripod shots of building interiors or landscapes where a small *f*-stop such as *f*16 or *f*22 is required to ensure sharpness in depth, and portraits where a particular aperture such as *f*8 gives the right degree of out-of-focus blur to the background with the chosen lens.

The disadvantages of working with "aperture priority" include the full steps involved in changing the shutter speed. The aperture can be set to half-stops, allowing you to centre the needle perfectly most times. The shutter can only be set in full steps, so you may then need to fine-tune by changing the aperture by half a stop, which is self-defeating.

We will encounter Aperture Priority again with the P30n, and you will see why it works very much better on an automatic camera. In fact, the P30n does not have shutter priority, despite the apparent advantages this method possesses.

## Exposure stability

Every time you re-compose a picture with the K1000, the needle's position will vary. If you look through the viewfinder, and pan the camera across a scene, you will see the needle move slightly up and down as different objects come into view. Does this mean you have to keep making fine adjustments to the controls? No!

The exposure meter will register changes such as a man in a dark suit walking across your picture. Clearly, there is no need to adjust for such minor variations. You do not have to change the exposure for every shot if the light stays constant, and you are shooting in the same general direction.

Take a reading from a typical scene; try to have around 1/3rd sky at the top of the picture, some grass, some concrete or stone, and maybe something like your camera bag in the foreground to add variety. Take this reading with the lens focused on infinity or around 15 feet/4m. Set the reading, and keep using this on all your shots until the light changes.

Here's when to meter again:

**If the light changes** – sun behind a cloud, or subject in shadow

**If you change camera-to-sun angle** – shooting into the light

**If the time of day changes** from within two hours of sunset or sunrise to the mid-day period. Readings taken in the late morning, mid-day and afternoon should be stable. Readings taken within the two-hour period from sunrise or before sunset should be re-taken every few minutes, as the light changes very rapidly.

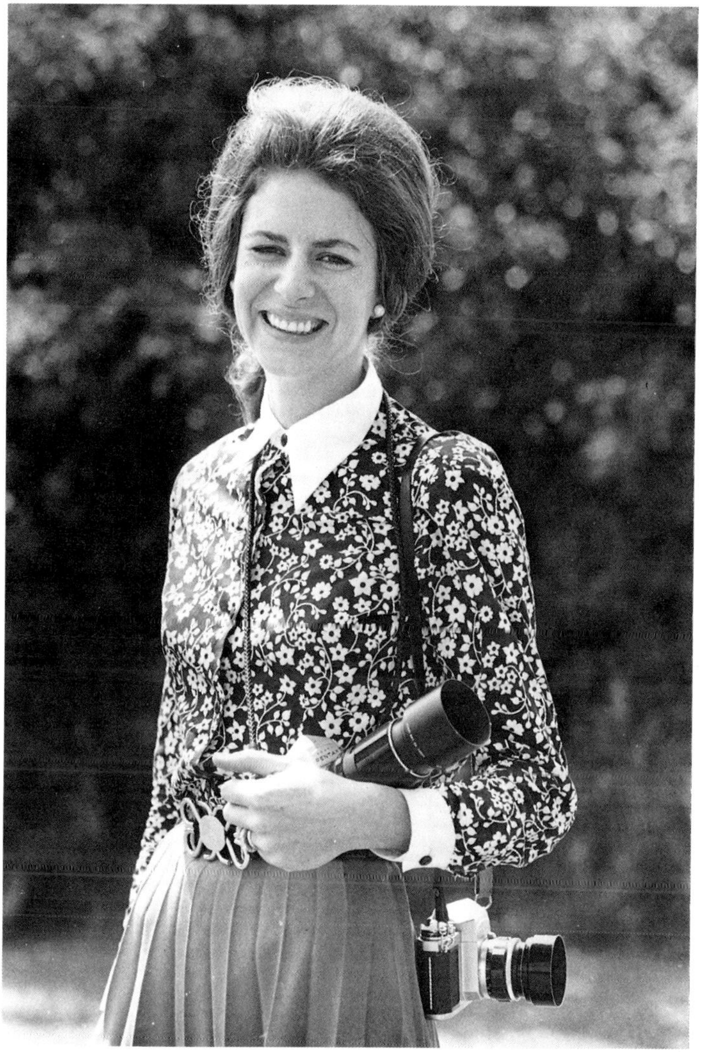

*Aperture priority exposure is ideal when the depth of field matters. This precise effect – the pattern created by the out-of-focus image – could only be achieved at f11 with a 105mm Pentax lens. A portrait of the Countess of Scarbrough, a professional photographer and Pentax user herself, by David Kilpatrick.*

**If you change from an open location** (fields, beach) to an enclosed location (street, woodland).

**If you move from outdoors to indoors**.

**If you change from taking distant views** to taking close-ups at arm's length (there is no change for close-ups at 3-5 feet).

**If you change from one film speed to another**.

There are some simple rules for outdoor exposure. In summer, with clear skies and bright sun, the exposure is *f*16 when the shutter speed is the same as the film speed. If you use Kodak Ektar 125 film, set 125 on the shutter dial, and the meter should read *f*16 from a front-lit open landscape in sunshine. Look at the leaflet or inside of the film box, and you will find a guide printed. Winter or hazy sun calls for *f*11; sun through clouds (bright overcast) for *f*8; overcast light for *f*5.6; stormy or heavy clouds for *f*4.

To this you can add "open up one stop for subjects under open shade", "open up two stops for subjects in heavy shade", "open up one stop for close-ups at 3ft/1m or less", and "open up one stop within 2 hours of sunrise/sunset". You will find that most of the time, your meter will confirm these rule-of-thumb calculations.

Sometimes, you need to take a reading for every shot. In side buildings, in shopping malls, in forest or woodlands, out in the street – these conditions can vary so much that is not safe to assume that the light has stayed the same, even if it looks this way to your eye.

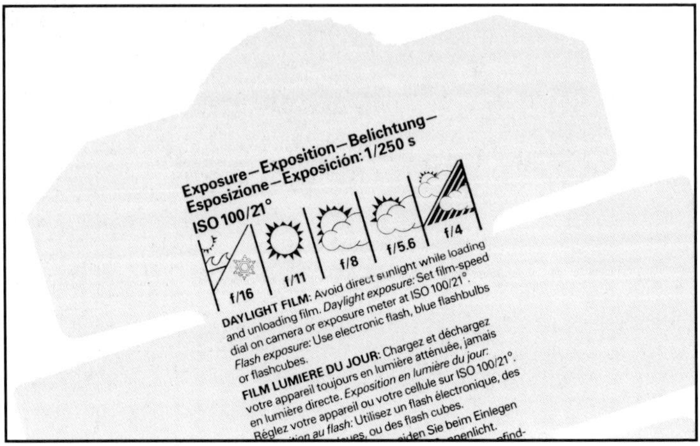


*These instructions may seem basic, but the film manufacturers use data proven over a long period. If your camera disagrees strongly with the recommendations on film leaflets, have it checked!*

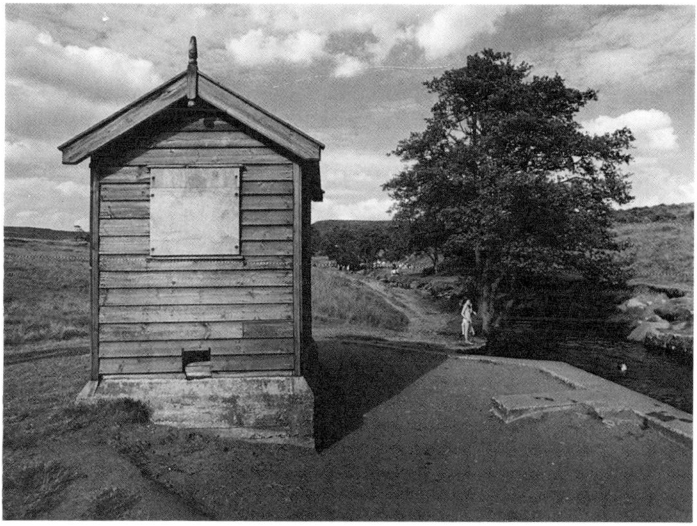

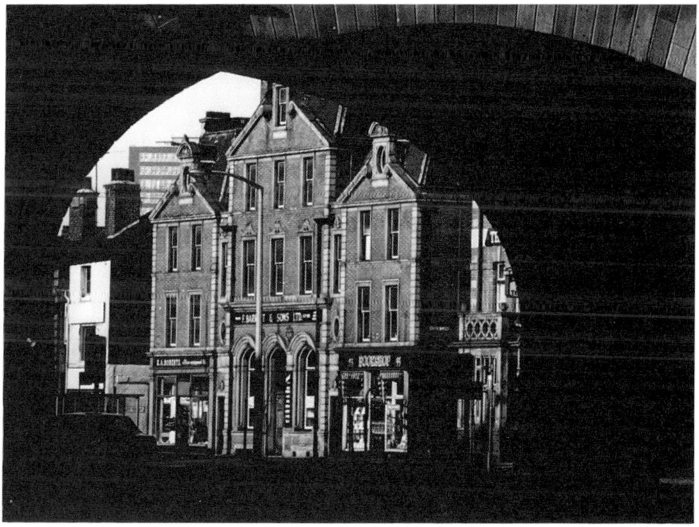


*Top: an open scene lit from behind the photographer should require 1/125 at ƒ16 in summer with ISO 100 film. Bottom: a street scene needs accurate metering, and rules of thumb don't work reliably.*

## Exposure modes with the P30n/P3n

The P30n offers both manual metering methods. Manual metering is selected when neither the camera nor the lens is set to "A"; a red "M" appears at the top of the viewfinder LED display. To use shutter priority manual metering, just set the shutter speed as required. You will see that the actual shutter speed set is displayed as a constantly illuminated figure on the left-hand edge of the viewfinder. Remember – with the P30n, the display always shows the speed set on the shutter dial as an unflickering, constantly-lit number.

Elsewhere on the scale, you will see a different shutter speed flashing rapidly. This indicates the shutter speed which WOULD be necessary at the aperture which is currently set. The difference between the constant setting and the flashing setting also shows the degree of exposure error which will result if you take the picture without further adjustment. If the flashing number is two speeds above the constant number, the picture would be two stops overexposed; if the flashing speed is one speed below the constant speed, the shot would be one stop underexposed.

To set correct exposure, adjust the aperture ring until the flashing speed coincides with the constant speed. You will see the flashing setting move up or down the scale as you turn the ring. When the two coincide, only a constantly-lit speed remains displayed.

You can tell when the P30n is giving a proper exposure at ANY time, regardless of the mode being used, by the display of a single, constantly-lit shutter speed.

Aperture priority manual metering on the P30n is undertaken in exactly the same way, but this time you leave the flashing setting unchanged, and turn the shutter dial so that the constantly-lit setting moves until it coincides.

## Slow speed warning

The P30n has one big advantage over the K1000 in metered manual mode. When you first pick up the camera, both the shutter speed set and the speed which would be required by the aperture currently set are displayed. You might have 1/250 set on the shutter dial, and *f*22 set on the aperture ring. If you go out on a dull day, the flashing speed may well be something like 15, 8 or 4 – all of these are speeds too slow to hand-hold. They are shown in the P30n viewfinder as ORANGE figures.

All the speeds between 1/30 and 1 second are orange, as it is not safe to hand-hold the camera with a standard 50mm lens at any of these settings. The speeds from 1/60 to 1/1000 are shown in green, to indicate that no tripod is needed.

You can easily see from the display how much you may need to alter

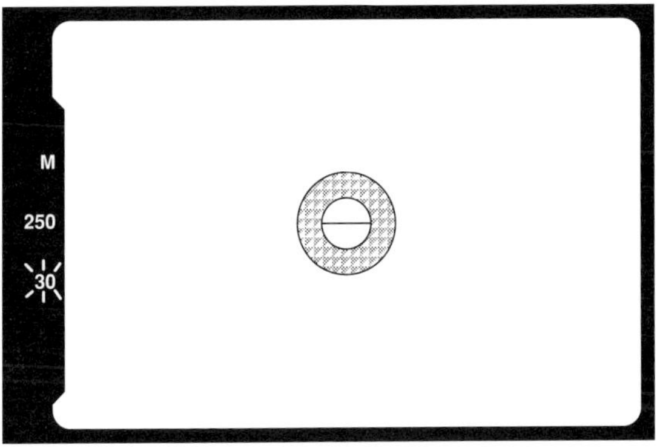


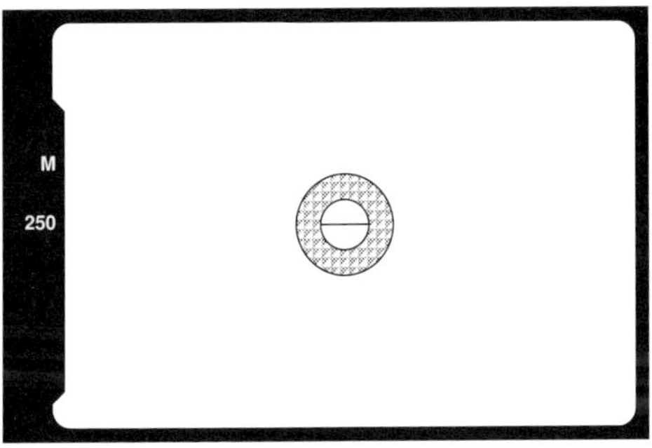


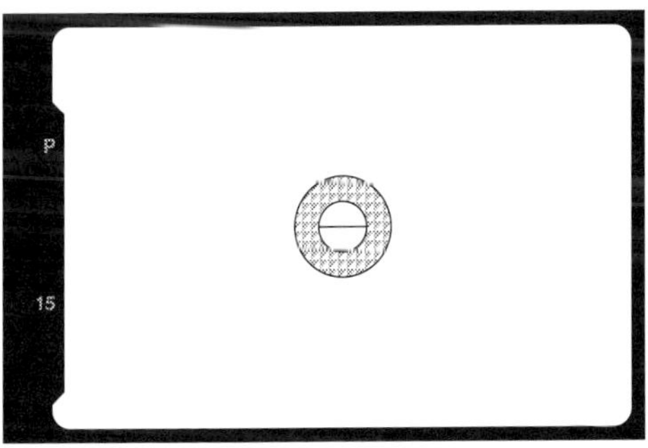


*Top: the display of the P30n for metered manual exposure – the "M" is illuminated at the top, with one shutter speed (1/250 in this case) constantly lit, and a second (1/30) flashing.*

*Centre: by adjusting the aperture ring, the flashing speed is moved up the scale until only one speed, 1/250, remains lit.*

*Bottom: the speeds from 1 to 30 are marked in orange to warn of the risk of camera shake in low light.*

**Note:** on the P30T screen the split-image indicator is diagonal, not horizontal.

your set shutter speed. If the flashing speed is near 1 second, change to 1/60. If it is already in the green range, you can usually select a fast shutter speed. Aim to have the final constant shutter speed (correct exposure) in the green range, never in the orange range. Only when you use a tripod with a static subject should you use a speed in the orange range.

## Aperture priority auto

The P30n can take auto exposure pictures with any Pentax lens using Aperture Priority Auto. To do this, you set the aperture on the lens as desired (say *f*8) and switch the shutter dial to A. The viewfinder display now shows just a shutter speed, constantly lit, and no other information.

To adjust the speed, just change the *f*-stop on the lens. You will see the shutter speed alter through the viewfinder, and as long as you are aware of where you started on the lens, you will know the overall combination in use. If you start at *f*8, and find the speed displayed is 30, then you will know that by twisting the aperture ring to *f*5.6 you will produce a speed of 1/60, which is better for hand-held shooting.

Why does aperture priority work well on the P30n, if it is not the best way to set the K1000?

There are two reasons – the control you set is the aperture ring, just in the same way that you adjust the aperture when using shutter-speed priority methods with the K1000. Only with the P30n, adjusting the aperture ring actually sets the shutter speed, because the camera itself ensures that the "needle is centered" (metaphorically speaking) all the time. You are no longer adjusting to get correct exposure, you are simply adjusting to get the settings you require.

The second reason is that the shutter on the P30n is stepless. Although the dial is marked in the normal steps, when the shutter is under the control of auto exposure it can be set by the camera to any intermediate speed. It is no longer restricted to 1/125 and 1/250, but can fire at 1/150, 1/175, 1/210 or any other exact time duration. If you use aperture priority by leaving the lens set to *f*8 (for example) and letting the shutter display wander up and down between 1/125 and 1/500, you will get even more accurate exposure than the half-stop steps on the lens can provide.

The P30n displays intermediate speeds by flashing between two adjacent speeds. Do not confuse this with the single flashing speed of metered manual displays.

A little earlier on, we asked the question – is it necessary to keep making fine adjustments? The answer on the K1000 was no, and it is also no with the P30n on metered manual. On Aperture Priority auto, the camera will make these fine adjustments whether you want it to or not. There is no harm in this, but be warned! If a very large object appears

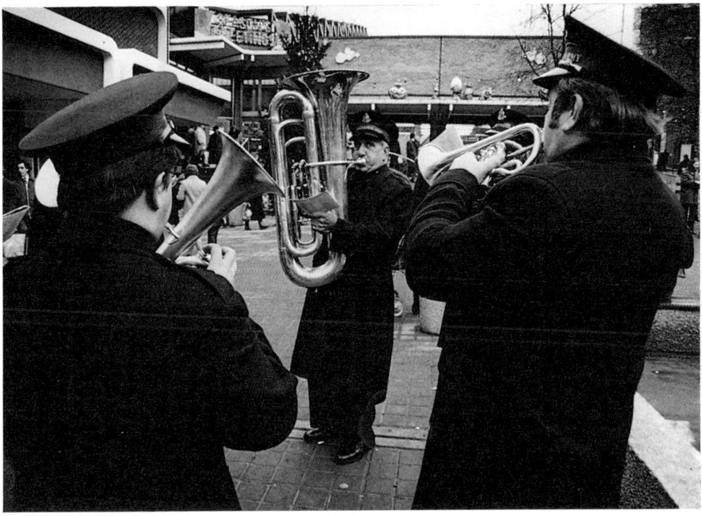

*An ideal subject for Aperture Priority auto – 24mm lens set to f11 for extra depth of field, and pre-focused to 8 feet for candid shots.*

in the viewfinder and dominates it with one shade, the exposure may change in a way which you do not want or need.

A good example would be this:

You are photographing a flotilla of sailing boats in sunshine, on a blue sea with a blue sky, and the boats are fairly distant. They are on the horizon, spread across the frame, sailing towards you. Exposure condition: 1/250 at *f*11, aperture priority. Exposure will be correct.

As the boats come closer, you zoom in and change the composition, so that a single yacht fills the frame. The yacht turns and its sail billows out, leaving the picture consisting mainly of white sail. Exposure condition: 1/750 at *f*11, aperture priority. Exposure will now be incorrect, over-influenced by the white sail, resulting in too dark a background of sky and sea, and a dirty-grey appearance to the sail.

This is an extreme example, but common enough. In another case, you might be tracking a rally-car by panning the camera as it comes down a track. The car passes from open fields as a background to a part of the track with dark pine trees immediately behind it. The shutter speed on Aperture Priority drops from 1/250 to 1/60 as you follow the car past these trees, although the car has remained evenly and equally lit by sunshine all the time. The result will be an over-exposed shot with a lack of detail in the car, and too much detail in the pines which should be a solid dark colour.

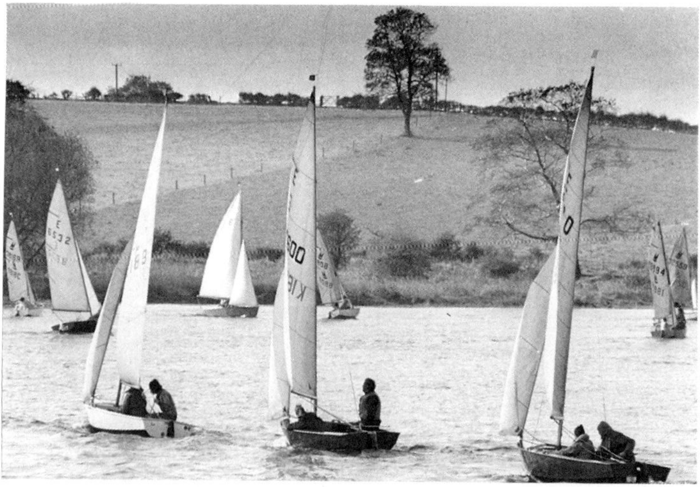

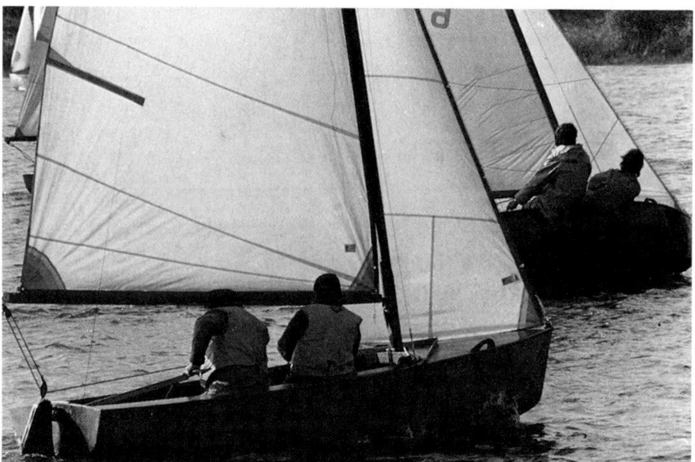

*Top: the general view is correctly exposed using Auto. Bottom: when a single boat and sail fills the frame, the exposure is reduced and the result is too dark. Photographs by Shirley Kilpatrick.*

*Right: Memory Lock or manual correction is necessary when your subject passes in front of a dark background with backlighting.*

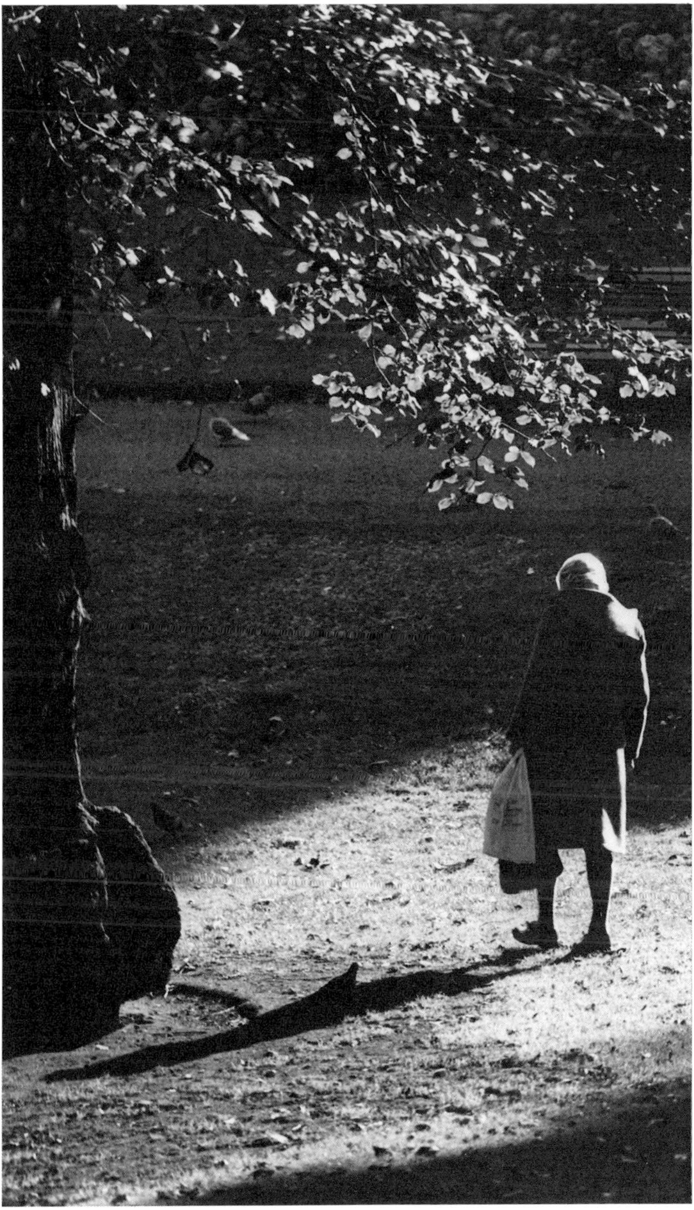

## Memory Lock or manual?

Before moving on to the final natural-light mode of the P30n, Programmed Auto Exposure, let's look at the solution to the problems above. The first solution is Memory Lock. When you are metering from a typical average part of the scene, lightly press the M L button. As long as you keep your finger on the shutter release, and do not take it off the release for more than 10 seconds at a time, the original exposure will be held as you follow the subject. The selected shutter speed will flash rapidly during the period of M L hold. However, once you fire the memory is lost, so a sequence of rapidly-wound pictures is hard to take this way.

Changing to Metered Manual is the solution. Set your exposure according to a typical part of the scene. Then, when a large white object or a heavy dark background happens to dominate a later shot, it will not have an adverse influence.

## Zooms & Metered Manual: P30n/P3n & K1000

There is one thing to watch closely when using manual metering on either the K1000 or P30n. Many Pentax zooms have a variable aperture – the popular 28-80mm, for example, is an *f*3.5-4.5 zoom. When set to 28mm, the maximum aperture is *f*3.5, and the minimum is *f*22, as marked. If you zoom to 80mm, however, the lens now has an *f*4.5 maximum aperture with an *f*32 minimum. Every single *f*-stop on the scale is reduced by one stop – if you set *f*8 at 80mm, you actually get *f*11.

There is no compensation built-in to the A-mount lens when used manually. This is easily checked by studying the display and zooming, when aiming at an even area of plain white (such as neutral wallpaper). The camera will compensate, of course, as the light entering is reduced. On auto exposure, zooming from 28mm to 80mm will change the automatically set shutter speed from 1/250 to 1/125 without any intervention from the user.

Using manual, to overcome the problems of "subject failure" which can occur in instances such as the sailing yachts and motor rally examples above, you may forget that zooming will alter the exposure. It is vital that you re-meter after zooming, or simply don't zoom when using a fixed manual exposure.

**Exactly the same applies to Memory Lock – if you lock the exposure, but then zoom, you may be locking in a wrong exposure.**

Not all zooms are like this. Many, especially telephoto zooms, have a fixed aperture which does not change. Some have a mechanism which ensures that only the maximum aperture is affected by zooming, so that if you set *f*8 it does not matter whether you are on 70mm or 210mm – but such lenses would fail to operate correctly with the Pentax metering

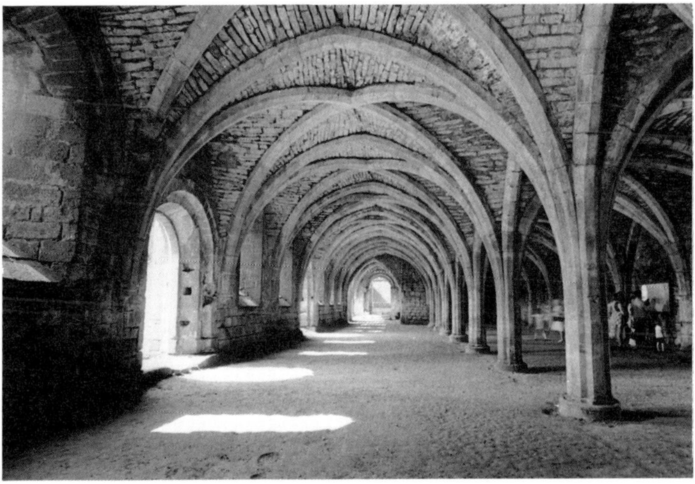

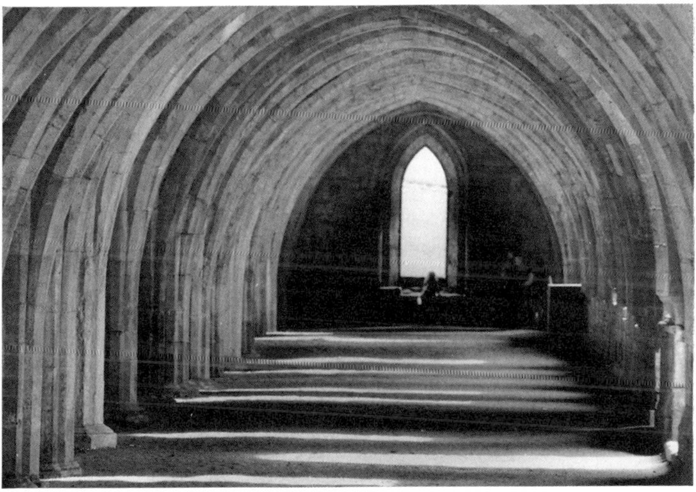

*Here are two pictures which demonstrate aspects of focusing, metering and lens choice. The top picture is taken with a 20mm lens on aperture priority automatic – the areas of bright light are too small to influence the exposure, and the depth of field is enough to give sharpness all the way at ƒ8. The bottom picture was taken with a 200mm, and needed one stop extra exposure; the far end of the undercroft is out of focus at ƒ8.*

system. Pentax lenses which have variable maximum apertures therefore have ALL their apertures variable, in proportion, all the way down the scale. The safe solution if you have any doubts is to use auto exposure or take a fresh meter reading.

## Programmed Auto Exposure with the P30n/P3n

The final natural-light mode on the P30n is **Programmed**. This is set by adjusting the lens aperture ring to "A" (press the small red button in to reach this position). If you own a K1000 or other manual camera as well, remember that the lens must be taken off "A" when transferred to your manual camera body! If you forget to do this, all your pictures on the manual-exposure body will be taken at the minimum aperture of the lens, and will almost certainly be under-exposed.

Setting "A" on the lens totally over-rides the shutter dial. *You do not have to set "A" on the camera as well.* It does not matter which shutter speed you are set to. The camera takes over, setting both the shutter speed and lens aperture itself according to a simple program.

This program changes the shutter speed only at low light-levels, working at the maximum aperture of the lens. With a fast lens, it will do this for speeds of 1/30 or longer – with most zooms, however, the program tries to keep the shutter speed faster than 1/125 unless the light is very low. If it uses a speed of 1/60 or 1/30 with a lens like the 28-80mm fitted, you can be sure that the lens is also working at full aperture. It is only after the camera finds itself able to set 1/125 that the lens even begins to close down to smaller apertures like *f*5.6 or *f*8.

In bright light, the camera will select increasingly fast shutter speeds, so that by the time the lens is closed down to *f*8 the shutter is guaranteed to be operating at 1/500, and all further adjustments are made by fine-tuning the shutter speed between 1/500 and 1/1000, and altering the aperture between *f*8 and *f*22.

This program ALWAYS favours freedom from camera shake, and action-stopping shutter speeds whenever the light permits. It is intended as a snapshot program eliminating most common faults in photographs. The program is able to adjust the exposure in half-stop steps, by changing both the shutter speed and the aperture by as little as a quarter-stop each. You only see the shutter speed in the readout in the viewfinder.

Programmed AE is ideal for outdoor photography in bright conditions with ISO 100 film. It is not so good for low-light tripod work, where you might prefer to use a smaller aperture and longer exposure; the program will always set full aperture, which is not the best in terms of performance.

Memory Lock functions on Programmed AE just as with Aperture Priority AE, but if you are using Programmed mode you're probably taking snapshots and will not have the time to consider exposure.

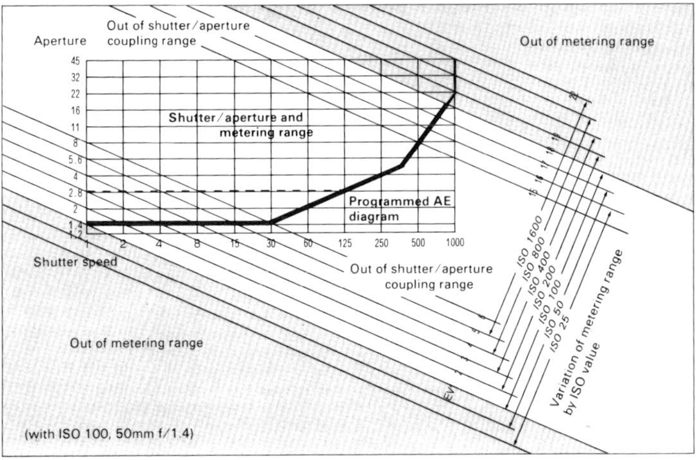


*Above: the program of the P30n when used on Programmed AE exposure. The grey areas indicate zones beyond the camera's metering range. The dotted line shows how the exposure is ajdusted when using a lens with a maximum aperture of ƒ2.8.*

*Below: a typical programmed exposure subject.*

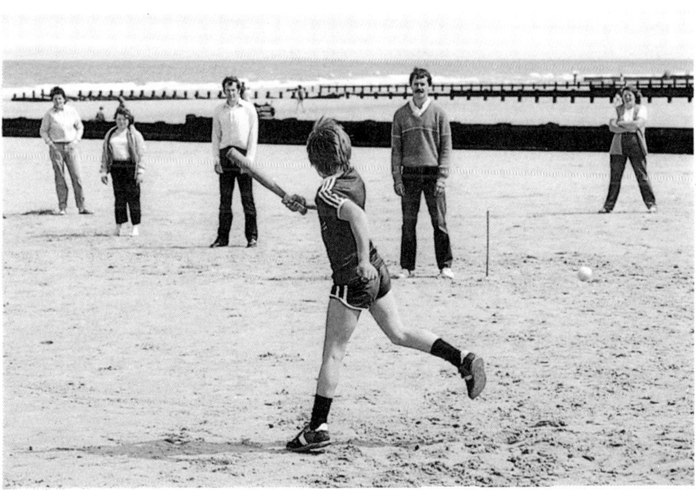

## Programmed Flash

The final mode on the P30n is Programmed Auto Flash. We will look at flash technique in the next chapter, as the K1000 is purely manual. The P30n hot shoe has two additional contacts – these are used to set the shutter speed and aperture, and to display flash-ready and exposure-check confirmation in the viewfinder.

Using a fully Pentax-dedicated flashgun such as the AF200T, AF280T or AF400T, all the functions are available. With other Pentax flashguns such as the AF200SA, AF240Z and AF160SA no variable aperture setting or flash exposure confirmation is given.

Once the flash is fitted and turned on, you can select an Auto Aperture setting on the flashgun itself – for example, a choice of *f*4, *f*8 or *f*11 at ISO 100 with the large AF400T flash unit. This is transferred electronically to the camera and set on the lens, as long as you have the lens on "A". If you load a faster or slower film, correspondingly smaller or larger apertures will be set.

As soon as the flash is ready to fire, a flash symbol will appear and glow at the top of the LED viewfinder display. This also shows that the shutter speed has been automatically set at 1/100. After you fire, the flash symbol disappears. With simpler Pentax flashguns, this is all that happens. With the T-series guns mentioned above, the flash symbol will briefly light up again to indicate that exposure has been verified as correct by the flashgun's own circuits, and then extinguish until the flash is ready to fire again a second or two later.

Unlike Programmed AE Flash in autofocus cameras, where the aperture is varied according to the distance set by the camera, the P30n requires the user to set the flash itself according to the general distance range. Thus you would set the AF400T to Red (*f*4 at ISO 100) for very large groups or outdoor shots at night, to Green (*f*8) for pictures of 2-3 people in a domestic interior, and to Yellow (*f*11) for close-ups of flowers, full-face portraits with a 50mm standard lens, and so on.

*A correctly-exposed shot using manual metering and a telephoto, with a high shutter speed (1/500) to ensure that camera shake is eliminated and the movement of the sail in the wind is frozen. Taken on Kodak Ektachrome 50HC film, a slow slide film, at f5.6, 300mm lens.*

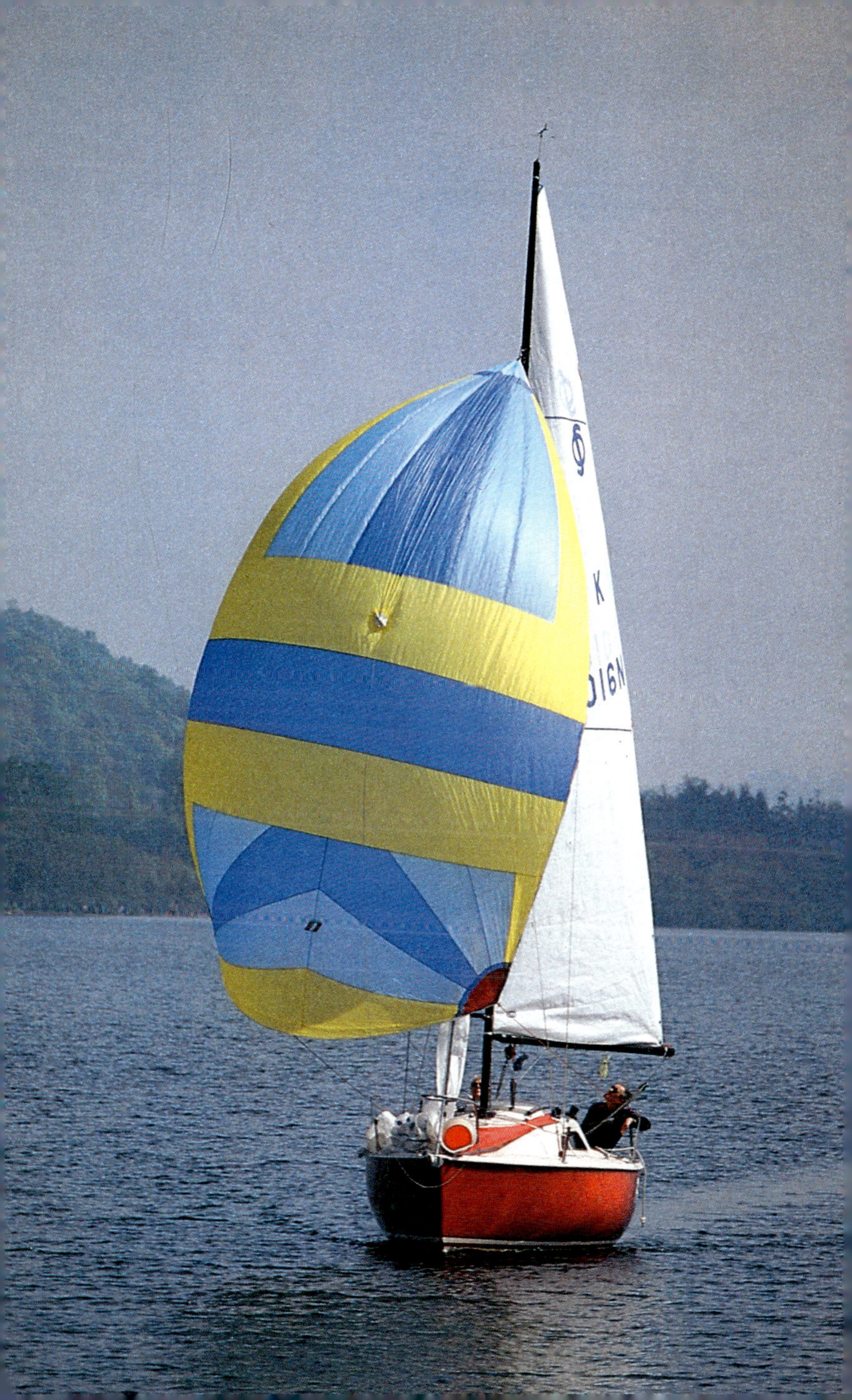

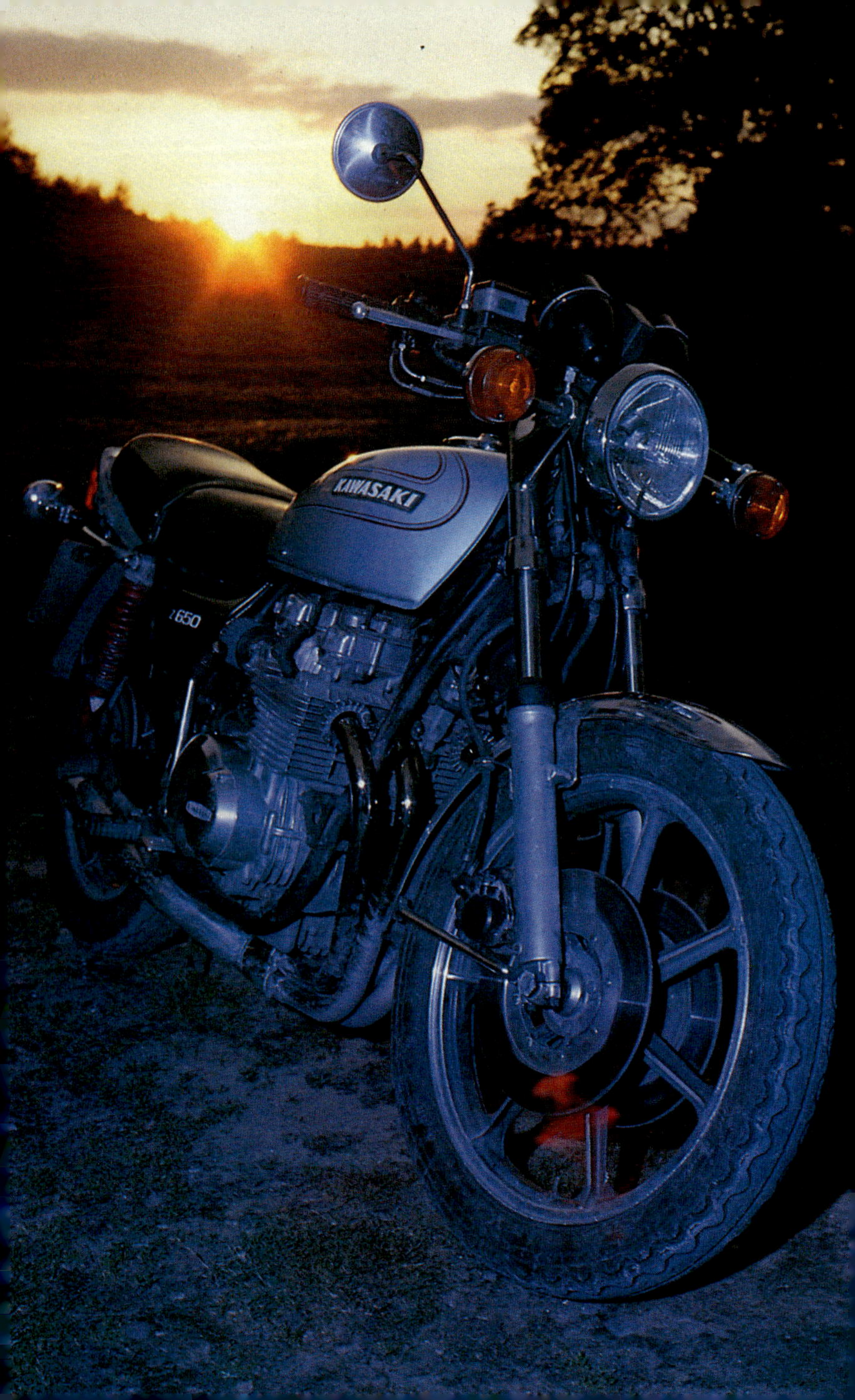
KAWASAKI
Z650

# Flash Photography

When the light falls below the level for hand-holding a camera or stopping the movement of your subjects, flash is the easy answer. It is not always the best answer, because the quality of light from flash leaves a great deal to be desired.

Flash has distinct advantages. Used on the camera, it is bound to illuminate the subject evenly as long as you do not use a lens with an angle view greater than the angle of illumination of the flash. Many of the smaller flashguns available, including Pentax models, cover the field of view of a 35mm lens; if you own a lens such as the 28-80mm zoom, be certain that you buy a flashgun intended to cover a 28mm wide-angle.

On the other hand, the direct illumination given by flash produces very little sense of depth. We normally judge the shape and size of everything in a picture by the way the light wraps round it, forming shadows and revealing texture. Flash hits the subject directly, leaving little apart from a thin shadow outlining some parts of the picture. At the worst, this shadow seems to be an extension of the person or object being photographed – as when you take a flash picture of someone with dark hair against a white background.

Flash reduces overall contrast as long as all the subject is at the same distance from the camera. If you double the flash distance, you end up with one-quarter of the illumination; in accordance with the Inverse Square Law, it's pretty easy to understand. At double the distance the flash is spread over four times the area. So if you need *f*11 at five feet distance, you will have to use *f*5.6 at 10 feet.

So what happens if your subject is five feet away, and the wall of the room is ten feet away, forming the background? Easy again – the wall ends up underexposed by two *f*-stops. So although flash has very low contrast in a single plane, a group of people at different distances – such as a shot taken down the length of a table at a banquet – may include foreground faces which are white and bleached out, and background faces which are dark and browner or redder than you might like.

The solution to getting good direct flash shots is to avoid very large rooms, because if you use flash in a small room with light decoration, much of the light is bounced round off the walls and ceiling. This lessens the severity of the fall off in illumination. Next, make sure you arrange people at a roughly equal distance from the camera, so that the flash lights them all equally. Bring them well away from any distracting background, and you will be rewarded by the background becoming fairly dark, and most of the detail being hidden. Don't let anyone step forward.

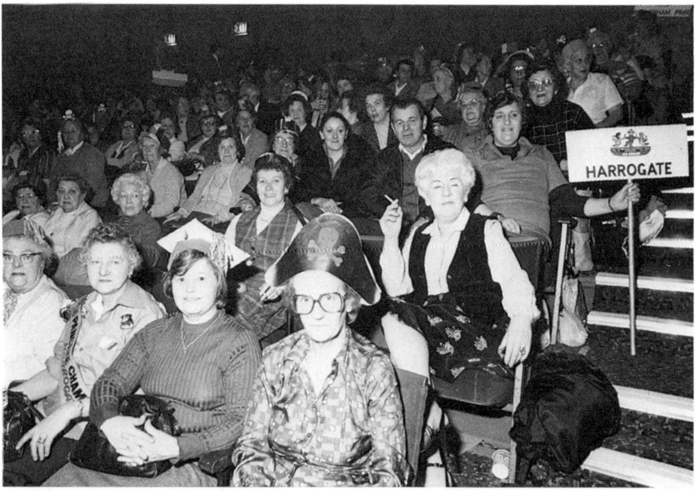


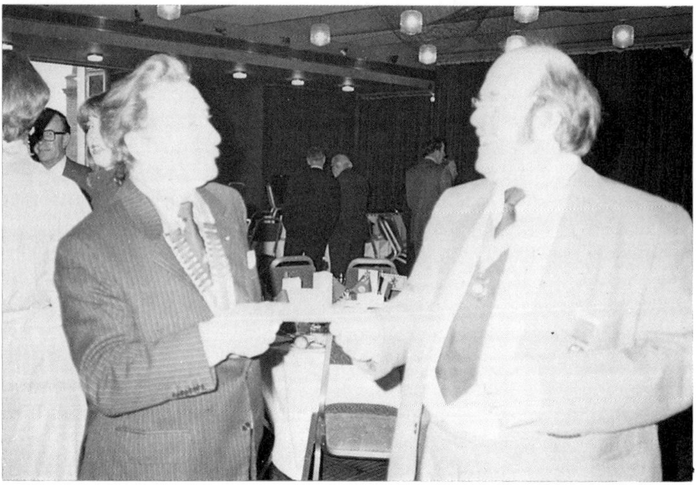

*Top: if you are photographing a group, try to keep everyone about the same distance from the camera to ensure even lighting. A picture with this kind of depth will never have even illumination, and distant faces will be darker than close ones. Bottom: watch out for a gap between your subjects. Here the people are over-exposed because the flash took its exposure from the space in between.*

# Auto flash

Your Pentax flashgun will probably be automatic, using a sensor cell on the flashgun itself. If you obtain a purely manual gun, you must read the distance off the focusing scale, consult a chart or calculator on the back of the gun, and then set the lens aperture according to this scale. An automatic flashgun turns even the Pentax K1000 into a point-and-shoot auto exposure camera! This is because auto flashguns work using aperture priority. You set a particular aperture on the flash, and match this on the camera lens. Every picture you take will have its exposure measured by the flash, which cuts off the light as soon as enough has been received by the subject. Camera controls have no further effect.

These auto (or "computer") strobe flash guns take their exposure reading from a fairly narrow angle in the middle of the picture – around 10 to 20°. So it is very important to have all or part of your subject occupying the central area. If you photograph two people, one at each side of the picture, with a gap between them and empty space beyond, they may be very badly over-exposed because the flashgun will try to read the exposure off a distant area, seen between the people.

The auto flash has a very responsive version of an ordinary light-meter cell as part of its circuit. As soon as the flash starts to emit light the cell starts to measure the cumulative light received back from the subject. This process is so rapid that durations as short as 1/50,000 of a second can be controlled. When a fixed amount of light has been received by the sensor cell, the power to the flashtube is diverted. In basic flashguns, a second "blank" tube called a quench tube is used – all the energy is simply channelled into a flashtube which is hidden inside the gun, and blacked out. Flash units like this are inexpensive to make, but use batteries quickly, and the interval between firing each flash is always fairly long, typically 5 to 10 seconds.

Thyristor flashguns use a different kind of circuit which retains the unused charge, instead of diverting it into a quench tube. The flash is still cut off after the correct exposure has been made, but only the required energy is actually drained from the capacitors. The battery circuit can then start re-charging the flash instantly, and in most cases the flash is ready to fire again in a fraction of a second. A thyristor flashgun may yield 100 to 400 flashes (or even more) from a set of batteries; a non-thyristor flash unit will give 40-80.

For this reason, it is well worth investing in a thyristor flash unit such as the Pentax AF280T if you intend to take many flash pictures. The thyristor circuit also enables the "exposure OK" signal to be shown in the P30n viewfinder, and also on the flashgun itself. A further reason for buying a good dedicated Pentax gun of this kind is that if you buy an autofocus Pentax SLR at a later date, the flashgun will be fully functional with this as well.

## Red Eye

All flash photographs are prone to the effect known as red eye, which is self-explanatory. It is produced by the flash being reflected off the retina of the eye. The more acute the angle at the eye between the flash and the lens, the greater the likelihood of the effect occurring.

As a photographic author, I receive many letters enclosing prints about red eye. At first, I used to make suggestions to do with removing the flash from the camera on a cable, using a bounce umbrella and many other things. However, people do not want to do this – they want to take pictures with the flash on the camera. Here is my reply which I now send to anyone asking about red eye:

> There is no sure way to avoid red eye when using built-in flash; you really have to invest in a larger flashgun which can be used with bounce illumination.
>
> However, we have a number of hints which may seem frivolous at first, but are quite genuine.
>
> a) Red eye is more likely when the subject stares directly at the camera
> b) It is most likely to happen at longer focal lengths, i.e. 80mm on a 35-80mm zoom
> c) It is worse when the room lighting is dim, or at night
> d) It is worse when the subject is slightly drunk, under five, a household pet, in love with the photographer – or just very happy (enlarged pupils)
>
> As photographs of subjects who are stone cold sober, adult, in brilliant room lighting, taken with a wide-angle lens and not looking at the camera are rather rare (and suffer from more serious faults than red eye) this information may not help, but at least you may understand why red eye is hard to avoid without a bounce flash unit.

All the things in this letter are perfectly true, and more often than not they are the real causes of red eye – you would be surprised how badly red eye affects baby pictures, and shots taken at parties with the lights turned down low.

Bounce flash is indeed the solution, and this calls for a larger flash unit such as the Pentax AF400T.

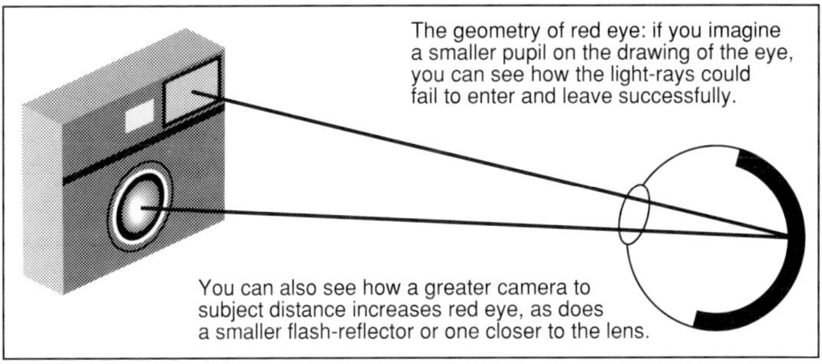


*Compact cameras are very prone to red eye because the flash is so close to the lens. Your Pentax SLR will not have as great a problem. Red eye can still occur, however – this diagram shows the geometry involved.*

## Flashgun power

At this point, we need to explain how flashguns are rated in terms of power. As a quick rule of thumb, any flashgun using only two batteries will not be powerful enough for bounce shots. Most flashguns using four AA cells (MN1500) will be adequate.

Flashguns have their power expressed as a "Guide Number". The GN is a simple factor which lets you work out the required aperture at any distance. Current Japanese strobes are normally named according to their guide number in metres at ISO 100.

A flashgun with a GN of 28 metres/ISO 100 has the lowest-power adequate for bounce, as an example which follows will show you. GN28m/ISO 100 means this:

Divide 28 by the distance in metres, flash to subject (direct flash) and you will find the *f*-number to set on your lens for correct exposure.

So, at 10 feet distance (3 metres):

$28 \div 3 = f9.3$

Nearest *f*-stops are *f*8 and *f*11

Set the half-stop between *f*8 and *f*11.

In Britain and the USA, guide numbers are often quoted in feet at ISO 100. Obviously, a GN28 flashgun (metric) is the same as a GN93 flashgun (feet). Do not be confused by this when buying a flash – always ask for the metric guide number, even if you do not often use metric measurements. All the Pentax flashguns have a model number based on their metric GN – AF200SA (GN20), AF400T (GN40) and so on. It is common to add a zero or a letter code to the model number of a flashgun, but nearly always it will indicate within the number the exact power output claimed for the gun.

# Bounce flash

The idea behind bounce flash is that you do not aim the flashgun at the subject, but at a white surface which acts as a reflector and scatters the light so that it no longer forms hard shadows. The ceiling is the most popular bounce surface, and bounce flash guns are made so that the flash-head can be angled upwards by 45°, 60°, 75° or 90° (usually with click stops at each position). With most models, the head can also be rotated, which is necessary when using the camera for a vertical (portrait) format composition. Avoid cheaper strobes which do not have this feature.

Guns which have no bounce facility can be removed from the camera and linked by an extension cord. K1000 owners need a standard PC-synch cable, which plugs into the coaxial synch socket; P30n owners need a dedicated Pentax off-camera cable set, which retains all the functions of the flash-to-camera linkage including programmed flash.

Be warned, however, that guns without any kind of bounce action on their flash-heads are NOT really suitable. Why? They are often used with autofocus SLRs, so why not with the P30n? The answer lies in the method used for controlling auto exposure. Pentax flashguns such as the AF280T are capable of controlling the exposure not only through a sensor cell on the flashgun, but also through the camera lens – when fitted to a camera with this function. Neither the P30n nor the K1000 operate in this way.

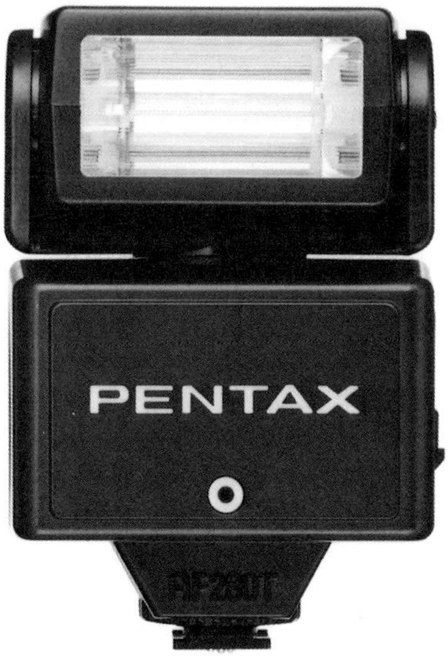


*The Pentax AF280T bounce flash gun, an ideal choice for the K1000 or P30n owner.*

If the flashgun has no bounce action on its flash-head, then aiming the flash itself at the ceiling will also aim the sensor-cell of the flash at the ceiling. The result would be perfect exposure for the ceiling, but you are photographing a group of people lit by reflected light OFF the ceiling. Using a non-bounce flash this way would result in 3-4 stops of underexposure.

The correct exposure for bounce flash off a white ceiling is determined as follows:

*Add up the distance of flash to ceiling and ceiling to subject.*

*Using the calculator dial or table on the flashgun, work out the correct aperture for this total distance (which may be twice the distance of camera to subject).*

*Set the lens to one-and-a-half stops WIDER than the f-stop you have just calculated. If the room is large, or the surroundings are dark, set the lens to two stops wider.*

Here is a specimen calculation:

Ceiling height **10ft / 3m**

Flash height **6ft / 2m** (mounted above the camera)

Group of people being photographed at eye level, **8ft / 2.5m** away.

Normal flash exposure at 8ft / 2.5m: ISO 100, AF280T flash: ***f*11**

Total flash>ceiling+ceiling>subject distance: **12ft / 3.6m**

Required *f*-stop at total distance: ***f*8**

Open lens by 1.5 stops: final exposure for bounce flash, ***f*4.5**

*This diagram shows the conditions described in the example above and is drawn to scale (in terms of the dimension lines). With direct flash, f11 would be needed – with bounce flash, f4.5.*

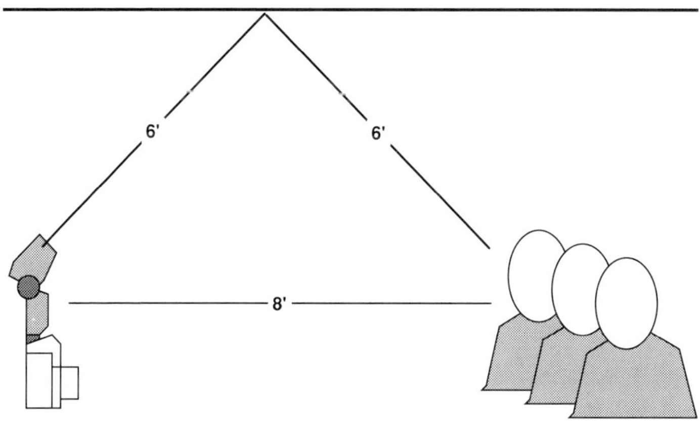

The diagram shows the actual distances involved. The difference between direct flash at *f*11 and bounce flash at *f*4.5 is considerable – in the first case, the lens is well stopped-down, with no focusing problems. Using bounce flash, the lens may well be at maximum aperture, and would be if the 28-80mm zoom was used at 80mm.

Bounce flash, though a fine solution to improving flash light quality and eliminating red eye, does call for a powerful flash and a good grasp of the light loss involved. The best solution here would be to switch to ISO 400 film, setting the lens to *f*8 and relying on auto exposure with a bounce flashgun of GN28 or higher. As you will see, it is not advisable to try to photograph anything further away than 10ft/3m in a room of normal size with ISO 400 film and a GN28 flashgun.

This demonstration will also show you why flashguns such as the AF400T have three aperture settings available – *f*4, *f*8 and *f*11 at ISO 100 in this particular case. With a medium-speed film (ISO 100) you would always select the widest aperture, *f*4, for bounce flash. With ISO 400 film, the flash automatically selects *f*8 instead of *f*4 – you still use the widest available setting.

Normally, you must keep to the widest aperture ALL the time when using bounce flash. There are rare exceptions. You can fit a bounce reflector attachment directly to the flash, which replaces the ceiling, and is much closer (about 1 foot). This does not provide such diffused illumination, but produces a complete absence of red-eye and a pleasant softened quality of light with gentle shadows falling underneath chins in the case of portraits (rather than a hard line). Larger reflectors or diffusion boxes, such as the Saunders "Soff'Shoulder" and Westcott Apollo flash diffuser systems, give very controllable results. These, however, call for the flash to be on an extension cable and often prevent the auto-sensor eye from pointing at the subject. They are aimed at the more experienced photographer who may well use a special flash exposure meter for measuring the flash from the subject position.

## Additional flashes

You can fire more than one flash from your Pentax camera. It is never a good idea to attach two strobes by using the hot shoe and X-synch socket of the K1000 simultaneously – the voltage and polarity of the strobes may be different, and serious damage could occur to one or both. At the worst, the synch contacts in the camera could be damaged.

So-called "peanut" adaptors, which branch off flash cables to add extra guns, are little better. You can add one or two extra Pentax flashguns to the P30n using Pentax dedicated extension cables and multi-way adaptors, but the best way to fire additional flashes with the K1000 is by slave units.

These are small light-sensor cells which attach to remote flashguns,

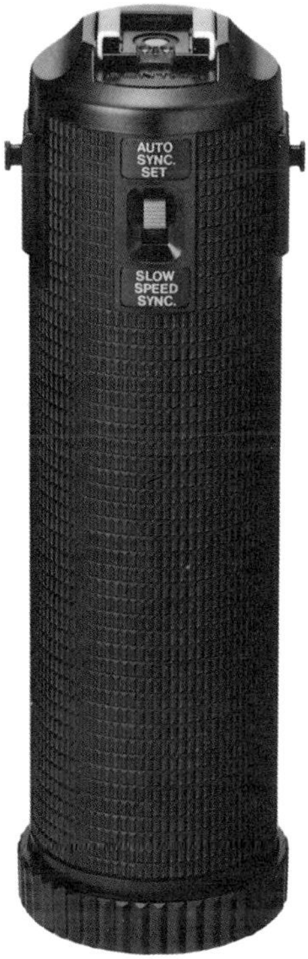


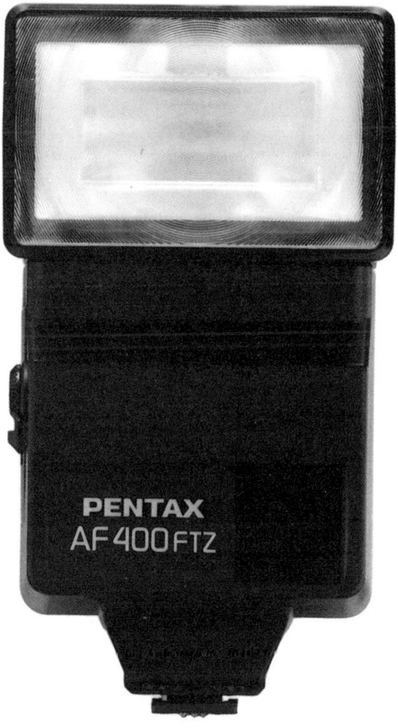


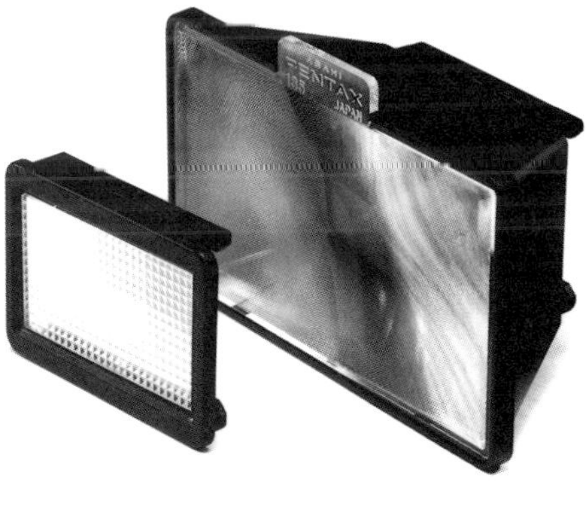

*Components in the Pentax flash system: the AF400FTZ flashgun, Hot Shoe Grip, AFW1 (wide) and AFT1 (tele) lens attachments to change the flash angle of coverage, and the 4P Synchro Cord B extension cable.*

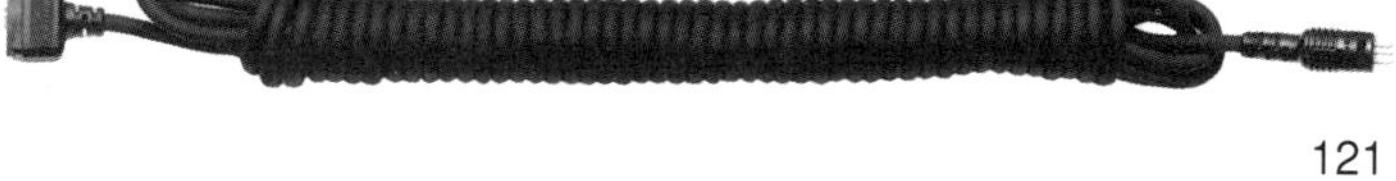

and trigger them the instant your main camera flash fires. You can use bounce flash on the camera, for general soft illumination, and add slave cell flashes for backlighting, coloured effects, a hairlight hidden behind a portrait sitter's head, a background light to iron out wrinkles in a paper seamless backdrop, or a texture light to skim across the surface of a subject with plenty of fine detail relief.

When used in combination, auto flashguns do not reliably take into account each other's contribution to the total exposure. Each flash will attempt to provide the full exposure. Backlights and hairlights do not count when adjusting exposure, but a textured "skim light" may add extra light. You might close the lens down by half a stop to compensate. This is very much a matter of experience – you should read a specialist book on flash work, such as *Understanding Flash Photography* by Tarrant and Braverman (Fountain Press).

## Close-up flash

Because of the short duration and even lighting provided by flash, it is ideal for close-up and macro (high magnification) photography. We will look at the special close-up flash equipment available for the Pentax cameras in the chapter on accessories.

For general close-ups, bear this in mind: the flash, particularly if it is a hammer-head or "cobra" type with the flashtube well above the camera top, may illuminate an area significantly out of line with the lens axis. This does not matter beyond 3ft/1m, but closer than this and it is possible that the bottom of the picture (horizontal format) will be darkened. Do not use ceiling bounce flash; the flash will merely go over the subject and illuminate whatever is behind it.

Diffusers and bounce cards can be used, with the flash aimed at a tilt. Some flashguns allow the head to be angled down by 15° to cope with close-ups. A better idea is to take the flash off the camera for any really close work, such as flower studies. Obtain an angle bracket with a tilting and rotating head, and use the synch cable or extension cord to remove the flash from the hot shoe, and place it on the bracket or handgrip. Then adjust it so that the flash aims obliquely across the subject. The three-dimensional quality of the lighting will be greatly improved, though in certain conditions the shadows created may be too strong.

## Slow synch flash

The K1000 allows flash synchronization at any speed slower than 1/60; the P30n also operates, when set to manual, at speeds of 1/60 or slower in place of the usually automatically set 1/100. You cannot use slow shutter speeds in Aperture Priority Auto or Programmed Flash modes. If you try to set a speed faster than 1/60, the camera will over-ride and

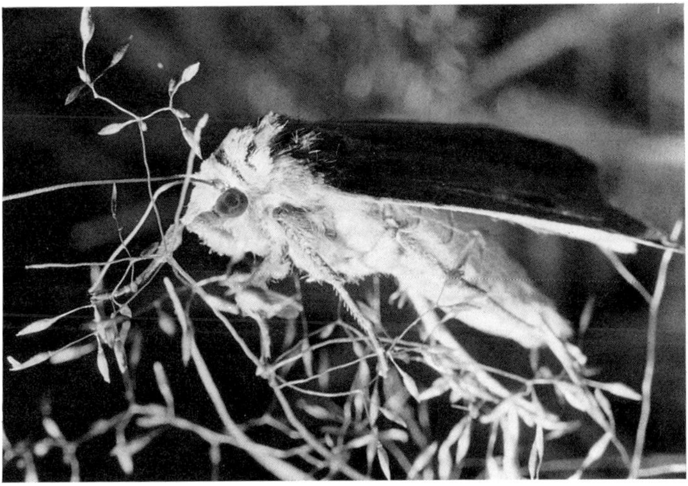

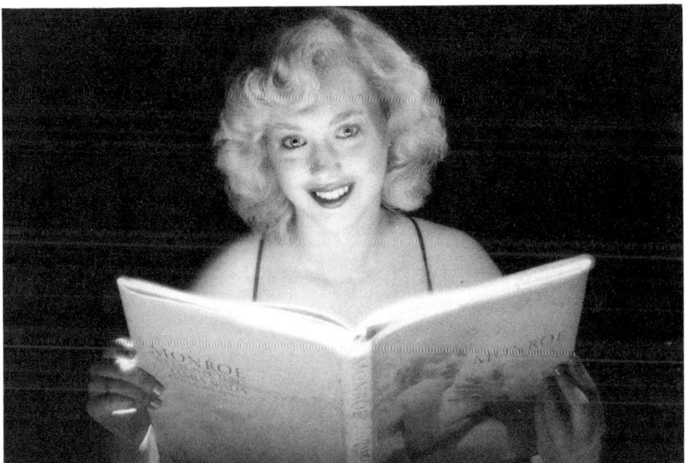

*Top: flash removed from the camera provided illumination for this close-up shot taken using a Pentax 55mm standard lens and extension tubes (Shirley Kilpatrick).*
*Bottom: a flash on an extension cable was placed behind the book, bounced off its pages, for this simple home studio photograph.*

keep the speed to 1/100. Be careful with the K1000, which has no such correction. You can set 1/1000 if you like; you'll get a strip of exposed frame and the rest blank. Always keep to speeds of 1/60 or longer!

You can combine flash with a pre-set shutter speed in several ways. First of all, you can fill in backlit daylight shots. If the sun is behind your subjects, especially with portraits and groups, the effect may be attractive but the shadows can be rather too heavy. Adding some flash from the camera position will improve the shot – many compact 35mm cameras do this automatically.

In this case, set the fastest shutter speed you can – 1/60 on the K1000, or 1/100 on the P30n. With ISO 100 film, you will find that the exposure required for a backlit group is around *f*11-16 (K1000) or *f*11 (P30n). Set your auto flash to the nearest available *f*-stop WIDER than this.

In the case of the AF200T, you would set it to green (*f*5.6) and the effect would be slight. You should aim to have the flash set on one *f*-stop wider than the camera setting. There is a way to cheat – obtain a small piece of grey neutral density filter, 2X density. Tape this over the sensor cell of the flash (the photo-eye). Three layers of cellulose adhesive tape will do the job adequately as a makeshift method. This fools the flash into putting out twice as much light.

With the AF280T or AF400T, you would simply set the flash to *f*8. this would give perfect fill-in results. If the flash was set to *f*11, the same as the actual exposure, then the effect would be to lighten the shadows to equal the bright background, producing an unnatural effect and risking over-exposure.

Using slower shutter speeds, the same technique can be applied to sunsets or pictures of people with interesting lighting in the background – Christmas lights, a bonfire, harbour lights or whatever. The secret is to set the camera for a normal full exposure of the background scene. A sunset might require 1/30 at *f*8 according to the camera's meter. Now set your flash to *f*5.6, and position your subjects as a silhouette against the sunset sky. The result will be just enough extra detail to work well. You can aim for a Hollywood effect, which looks as if the subject is in spotlighting against the sunset, by using the same aperture on your auto flashgun as you have set on the camera.

Against after-dark light sources such as city illuminations, you will find yourself using much longer shutter opening times such as 1/4 or even 1 second. The same technique can apply, but this time give your subject the same flash exposure as the aperture set on the camera. Make sure, too, that the subject does not MOVE – otherwise, some of the lights in the background will "ghost" through the space where the subject has moved away. In all these cases it pays to use a tripod, and it pays to take several different exposures at various settings and combinations. Try each different power on your flashgun. Results are unpredictable but can be superb when they work well.

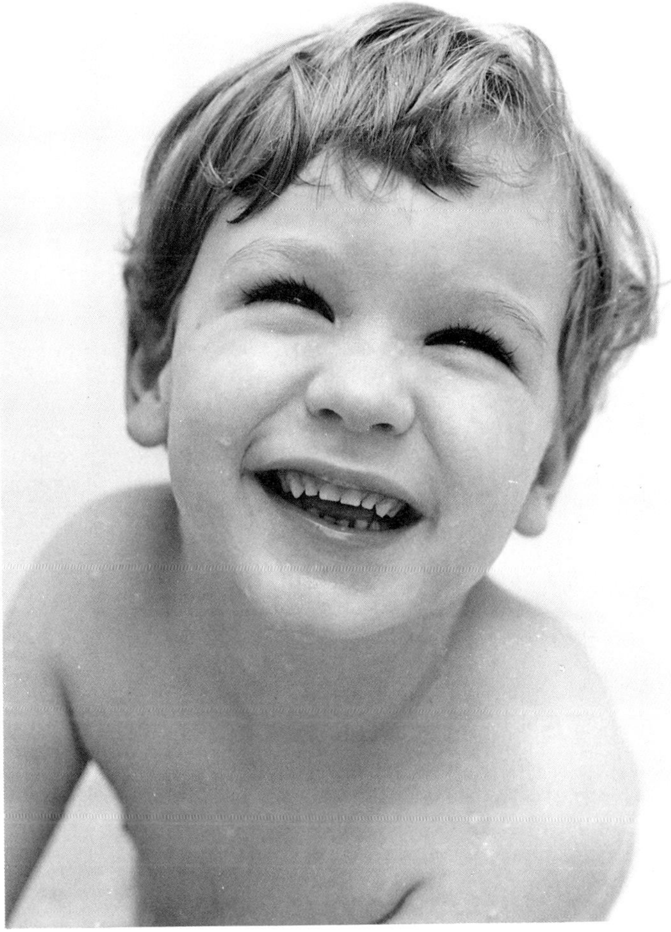

*Bounce flash provides very even lighting, as shown in this example by David Kilpatrick. In this case a high power flash was used in a small, bright room to photograph the author's nephew.*

# Pentax lenses

## Pentax-K lenses

Lenses in the original Pentax-K range, Pentax-M range and Takumar-K range will all work on any current Pentax SLR, including autofocus models. They provide all the couplings necessary for the K1000, and will work on Metered Manual and Aperture Priority Auto with the P30n.

There are literally dozens of designs of K-mount Pentax lenses available in good used condition, with specifications different from those listed here. A complete range of compact M-series lenses was launched to accompany the M-range SLRs, and there have been both regular K and budget-priced Takumar models of many focal lengths since the mid-1970s.

One major advantage of the K-mount is that it is impossible to buy an old lens in terms of optical design. The mount was introduced after the major advances in optics had been made – superior assembly methods, better zoom design using computers, and multi-coating. You may therefore find a lens such as the 45-125mm *f*3.5 Pentax K zoom, and see that it is not listed here and was clearly discontinued some time ago; will it be a decent lens? The answer is a very firm "yes". The sheer number of genuine Pentax lenses in existence is one of the big advantages of K1000 or P30n ownership.

As the Pentax autofocus range develops, many of the K (and indeed A) series lenses are being discontinued. Because the replacement lenses are not always an ideal choice for the K1000 or P30n owner – although they work perfectly well – we have retained in this section details of several recently obsolete K and A designs.

**18mm *f*3.5 Pentax-M**
*Minimum aperture: f22*
*Closest focus: 25cm*
*Dimensions: 62 x 63mm*
*Weight: 295g*
*Filter thread: dial-in filters*

A true wide-angle free from curvilinear distortion, this K-mount lens was discontinued in 1989, but has not at the time of writing been replaced by any equivalent focal length in the A or F ranges. It's therefore worth including here, as it is the widest angle lens (covering 105°) in the K-mount range apart from the very much more expensive 15mm Pentax-A. Good used examples should be available at a reasonable price

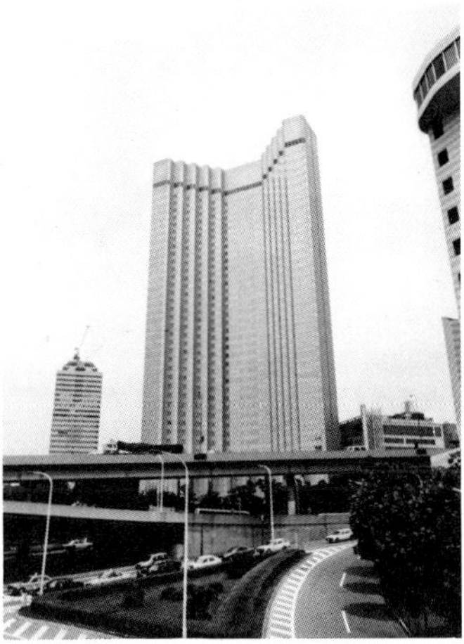 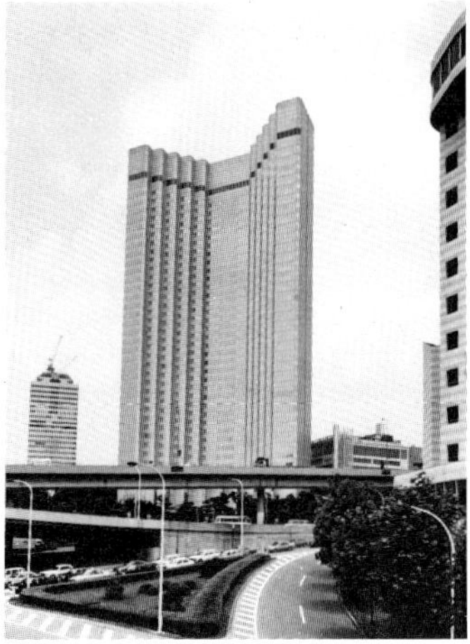

*Above: the Pentax K-mount 28mm shift lens is an unusually wide-angle perspective control lens, giving your 35mm SLR some of the capabilities of a large format camera. A normal 28mm lens angled upwards to include a building from ground-level produced a result with converging verticals (left). The 28mm Shift can be adjusted so that the camera remains parallel to the building, but the image is brought into line, retaining perfect verticals (right). Photographs by Asahi Optical Co. Ltd, Japan.*

**28mm *f*3.5 Shift**
*Minimum aperture: f32*
*Closest focus: 30cm*
*Dimensions: 92 x 80mm*
*Weight: 610g*
*Filter thread: dial-in filters*

A lens for architectural and industrial photographers wanting perfect parallel verticals even when looking upwards at tall buildings. A mechanism in the mount allows the entire lens to be shifted off-centre, enabling the camera to remain perfectly parallel to the subject, while changing the field of view to place the horizon at the bottom of the picture instead of the middle. The results show a dramatic perspective with graphic accuracy. This lens is not coupled to the metering, but operates using the stop-down principle, and works well with either the K1000 or P30n. When used with a limited shift movement, it will function on Aperture Priority Auto with the P30n, but exposures will be inaccurate when the lens is fully shifted.

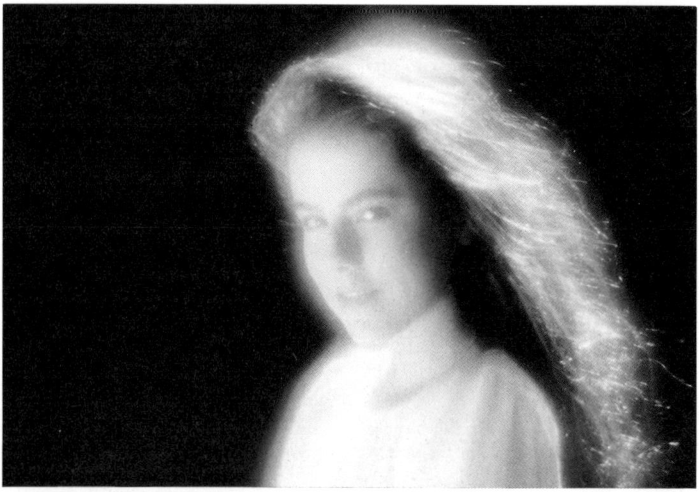

**85mm *f*2.2 Soft Focus**
*Minimum aperture: f5.6*
*Closest focus: 50cm*
*Dimensions: 72 x 52mm*
*Filter thread: 77mm*

An unusual lens with its corrections deliberately adjusted to produce a soft focus halo effect. The aperture range is limited, as the lens uses an unconventional *f*-stop arrangement to produce its soft focus, and is much larger than you would expect from an *f*2.2 design – this is a result of the baffle which produces the special softening effect. For portraiture; *photograph above – courtesy of Asahi Optical Co. Ltd.*

**100mm *f*4 SMC Macro**
*Minimum aperture: f32*
*Closest focus: limited by bellows*
*Dimensions: 78 x 64mm*
*Weight: 340g*
*Filter thread: 49mm*

This K-mount lens is purely a lens "head" with no focusing mechanism. It is intended for use with the Pentax K-mount automatic extension bellows for close-up and macro (high magnification) photography. It is not particularly expensive, and offers the highest standard of image sharpness; when mounted on the bellows, it will permit focusing from infinity to larger than life size on film.

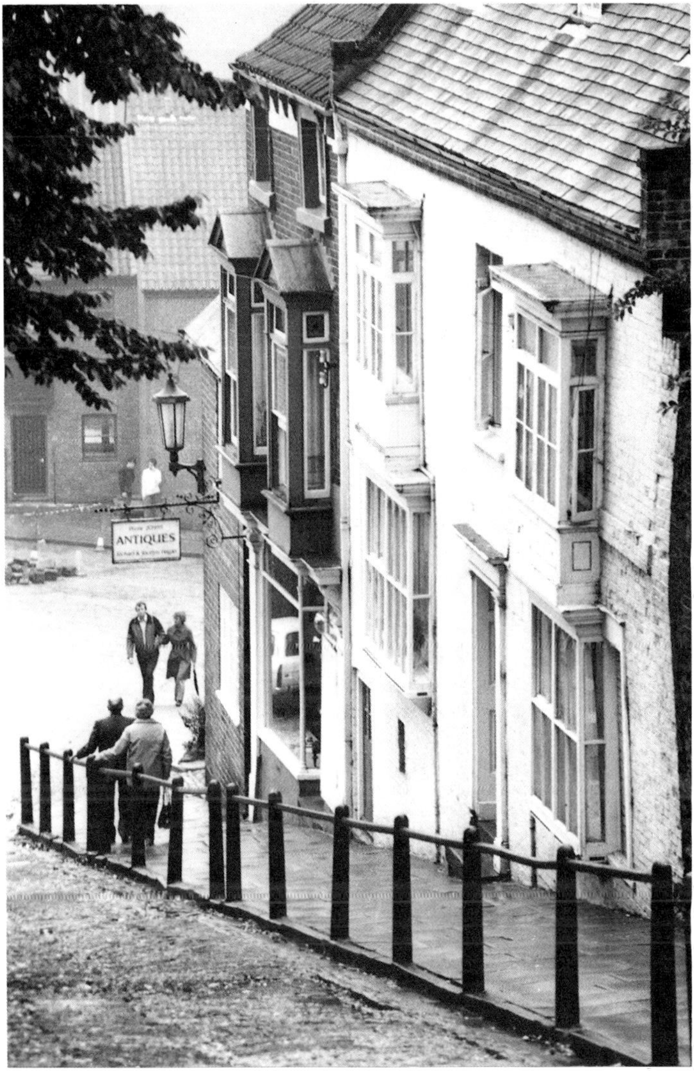


*The restricted angle of view of the 135mm telephoto cuts out unwanted sky area, and the compressed perspective gives the impression of a visual corridor. Steep Hill, Lincoln, photographed by David Kilpatrick using a 135mm f3.5.*

**135mm *f*3.5 Pentax-M**
*Minimum aperture: f32*
*Closest focus: 1.5m*
*Dimensions: 66 x 63mm*
*Weight: 270g*
*Filter thread: 49mm*

**135mm *f*2.5 Pentax-M**
*Minimum aperture: f32*
*Closest focus: 1.5m*
*Dimensions: 86 x 68mm*
*Weight: 480g*
*Filter thread: 58mm*

These two popular designs are now discontinued but may be available used. The *f*3.5 is the smallest and lightest 135mm ever made for the system, and the *f*2.5 is a very fast telephoto at a reasonable cost in terms of size, weight and financial outlay.

**135 - 600mm *f*6.7 SMC**
*Minimum aperture: f45*
*Closest focus: 6m*
*Dimensions: 588 x 105mm*
*Weight: 4070g*
*Filter thread: 98mm*

This original K-mount monster is one of those lenses which is probably "still on the books" because its focal length range is unique and remarkably few are sold – the price would buy three or four 400mm Pentax-A lenses or ten selected zooms! With an integral tripod mount and twin-ring zooming, the weight alone calls for the heaviest professional tripod. There is a very specific use for this lens in covering field sports which involve cross-field movement, from the sidelines. Ordinary Pentax owners are unlikely to need it.

**400 - 600mm *f*8 ~ 12 Reflex**
*Minimum aperture: f8 ~ 12*
*Closest focus: 3m*
*Dimensions: 108 x 82mm*
*Weight: 725g*
*Filter thread: 40.5mm rear-mounted (6 supplied)*

An expensive but unique lens, the 400-600mm mirror zoom is the only such design from any camera manufacturer. It overcomes many restrictions of a fixed focal length 500mm mirror lens by allowing some re-framing of the subject, which otherwise calls for major changes in camera position. The close focus limit allows you to shoot fairly small garden birds or rodents with flash. All in all, a good choice if you want a mirror lens – which means a fixed aperture, exposure is controlled by fitting neutral density filters (a set of colour and ND filters is included with the lens). Fully functional on the K1000, the 400-600mm also works in Aperture Priority Auto mode with the P30n.

### 500mm *f*4.5 Pentax-M

*Minimum aperture: f45*
*Closest focus: 10m*
*Dimensions: 440 x 126mm*
*Weight: 3370g*
*Filter thread: rear 52mm*

A very large conventional telephoto with a moderately fast maximum aperture, the 500mm is not very portable compared to the 400-600mm, and has the disadvantage of being intended as a long-range lens – if anything is closer than 33 feet (10 metres) it won't be possible to focus on it. Mainly used by sports and news photographers for distant events, as with the 135-600mm zoom. Works normally with the K1000, cannot be used on Programmed Auto Exposure with the P30n.

### 1000mm *f*8 Pentax-M

*Minimum aperture: f45*
*Closest focus: 30m*
*Dimensions: 738 x 143mm*
*Weight: 5290g*
*Filter thread: rear 52mm*

A big brother to the 500mm *f*4.5, most of the same comments apply. Extremely expensive, large and heavy – all to achieve a maximum aperture of *f*8, one *f*-stop more than the mirror version below. Most users would find it preferable to use a 2x converter on the 400mm *f*2.8, resulting in a much faster 800mm *f*5.6 combination.

### 1000mm *f*11 SMC Reflex

*Minimum aperture: f11*
*Closest focus: 8m*
*Dimensions: 119 x 241mm*
*Weight: 2300g*
*Filter thread: 81mm*

### 2000mm *f*13.5 SMC Reflex-M

*Minimum aperture: f13.5*
*Closest focus: 20m*
*Dimensions: 530 x 180mm*
*Weight: 8000g*
*Filter thread: internal*

Mirror lenses in a plain K-mount, these very powerful telephotos have fixed (and limited!) maximum apertures. Housing and tripod mount contribute to substantial overall weight despite the simplicity of mirror-lens design. Strictly for natural history and distant (sideline) close-ups of sports. Panning, rapid refocusing and quick lining-up on an unexpected subject are out of the question. You require a very good tripod and a film fast enough to allow the fastest shutter speeds. In many areas of Europe, it is simply not possible to secure good photographs with a lens of this focal length on 360 days out of the year; in the USA conditions can be better, but anywhere close to cities the air is not clear enough.

# Pentax-A lenses

The A-series lenses, which have electrical contacts allowing programmed exposure and flash, are fully functional with both the K1000 and P30n in all modes. They also work to a greater degree with autofocus Pentax SLRs, and in the case of most wide-angles are the recommended (only) option for use with the AF bodies.

The A-mount lenses are all designs of the 1980s or later, and offer an exceptionally good performance-to-size ratio. Most A-series lenses are lighter, shorter and take smaller filters than their K-series counterparts.

Be warned, however; to achieve this economy of size, many A-series zooms have variable maximum apertures. Very few have constant maximum apertures. As you zoom from (say) 70 to 200mm with one of these lenses, the aperture actually changes from (say) *f*8 to *f*11. There is no external indication that this is happening.

This is fine with an auto or programmed camera, as all the cameras built specifically to accept the A-mount lenses are. The P30n works well with this type of lens. If you switch to manual, however, your exposure will change when you zoom – using programmed or auto exposure compensates for this. Such lenses are NOT the best choice for a manual-only camera like the K1000, as you would need to keep adjusting the aperture with every change of focal length. Not only this, but with a manual camera it can be useful to zoom in on a small area to take a meter reading – this is not reliable if the zoom changes aperture as you do so.

You should therefore study the specification of the A-mount zooms carefully, and consider choosing those lenses with constant maximum apertures for your K1000, even if they are bigger and heavier.

**15mm *f*3.5 SMC-A**
*Minimum aperture: f22*
*Closest focus: 30cm*
*Dimensions: 62 x 83mm*
*Weight: 595g*
*Filter thread: dial-in filters*

This is a true wide-angle lens covering a 110° field of view (diagonal) without any distortion. It has a large, curved front element and "wings" which act as a lens-hood, so filters cannot be attached to the front of the lens. Instead, there are four built-in filters which cope with most requirements for black-and-white and colour photography.

The 15mm is a specialized lens, normally used by architects and real-estate agencies to show interiors to their full extent. It is very difficult

*Right: the sweeping view given by the Pentax 15mm ultra-wide. Photograph by David Kilpatrick.*

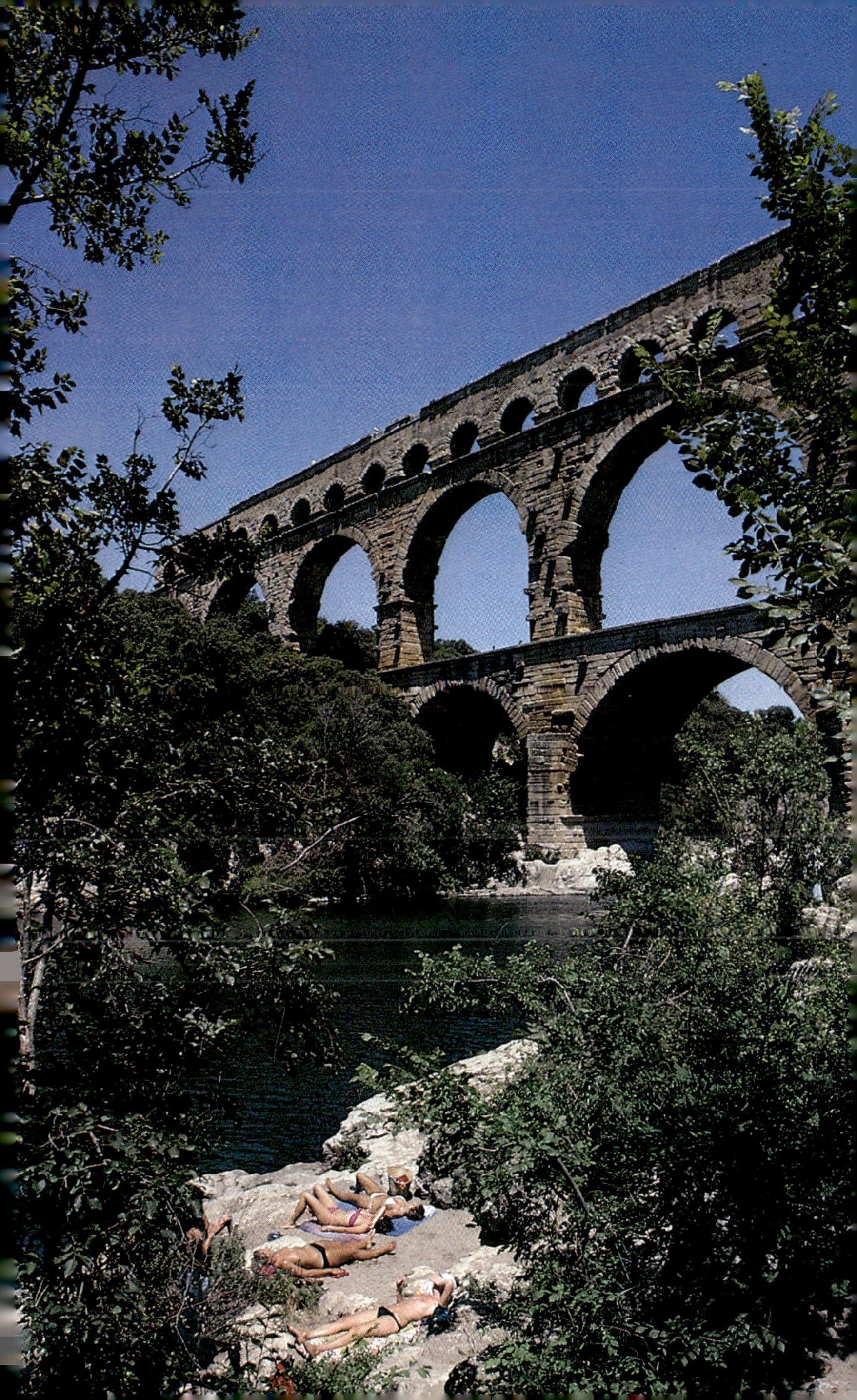

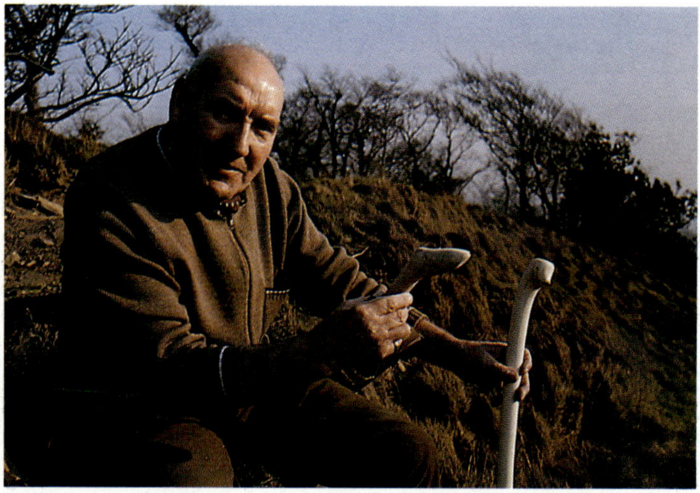

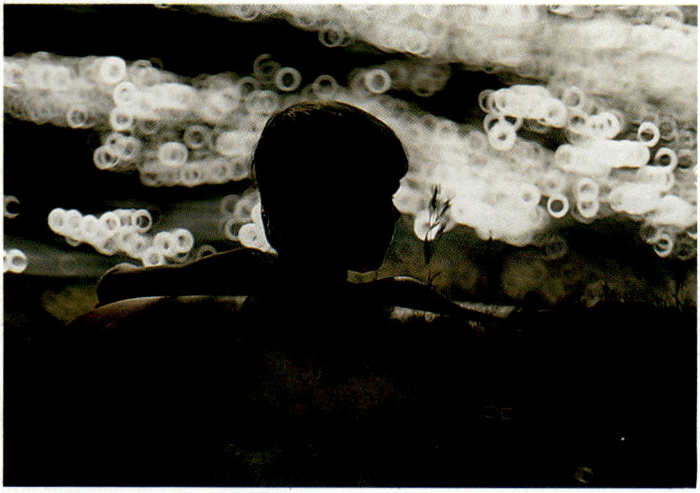

to use properly, as the camera must be held absolutely horizontal – otherwise, the picture will seem to lean strongly. It is also suitable for landscapes, and especially effective with dramatic skies. Performance is excellent, though distortion will be noticed at the edges of the field if you make the mistake of using this lens close to groups of people.

**16mm *f*2.8 A**
*Minimum aperture: f22*
*Closest focus: 20cm*
*Dimensions: 64 x 82mm*
*Weight: 320g*
*Filter thread: dial-in filters*

The 16mm, unlike the 15mm, is a curved-image fisheye lens. It shows straight lines as increasingly curved the closer they are to the edge of the picture. The angle of view is a full 180°, horizon to horizon, corner to corner of the picture. Unlike shorter fisheyes (Pentax do not make one) the image does cover the entire film frame – a fisheye of 8mm focal length will only cover a 24mm circle. This lens has a strongly curved front element and uses a set of built-in filters.

**20mm *f*2.8 SMC-A**
*Minimum aperture: f22*
*Closest focus: 20cm*
*Dimensions: 48 x 70mm*
*Weight: 320g*
*Filter thread: 67mm*

This is the widest wide-angle lens you are likely to want to own for normal photography. Covering an angle of 88°, the 20mm can even be used for group photographs with care. It is ideal for architecture, landscapes, creative still life, and sports action photography handled as close range. It can also be a very useful lens for candid, news and travel photography, with a wide maximum aperture but great depth of field if stopped down to *f*8 or *f*11. Like the 15mm, the 20mm will show up any poor camera alignment by emphasizing converging verticals. The 20mm makes an ideal choice of wide-angle if you already own a 28mm lens, or a 28-80mm zoom.

*Top left: the 24mm lens is ideal for putting a subject into perspective – to show the environment, for example, in a portrait.*

*Bottom left: the 400-600mm Reflex and longer mirror lenses produce an image with characteristic out-of-focus "doughnut" effects like this. Both photographs by David Kilpatrick.*

Right: the 20mm *f*2.8 SMC-A lens is a typical wide-angle, with a large front element though compact in size.

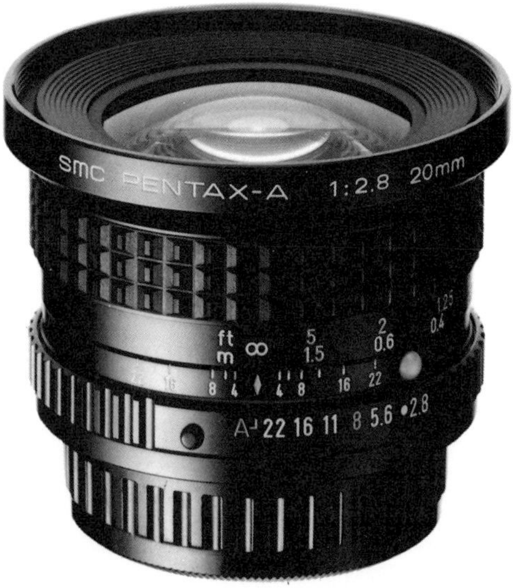


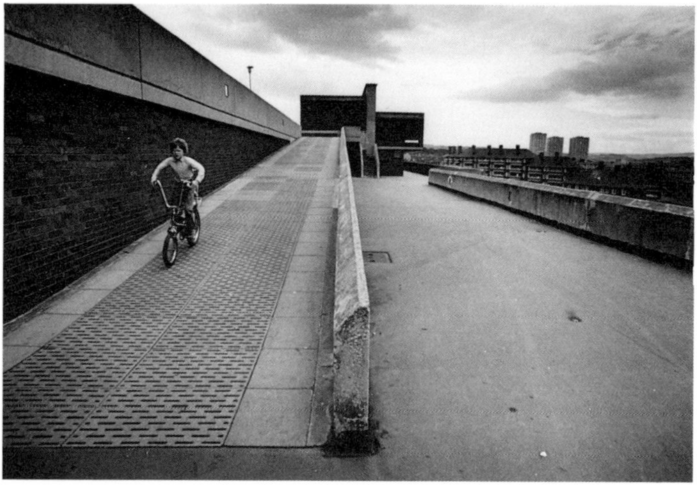

*The perspective given by a 20mm wide-angle can be dramatic, especially when straight lines are used to emphasize it. This picture by Shirley Kilpatrick shows how distance is exaggerated, the foreground is emphasized, and the sky (here burned-in on the original print) shows greater detail because the scale of clouds is reduced.*

### 24mm *f*2.8 SMC-A

*Minimum aperture: f22*
*Closest focus: 20cm*
*Dimensions: 48 x 58mm*
*Weight: 205g*
*Filter thread: 52mm*

The 24mm *f*2.8 is a versatile all-round wide angle, much easier to use correctly than the 20mm. It covers an angle of 84°, which is adequate to allow a good photograph in most domestic or office interiors. Outdoors, the 24mm offers fewer problems with the inclusion of your own shadow or unwanted intrusions than the 20mm, and may produce more attractive sky tones when used with a polarizing filter. It is also extremely small and light, and performs to a high standard even when used at its closest focus. This is a semi-macro distance of just eight inches or 20cm, so the 24mm can be used for shots of small flowers or objects despite its wide-angle design. A good lens to team up with a 50mm standard, or an outfit based on any zoom which starts at 35mm (such as the 35-135mm).

### 28mm *f*2 SMC-A

*Minimum aperture: f22*
*Closest focus: 30cm*
*Dimensions: 42 x 63mm*
*Weight: 215g*
*Filter thread: 49mm*

A fast wide angle lens favoured by newspaper photographers. For ordinary photography, it is not necessary to buy the *f*2, as speed is rarely needed with a wide-angle lens unless you are working in low light.

### 28mm *f*2.8 SMC-A

*Minimum aperture: f22*
*Closest focus: 30cm*
*Dimensions: 34 x 63mm*
*Weight: 170g*
*Filter thread: 49mm*

A good all-round wide-angle, the perfect choice if you own a 50mm lens already. With a 75° angle of view (diagonal) the 28mm lens is easy to use, but gets in sweeping landscapes with attractive depth to the sky, and can be used in many room interiors. A house must be in cramped surroundings if the 28mm will not "get it in" from the road or garden. The SMC-A version is a high performance modern 28mm.

**28mm *f*2.8 Takumar-A**
*Minimum aperture: f22*
*Closest focus: 30cm*
*Dimensions: 34 x 63mm*
*Weight: 170g*
*Filter thread: 49mm*

Very similar to the Pentax-A, the Takumar-A has a slightly reduced specification (in design terms) but is identical in use. It may theoretically have slightly inferior sharpness, more tendency to flare when used into the light, and be less well-corrected for close-ups. You are unlikely to notice any of this, and it is a fine choice of wide-angle for the budget K1000 outfit, costing little more than a standard lens.

**35mm *f*2 SMC-A**
*Minimum aperture: f22*
*Closest focus: 30cm*
*Dimensions: 42 x 63mm*
*Weight: 205g*
*Filter thread: 49mm*

The 35mm lens is very useful alternative to your 50mm standard, with a wider angle of view. It is ideal for photographing groups of people, gardens, cars, and children (not too close up). It is an unusual choice as an extra lens, because most mid-range zooms function very successfully at 35mm. If you have the choice when you first buy a Pentax, the 35mm *f*2 would be worth getting in place of the 50mm *f*2, but the price is considerably higher. Liked by photojournalists, sports and theatrical photographers. A K-mount version, the Pentax-M 35mm *f*2, is now discontinued. Expect the highest optical standard from 35mm designs.

**35mm *f*2.8 SMC-A**
*Minimum aperture: f22*
*Closest focus: 30cm*
*Dimensions: 36 x 63mm*
*Weight: 170g*
*Filter thread: 49mm*

Reasonably priced, the 35mm *f*2.8 is a slower version of the *f*2. It has exceptional image-quality, but is not a very popular lens today, being neither a true wide-angle nor a fast standard lens.

*Right: the 35mm lens is capable of the highest quality results. This picture was taken with one of the very first Pentax 35mm lenses ever made (inherited by the author!), using fine-grain ISO 32 film.*

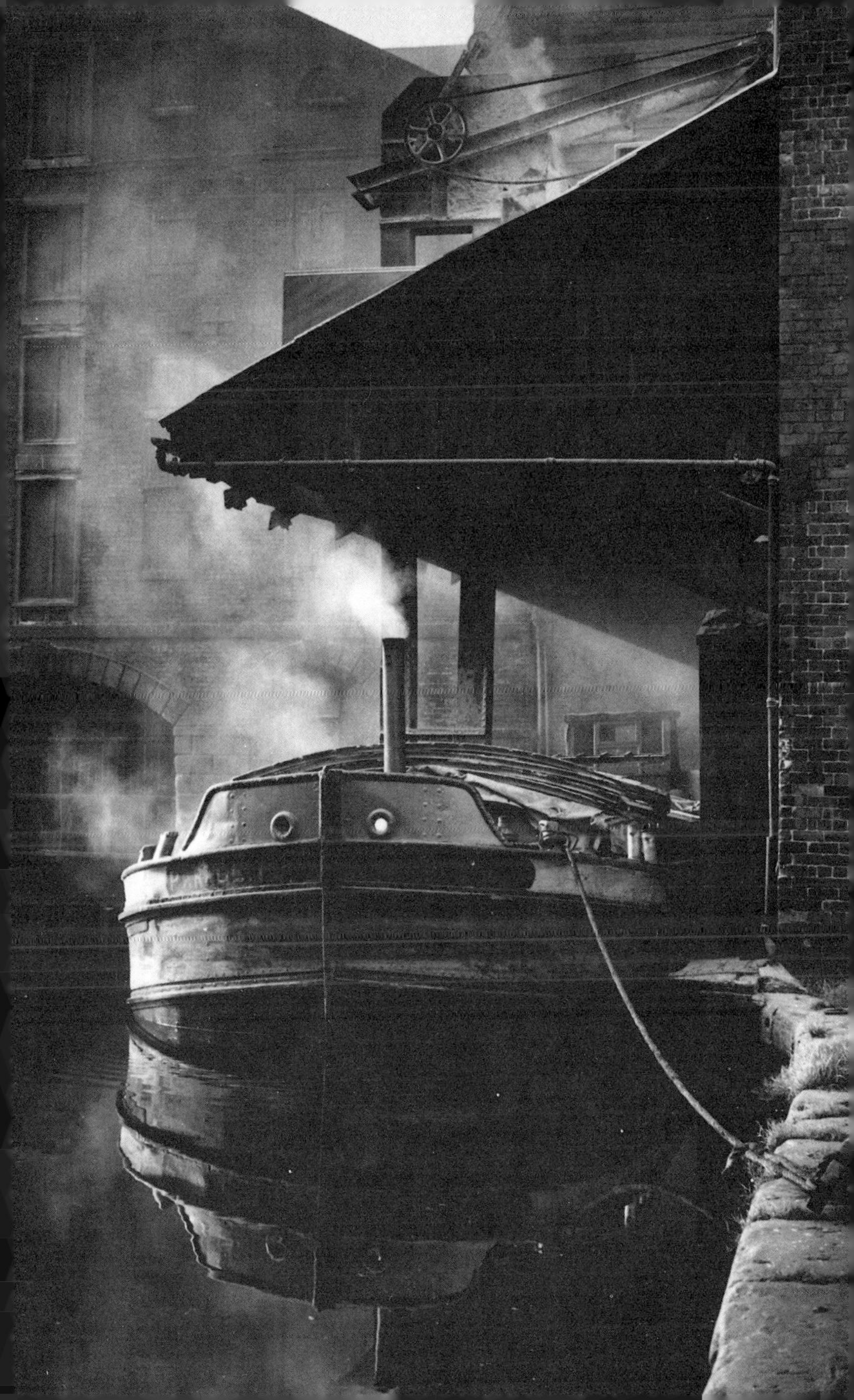

*Right: the 50mm Macro-A lens is a good alternative to the standard 50mm if you obtain it with your camera body. It allows very effective close-ups without requiring any accessories. However, if you already own a 50mm standard, you may prefer to buy a set of extension tubes (see the next chapter on accessories).*

**50mm *f*1.2 SMC-A**
*Minimum aperture: f22*
*Closest focus: 40cm*
*Dimensions: 48 x 65mm*
*Weight: 345g*
*Filter thread: 52mm*

An expensive super-fast standard lens, usually purchased as a status-symbol rather than a working lens. There are very few advantages to owning an *f*1.2, at four times the price of an *f*2, 50mm. The viewing screen is brighter, and focusing is easier in low light. Performance is improved at *f*1.4 and *f*2 compared with slower lenses – but close-ups may show loss of sharpness at the edges, and the lens is slightly lower in contrast.

**50mm *f*1.4 SMC-A**
*Minimum aperture: f22*
*Closest focus: 40cm*
*Dimensions: 37 x 63mm*
*Weight: 235g*
*Filter thread: 49mm*

If you want a fast lens for bright viewing and occasional low-light candid shots, this is the best choice – it's half the price of the *f*1.2, and only half a stop slower. It is still more expensive than the *f*1.7 or *f*2, and in practical terms very few people make use of *f*1.4. Now discontinued.

**50mm *f*1.7 SMC-A**
*Minimum aperture: f22*
*Closest focus: 40cm*
*Dimensions: 31 x 63mm*
*Weight: 165g*
*Filter thread: 49mm*

Small, light and excellent – the *f*1.7 SMC Pentax-A is the best all-round standard lens. The SMC (Super-Multi-Coating) gives better colours, contrast and freedom from flare, when compared to 50mm *f*2 non-SMC. The *f*1.7 is normally supplied with the P30n, or on request with the K1000.

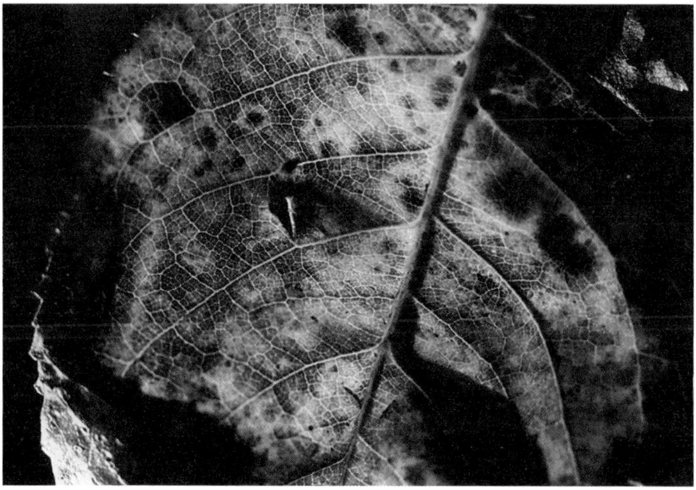

**50mm *f*2 A**
*Minimum aperture: f22*
*Closest focus: 40cm*
*Dimensions: 31 x 63mm*
*Weight: 145g*
*Filter thread: 49mm*

Multicoated, but not Super-Multi-Coated; a budget Pentax standard lens, the 50mm *f*2 is the standard lens for the K1000. It performs impeccably, as any 50mm lens should today, and is very small and light. If you own this lens, do not think you need to upgrade to one of the faster 50mms. It is capable of resolving finer detail than most people can see in a print or a projected slide, and at *f*2 it does not need the SMC coating which is vital in an *f*1.4 or *f*1.2 lens.

**50mm *f*2.8 Macro-A**
*Minimum aperture: f22*
*Closest focus: 1:2*
*Dimensions: 50 x 63mm*
*Weight: 220g*
*Filter thread: 49mm*

A special close-focusing, high quality 50mm lens which allows pictures half life-size on the film, with continuous focusing between this setting and infinity. Free from linear distortion and with a very flat field, the Macro-A is ideal for copying paintings and engravings, or stamps; it is also a good natural history lens, and performs perfectly at middle and far distances. It is a little less expensive than, for example, the 50mm *f*1.2; it gives the photographer considerably more in added features. The *f*2.8 maximum aperture is perfectly adequate and the focusing is very crisp and responsive. If you can afford it, the best all-round standard lens to own. Now discontinued and replaced by the similar SMC-F lens.

**85mm *f*1.4 SMC-A**
*Minimum aperture: f22*
*Closest focus: 80cm*
*Dimensions: 66 x 74mm*
*Weight: 555g*
*Filter thread: 67mm*

Lenses of this focal length are traditionally supposed to be ideal for portraits. Some find slightly longer lenses such as the 100mm and 135mm better. The 85mm *f*1.4 is a super-fast lens aimed at news and sports photographers, and is popular for shots of ballet, gymnastic displays and opera – anything where the entire stage may need to be photographed from the back of the auditorium, and then an individual portrait from on-stage. Too heavy for use as a general outdoor lens, and rather vulnerable too.

**100mm *f*2.8 SMC-A**
*Minimum aperture: f22*
*Closest focus: 1m*
*Dimensions: 56 x 63mm*
*Weight: 260g*
*Filter thread: 49mm*

One of the smallest and lightest of all Pentax lenses, this short telephoto is an ideal general lens for family portraits, travel and landscape shots (especially if you hike or climb). It is little larger than a 50mm standard lens and provides a bright focusing image for manual cameras. It is more expensive than the 135mm *f*2.8 (see below) but considered by serious photographers to be a more useful lens. However, you can imitate the 100mm *f*2.8 by using the Pentax Takumar-A 2x converter on your standard 50mm lens, and if you own a 35-105mm or similar zoom you already have access to the 100mm focal length. If you like this lens, you'll want it. Makes a good compact outfit if teamed up with a 50mm and 28mm.

*Right: the 100mm lens is one of the author's favourites. This picture was taken with an earlier 105mm Super Takumar on a screw-thread Pentax Spotmatic, the K1000's predecessor.*

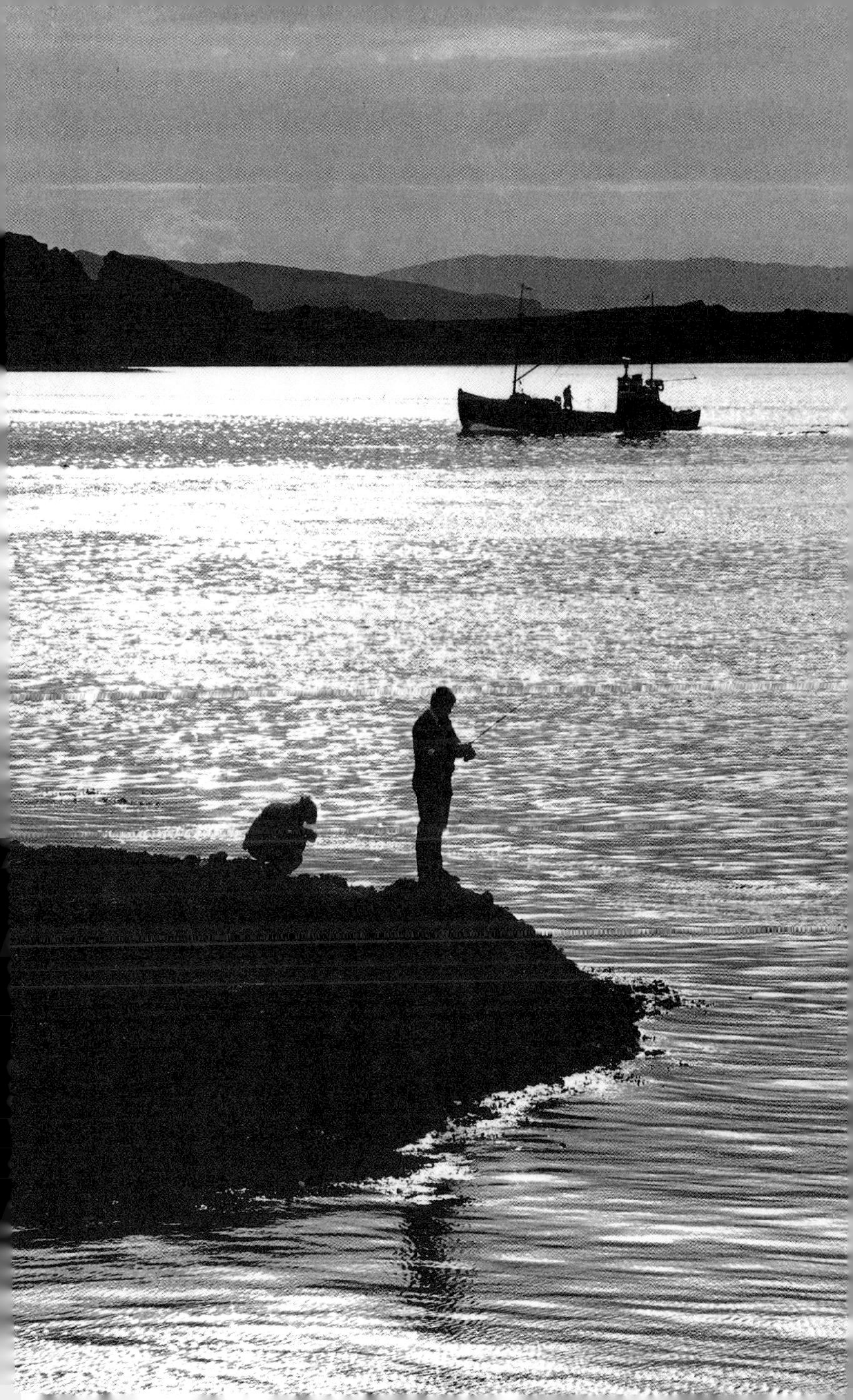

### 100mm *f*2.8 Macro-A

*Minimum aperture: f22*
*Closest focus: 1:2 (30cm from lens front)*
*Dimensions: 93 x 74mm*
*Weight: 470g*
*Filter thread: 58mm*

Focusing to life size in a continuous action from infinity, this is a superb all-round 100mm lens capable of portrait, landscape, still life, natural history and copying work as well as frame-filling close-ups of subjects as small as 1 x 1.5". Only buy this in place of the standard 100mm if you need the macro facility. There is a discontinued *f*4 version which is lighter and focuses to half life size, requiring an additional extension tube for life-size shots. Both A lenses are now replaced by F type.

### 135mm *f*2.8 SMC-A

*Minimum aperture: f32*
*Closest focus: 1.2m*
*Dimensions: 65 x 77mm*
*Weight: 340g*
*Filter thread: 52mm*

The obvious telephoto to buy if you want a fast lens for easy focusing. It costs less than a zoom, and performs better; it is pocketable, light and takes a small filter; it focuses close enough to allow frame-filling shots of flowers and portraits of small animals like cats. This lens is very quick to use, and although rather unfashionable today (most people prefer a zoom) the 135mm *f*2.8 is a classic choice which goes well in almost any outfit. You may even want this lens as well as a 70-200mm zoom, as the extra speed lets you shoot at concerts, by theatre spotlights, or by sports floodlighting.

### 135mm *f*1.8 SMC-A

*Minimum aperture: f22*
*Closest focus: 1.2m*
*Dimensions: 98 x 80mm*
*Weight: 865g*
*Filter thread: 77mm*

For a considerable extra outlay, the *f*1.8 version of the 135mm gives over a stop more in maximum aperture. It is specifically intended for low-light work at *f*1.8, where focusing may be difficult and every ounce of speed must be used. Chosen by news photographers who take portraits in conferences or candid pictures of people in places where flash may not be used, and ideal, of course, for all floodlit spectator events.

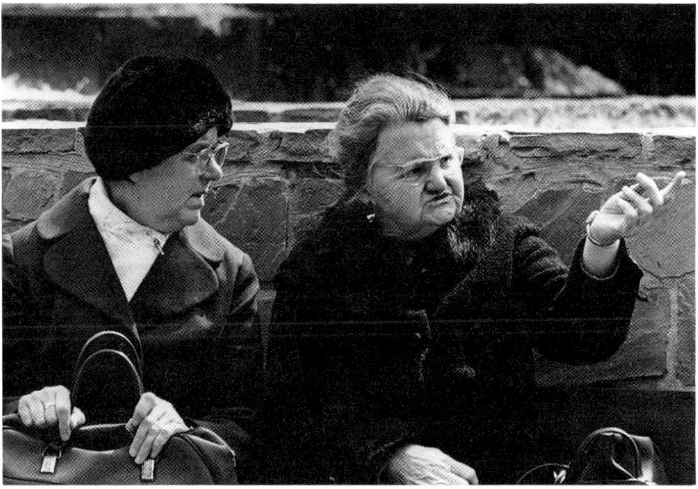

*Sitting on another bench in a town square, Shirley Kilpatrick picked out these old ladies using a 200mm f4, which helped her shoot a whole series of candids showing hand gestures in a few minutes.*

**200mm *f*4 SMC-A**
*Minimum aperture: f32*
*Closest focus: 1.9m*
*Dimensions: 64 x 111mm*
*Weight: 410g*
*Filter thread: 52mm*

If you prefer prime lenses to zooms, this is a superb lightweight long telephoto small enough to slip into a pocket. A good companion lens to the 135mm, it can be used for portraiture outdoors, candid photojournalism, landscapes, sports, architecture and almost any subject.

**200mm *f*2.8 A ED**
*Minimum aperture: f32*
*Closest focus: 1.8m*
*Dimensions: 137 x 91mm*
*Weight: 850g*
*Filter thread: 77mm*

A fast high quality telephoto suitable for sports, fashion and portraiture – it is light enough for travel and landscape work, too. A lens like this will cost twice as much as a good zoom but the results are worth it.

**200mm *f*4 Macro ED**
*Minimum aperture: f32*
*Closest focus: 55cm from lens front*
*Dimensions: 145 x 70mm*
*Weight: 880g*
*Filter thread: 58mm*

A long macro lens, focusing to life-size at 55cm (1.8ft) distance, has a specific use – in hospitals. This lens is often termed a medical lens, because it allows close-ups of patients to be taken from a distance which avoids interfering with a surgeon at work. It is also ideal for photographing insects without disturbing them, for the same reason – a longer than normal working distance. Exceptional performance, at a price; best teamed up with a ring-flash unit. An unusual optic, unique to Pentax.

**300mm *f*4 A**
*Minimum aperture: f32*
*Closest focus: 4m*
*Dimensions: 132 x 84mm*
*Weight: 850g*
*Filter thread: 77mm*

A lightweight 300mm general-purpose telephoto in the Pentax-A series, this lens does not use any special glasses. It has now been replaced by the 300mm *f*4.5 ED-IF SMC Pentax-F, but remains an excellent secondhand purchase for K1000 and P30n owners.

**300mm *f*2.8 SMC-A ED-IF**
*Minimum aperture: f32*
*Closest focus: 3m*
*Dimensions: 236 x 133mm*
*Weight: 2970g*
*Filter thread: 49mm rear thread*

Much heavier than the 300mm *f*4, the *f*2.8 offers greater sharpness and an extra stop in aperture. The penalty is a more than threefold increase in weight and bulk. Once tripod-mounted, the internal focusing makes this lens much easier to use than the *f*4, which has a comparatively large focusing collar. Essentially a professional lens for news, sports, theatrical and concert photography.

*A fast long lens like the 200mm or 300mm f2.8 will enable you to take pictures without flash at concerts or during theatrical productions. The K1000 and P30n are ideal cameras for this, as they have no motor winders and make less noise than many SLRs.*

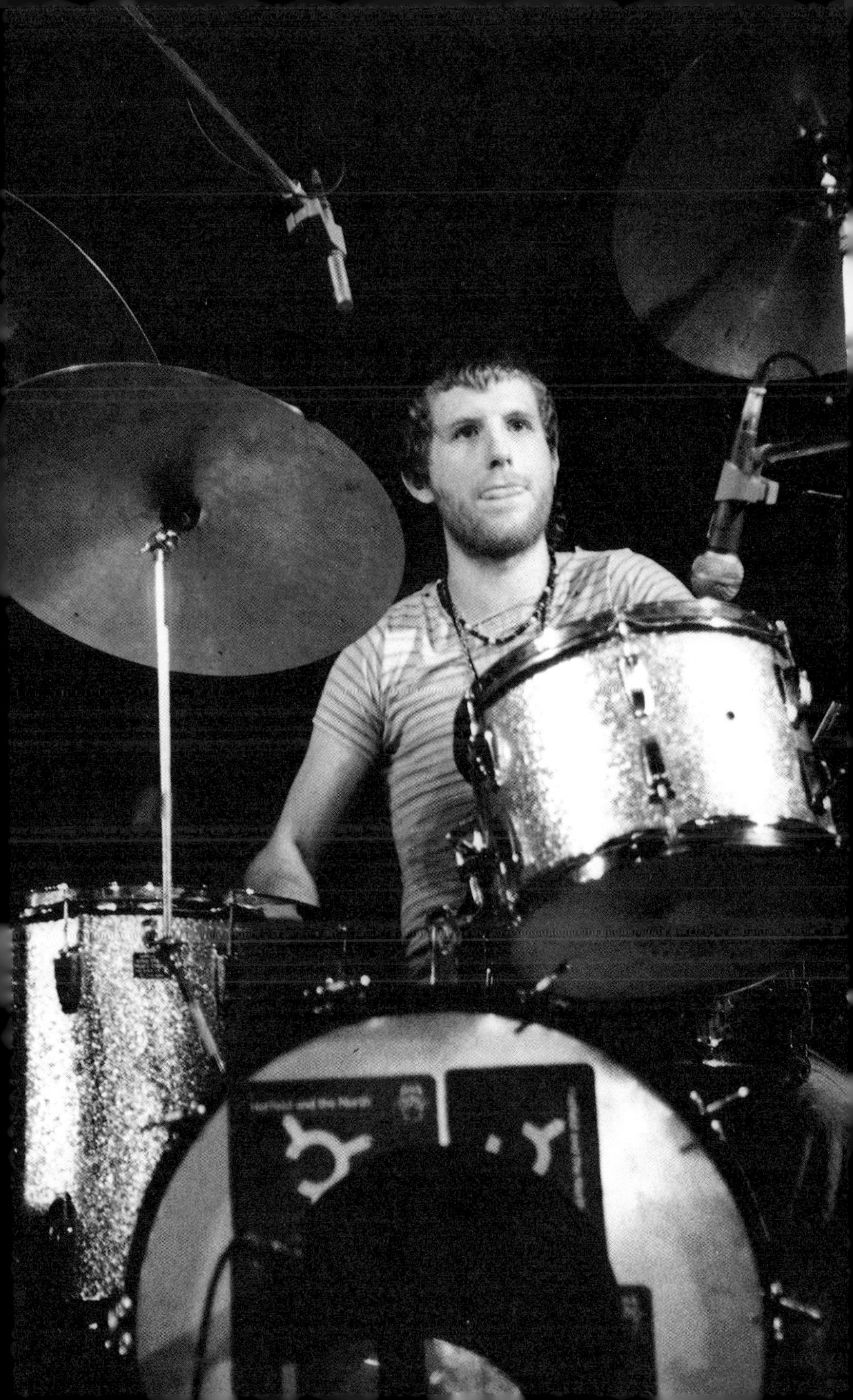

**400mm *f*5.6 SMC-A**
*Minimum aperture: f32*
*Closest focus: 2.8m*
*Dimensions: 220 x 80mm*
*Weight: 1240g*
*Filter thread: 77mm*

Another competitively-priced straightforward telephoto, of modern design with a reasonable aperture, allowing a relatively light weight and compact size. A good lens for wildlife photography which can also produce some surprisingly powerful landscape and city scenes. Often chosen for motor-racing and motocross event photography, as this is the ideal length to ensure a safe working distance, and is small enough to hand-hold as long as a shutter speed of 1/500 or 1/1000 is used. A good choice if you already own a 70-200mm zoom, as the jump to double the focal length makes a noticeable difference. Can be used with the 2X-L converter, as an 800mm *f*11 combination.

**1200mm *f*8 A ED-IF**
*Minimum aperture: f45*
*Closest focus: 8m*
*Dimensions: 684 x 170mm*
*Weight: 8580g*
*Filter thread: 49mm rear-mounted*

Unusually long in terms of focal length, and almost a yard long physically, this is a rare example of a modern conventional telephoto using new extra-low dispersion glasses and internal focusing. High performance can only be ensured by using a very strong tripod and working in atmospheric conditions free from rising heat, aerial dust or haze, or excess humidity. A lens for the specialist!

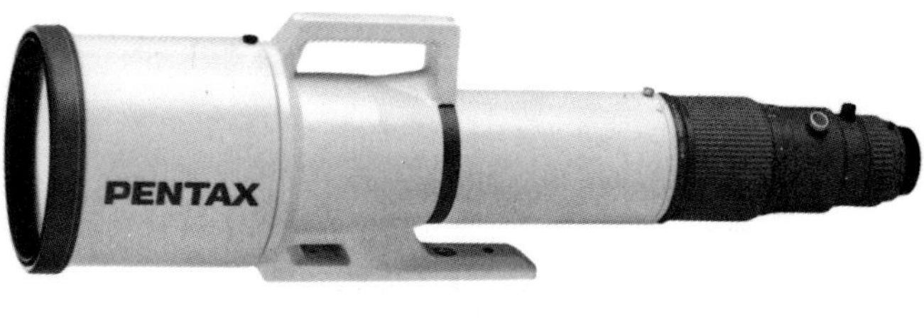


*The 1200mm f8 is one of the longest lenses you are ever likely to see – virtually a telescope, complete with carrying handle.*

# Pentax-A zooms

### 24 - 50mm *f*4 A

*Minimum aperture: f22*
*Closest focus: 40cm*
*Dimensions: 68 x 64mm*
*Weight: 375g*
*Filter thread: 58mm*

With the advantage of a constant maximum aperture, this zoom covers the entire range of shorter focal lengths which you are likely to need, in a compact and light form. It performs moderately well – not up to the same standard as either the 24mm *f*2.8 or 50mm *f*1.7 taken individually – and scores highly on convenience and handling. From *f*8 downwards, it is indistinguishable in performance from the other lenses within its range. It also focuses to a useful minimum distance of 15" (40cm).
**Constant aperture design – recommended for the K1000**

### 28 - 80mm *f*3.5 ~ 4.5 Takumar-A

*Minimum aperture: f22 ~ 32*
*Closest focus: 80cm*
*Dimensions: 82 x 69mm*
*Weight: 450g*
*Filter thread: 58mm*

The Takumar-A lens is a budget priced standard zoom, costing around half the price of the regular Pentax-A 28-80mm. Otherwise the specifications are similar. The performance is marginally inferior – to a degree which few would ever notice – and the lens is a little heavier and bulkier. A very versatile range of focal lengths, strongly recommended if you intend to own just one lens.

### 28 - 80mm *f*3.5 ~ 4.5 A

*Minimum aperture: f22 ~ 32*
*Closest focus: 80cm*
*Dimensions: 77 x 63mm*
*Weight: 355g*
*Filter thread: 58mm*

A state-of-the-art design, the Pentax-A 28-80mm is lighter and smaller than the Takumar-A. It intended for professional photographers or those who want to make large prints (over 10 x 8"). It also has a very good macro close-up feature which retains sharpness and flatness of field.

**28 - 135mm *f*4**
*Minimum aperture: f22*
*Closest focus: 1.7m*
*Dimensions: 113 x 80mm*
*Weight: 820g*
*Filter thread: 77mm*

If you want this range, you pay heavily in weight and bulk, with a 77mm filter thread making life expensive should you want a polarizer or a soft-focus filter. The Pentax 28-135mm is far bigger than most independent lenses of a similar range, because it has a fixed maximum aperture of *f*4 at all focal lengths and offers exceptionally high performance. It is correspondingly expensive. The focusing range is restricting, as you are unable to get any closer than 1.7m (nearly six feet) without switching to the special macro range. Although this minimum distance is adequate for a portrait at 135mm, it is too far for comfort when you have the lens set to 28 or even 50mm. Small children and pets will come closer to the lens and you will be unable to focus and zoom (though as a quick remedy, switching to the macro range enables you to catch subjects which do move too close when you are using the 28mm end of the zoom).
**Constant aperture design – recommended for the K1000**

**35 - 105mm *f*3.5**
*Minimum aperture: f22*
*Closest focus: 1.5m*
*Dimensions: 98 x 70mm*
*Weight: 615g*
*Filter thread: 67mm*

A substantially larger lens than the 28-80mm, the range of the 35-105mm is better suited to photographing people. The 28-80mm is ideal for landscapes, interiors and general scenes; the 35-105mm superior for groups, portraits and candids. It has the benefit of a fixed *f*3.5 maximum aperture, which is very fast for a lens of this type, and is responsible for the weight and bulk of the type A 35-105mm. A good macro close-up facility is provided, capable of just under one-quarter life size on film. This lens provides a very bright and crisp focusing image at all focal lengths when used with the K1000 or P30n – see the notes under the details of the autofocus SMC Pentax-F version, which is not a good choice for manual camera owners. We have therefore included this lens although it was removed from the range shortly before preparation of our lens list. It is better suited to manual cameras than the autofocus version which replaces it in the range.
**Constant aperture design – recommended for the K1000**

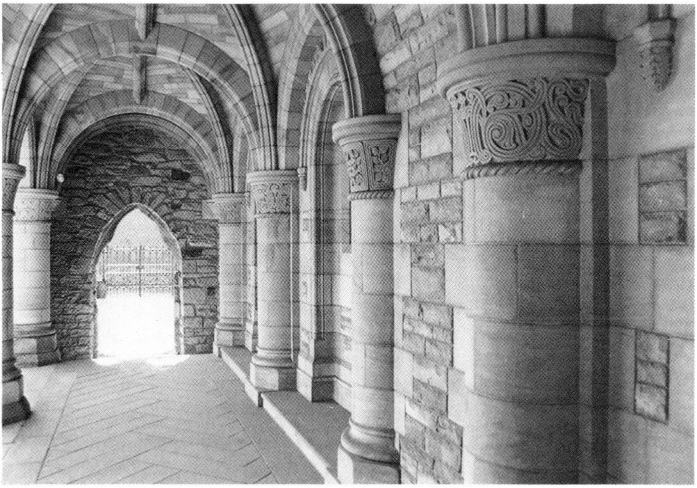

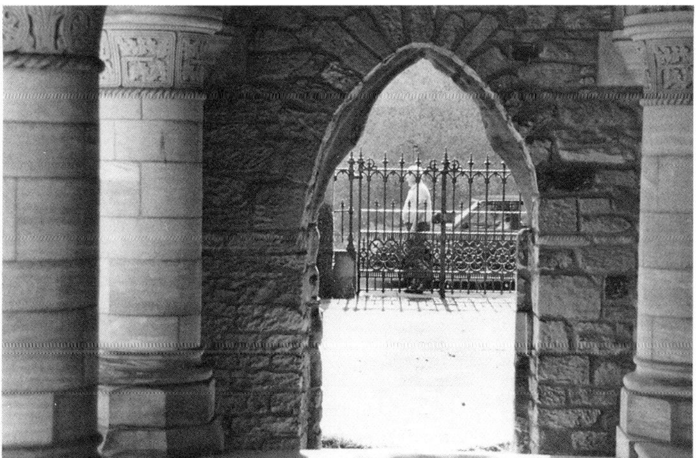

*The 28-80mm is the most popular current choice of zoom to replace the standard 50mm lens. The change between 28mm and 80mm is much greater than you would imagine, as these two pictures show. The top shot is taken at 28mm, the bottom one at 80mm. Photographed with the P30n and Pentax-A 28-80mm lens.*

**35 - 135mm *f*3.5 ~ 4.5**
*Minimum aperture: f22 ~ 32*
*Closest focus: 75cm*
*Dimensions: 92 x 63mm*
*Weight: 450g*
*Filter thread: 58mm*

A wider range than the 35-105mm, but with a small penalty in the loss of constant maximum aperture. The viewing image remains bright enough for either the K1000 or P30n at any focal length. If you want this range of focal lengths, buy this version rather than the autofocus SMC Pentax-F equivalent – the Pentax-A 35-135mm focuses much closer (70cm as opposed to 1.6m) and this alone makes it considerably more versatile. However, this a focal length range which offers few advantages in size and weight; the regular 135mm telephoto is both faster and smaller. The 35-135mm is a standard-lens replacement with the benefit of extra telephoto reach. You may find it a good choice if you take photographs at field sports events, of weddings, portraits and groups, or for fashion and human figure studies.

**70 - 200mm *f*4 Takumar-A**
*Minimum aperture: f32*
*Closest focus: 1.2m*
*Dimensions: 102 x 62mm*
*Weight: 623g*
*Filter thread: 58mm*

The basic Pentax tele zoom, the Takumar version is an earlier design than the Pentax-A version which follows. It has the advantage of a fixed maximum aperture, which gives it a larger front element and filter thread, but the overall size and weight are similar. There is really nothing to choose between the two. The focal length range is by far the most popular and covers 90% of your requirements for long-range, middle-distance and portrait tele photography. It dovetails neatly with either the 35-70mm or 28-80mm, and goes well with a 50mm, leaving very little by way of gap as the focal lengths between 50 and 70mm are not widely used. If you own two camera bodies, it can sometimes be useful for have both with the same focal length – and this is something you can do with a mid-range zoom and the 70-200mm, by setting both 70mm (or 80mm, etc).
**Constant aperture design – recommended for the K1000**

*Right: the 70-210mm SMC Pentax-A is a slide action (one-touch) rather than twin ring zoom. The lens remains the same physical length as the barrel is moved from 70mm (left) to 210mm (right).*

**70 - 210mm *f*4 ~ 5.6 Pentax-A**
*Minimum aperture: f22 ~ 32*
*Closest focus: 1.1m*
*Dimensions: 103 x 61mm*
*Weight: 628g*
*Filter thread: 49mm*

This Pentax-A lens takes a smaller filter, closer focusing and more modern overall design. It also has a variable maximum aperture, so if you intend to use manual exposure on the P30n, or to use it with a K1000, consider the Takumar first. There is very little difference in performance or price. A previous Pentax-A 70-210mm with a fixed *f*4 maximum aperture and 58mm filter thread, similar to the current Takumar but of higher performance, is now discontinued. This lens was more suited to use with the K1000. Both lenses will be replaced by the SMC-F.

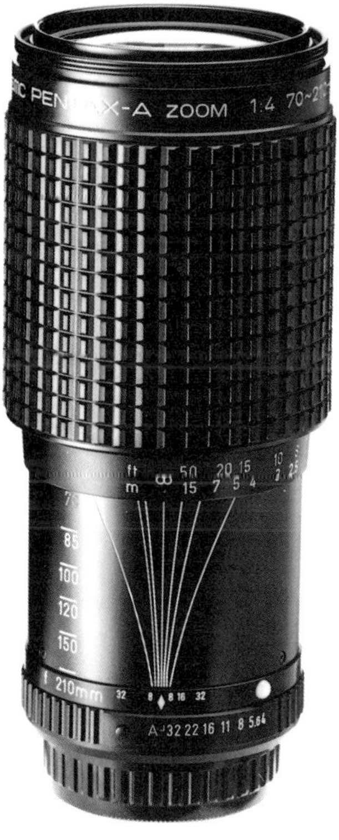


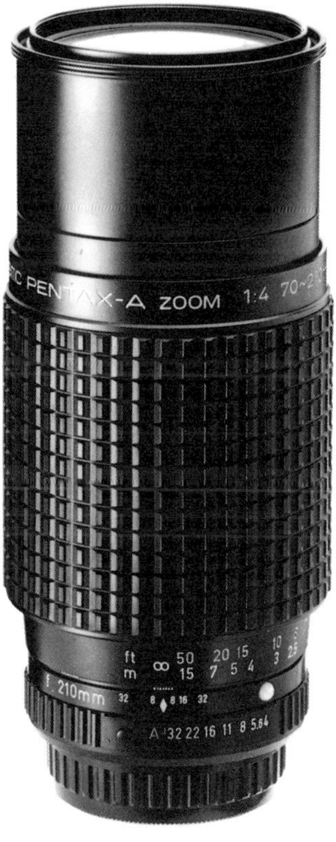

## Pentax-F lenses

Pentax-F lenses are intended for the autofocus SLR range, but will function perfectly well on every other K-mount or KA-mount Pentax SLR. The focusing ring is generally rather small and its action lacks "feel", as it has so little resistance. There is no need to buy these lenses for your K1000 or P30n, but if you do pick from this range, you can change to an AF SLR later and keep your lenses with full AF operation. If you buy K or KA mount lenses, these will still work perfectly on the AF body, but without autofocus. F-designs are the future standard.

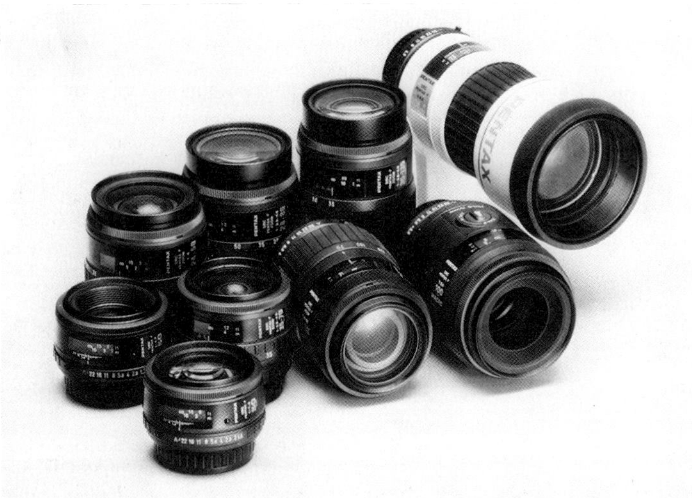

*The Pentax-F autofocus range is constantly growing, and most new lenses will be introduced in this mount. Right: a 300mm lens provides a strong close-up at the Scottish School of Falconry.*

### 28mm *f*2.8 F

*Minimum aperture: f22*
*Closest focus: 30cm*
*Dimensions: 37 x 64mm*
*Weight: 182g*
*Filter thread: 49mm*

The only autofocus wide-angle in the Pentax range at the time of writing, the 28mm is competitively priced but offers no advantage over the Takumar-A or Pentax-A versions for the K1000 or P30n owner.

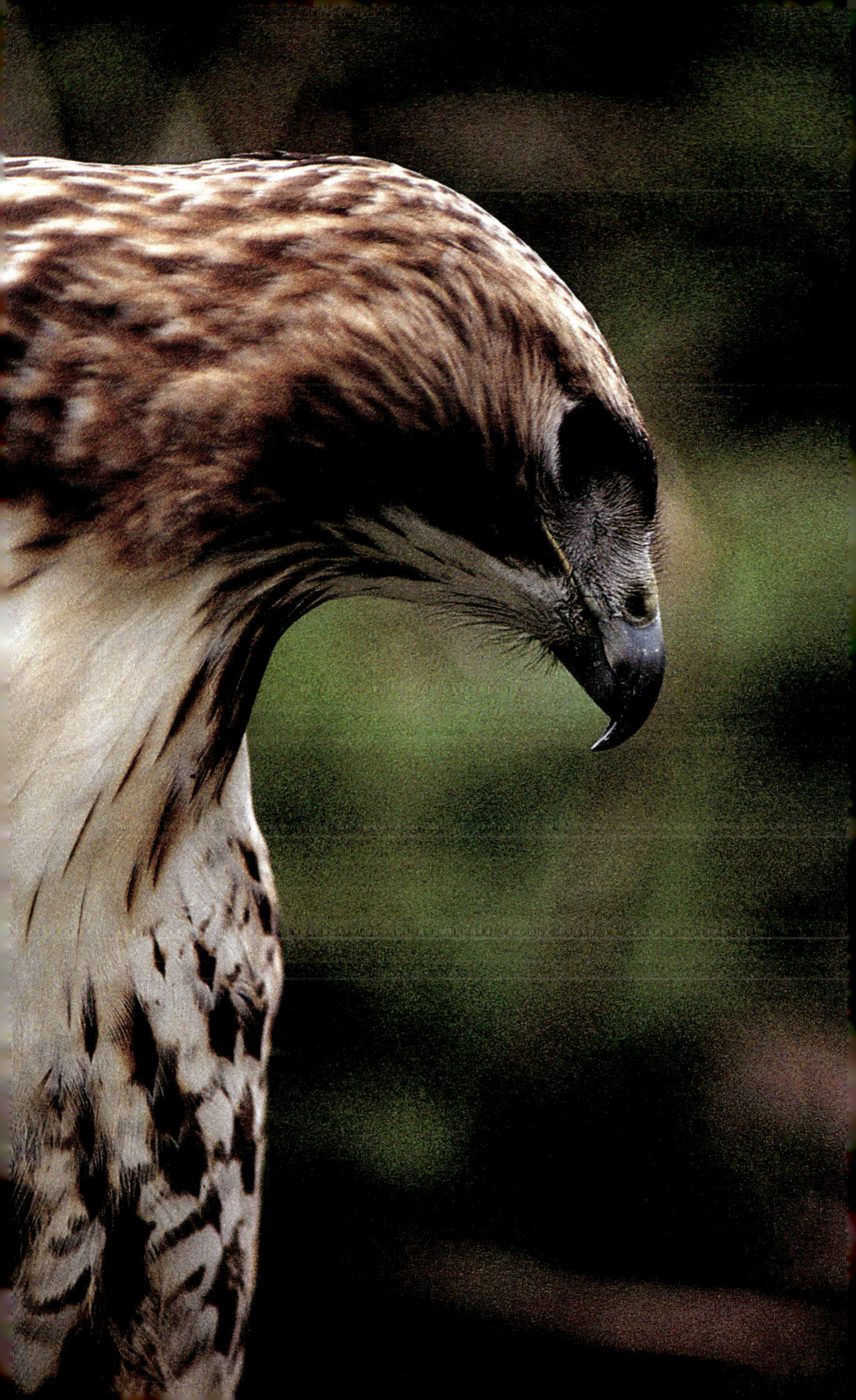

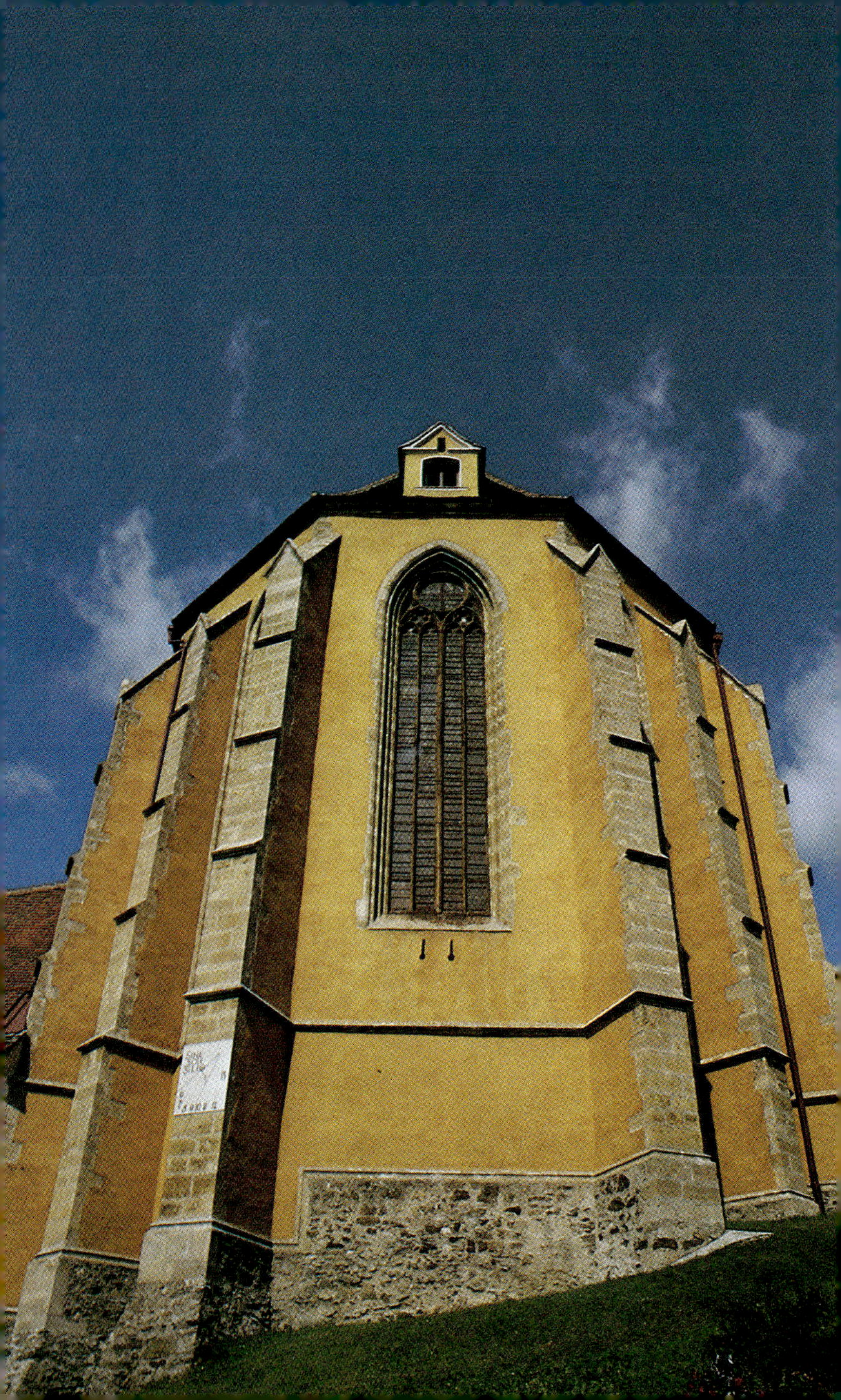

**50mm *f*1.7 SMC-F**
*Minimum aperture: f22*
*Closest focus: 40cm*
*Dimensions: 37 x 65mm*
*Weight: 200g*
*Filter thread: 49mm*

**50mm *f*1.4 SMC-F**
*Minimum aperture: f22*
*Closest focus: 40cm*
*Dimensions: 37 x 65mm*
*Weight: 230g*
*Filter thread: 49mm*

The autofocus standard lenses – not normally supplied with K1000 or P30n bodies, and not necessary. The prices are virtually identical, and autofocus merely adds a little weight.

**50mm *f*2.8 Macro F**
*Minimum aperture: f32*
*Closest focus: 1:1*
*Dimensions: 70 x 68mm*
*Weight: 385g*
*Filter thread: 52mm*

The autofocus version of the 50mm macro lens is larger and heavier than the Pentax-A macro, principally because it focuses to life size. This lens replaces the A-series macro.

**100mm *f*2.8 Macro F**
*Minimum aperture: f22*
*Closest focus: 1:1*
*Filter thread: 58mm*

The autofocus version of the 100mm macro lens, and not necessary unless you plan to buy an AF body. Once again, the F-series replaces the A-series lens in this focal length.

**135mm *f*2.8 Pentax-F**
*Minimum aperture: f32*
*Closest focus: 40cm*
*Dimensions: 80 x 68mm*
*Weight: 400g*
*Filter thread: 52mm*

The autofocus version of the 135mm *f*2.8 – comments as for 28mm F.

*When you buy lenses, try to keep the filter size the same throughout your outfit. This shot is taken with a polarizer, and it's useful to be able to buy just one filter like this to use on several lenses. If you buy one to fit your largest lens, an adaptor ring can be used to match it to other lenses.*

### 300mm *f*4.5 SMC Pentax-F ED-IF

*Minimum aperture: f32*
*Closest focus: 4m*
*Dimensions: 212 x 75mm*
*Weight: 880g*
*Filter thread: 67mm*

A 300mm lens with fine performance at a reasonable price. *f*4.5 is more than adequate for a 300mm; filter size and bulk are all kept to a minimum. The design uses internal focusing and extra-low dispersion glass. The 400mm *f*5.6 Pentax-A is substantially lower in cost, so consider the longer A lens as an alternative.

### 400mm *f*2.8 SMC Pentax-F ED-IF

*Minimum aperture: f32*
*Closest focus: 4.5m*
*Dimensions: 325 x 165mm*
*Weight: 6000g*
*Filter thread: 49mm rear-mounted*

The basic features of the 300mm *f*2.8 and 400mm *f*5.6 A-mount lenses are combined in this very fast long telephoto, with the addition of autofocus. The 400mm *f*2.8 is far to heavy to use hand-held.

### 600mm *f*4 SMC Pentax-F ED-IF

*Minimum aperture: f32*
*Closest focus: 5m*
*Dimensions: 413 x 181mm*
*Weight: 5800g*
*Filter thread: 43mm rear-mounted*

A lens with exactly the same uses as the 600mm *f*5.6, but substantially faster and offering even higher image quality. Very much larger and heavier, and best reserved for tripod use.

### 24 - 50mm *f*4 Pentax-F

*Minimum aperture: f22*
*Closest focus: 40cm*
*Dimensions: 62 x 80mm*
*Weight: 380g*
*Filter thread: 58mm*

Most of the comments on the Pentax-A 24-50mm also apply to this lens, which is slightly larger as a result of autofocus design. There is no advantage in owning the AF version for use on a P30n or K1000.

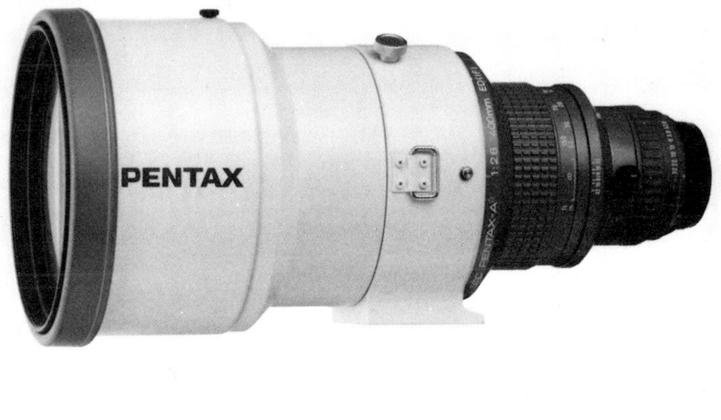


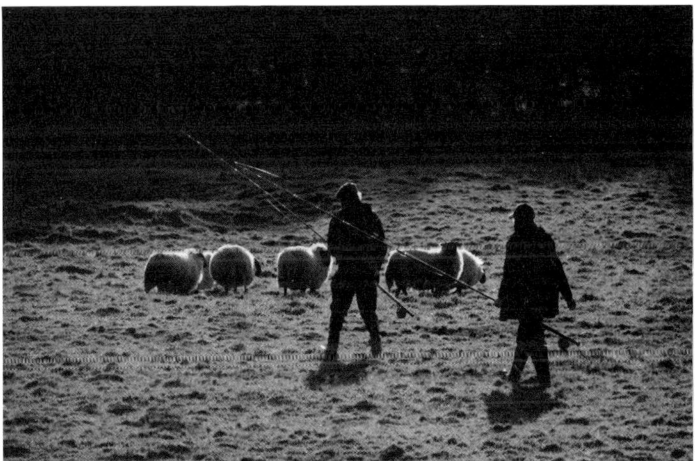

*Top: the Pentax 400mm ƒ2.8 is a very substantial lens intended for the professional sports and news photographer. Bottom: using the 400mm ƒ5.6, hand-held shots like this against-the-light study are possible on medium speed film. I gave one stop less exposure than the meter indicated, to compensate for the dark background.*

**28 - 80mm *f*3.5 ~ 4.5 Pentax-F**
*Minimum aperture: f22 ~ 32*
*Closest focus: 80cm*
*Dimensions: 68 x 72mm*
*Weight: 395g*
*Filter thread: 58mm*

Very similar to the Pentax-A 28-80mm lens in size and weight, with the standard medium-sized 58mm filter thread, this autofocus lens is priced between the Takumar-A and Pentax-A in price.

**28 - 80mm *f*3.5 ~ 4.5 SMC Pentax-F**
*Minimum aperture: f22 ~ 32*
*Closest focus: 80cm*
*Dimensions: 85 x 70mm*
*Weight: 395g*
*Filter thread: 58mm*

The **SMC** Pentax-F version of the 28-80mm uses Pentax Super-Multi-Coating for better contrast and colour saturation. It is the most expensive 28-80mm of the four alternatives available.

**35 - 70mm *f*3.5 ~ 4.5 SMC Pentax-F**
*Minimum aperture: f22 ~ 32*
*Closest focus: 70cm*
*Dimensions: 58 x 65mm*
*Weight: 214g*
*Filter thread: 49mm*

Part of the top grade SMC Pentax range, this mid-range zoom is very small and light – little bigger than a standard lens. An ideal choice as an alternative to the 50mm when buying a P30n, it costs more than the 28-80mm Pentax-F. For versatility on a budget, choose the 28-80mm. An earlier 35-70mm with an *f*2.8 maximum aperture, physically larger, remains an attractive buy for owners of manual focusing cameras.

**35 - 105mm *f*4 ~ 5.6 SMC Pentax-F**
*Minimum aperture: f22 ~ 32*
*Closest focus: 1.4m*
*Dimensions: 81 x 70mm*
*Weight: 345g*
*Filter thread: 58mm*

Combining very good performance with light weight and compact dimensions, this relatively expensive lens achieves its performance and size at the expense of a variable maximum aperture which is half a stop slower than the A-mount version at 35mm focal length, and one-and-a-half stops slower at 105mm. The focusing screen of a K1000 looks decidedly dim with an *f*5.6 105mm lens in use, and even the split-image finder of the P30n can black out in one half very readily unless you eye is exactly centred. For these reasons, you are better off with the larger and heavier 35-105mm *f*3.5 Pentax-A lens, with its brighter image for manual focusing, if you can obtain one.

### 35 - 135mm *f*3.5 ~ 4.5 SMC Pentax-F

*Minimum aperture: f22 ~ 32*
*Closest focus: 1.6m*
*Dimensions: 92 x 71mm*
*Weight: 485g*
*Filter thread: 58mm*

Although rated as a top performance lens and priced accordingly, the 35-135mm has the disadvantage of a close focus limit of 1.6 metres without using the macro facility. A compromise between focal length ranges which does not fulfil the all-round potential of a 28-135mm, yet lacks the convenience of a 35-105mm.

### 35 - 210mm *f*3.5 ~ 4.5 SMC Pentax-F

*Minimum aperture: f22 ~ 32*
*Closest focus: 1.1m*
*Dimensions: 80 x 130mm*
*Weight: 815g*
*Filter thread: 67mm*

A zoom with a phenomenal range, capable of covering everything from landscapes to telephoto action pictures. This lens has a good close-focus limit which enables it to reproduce small subjects such as flowers at 1:3.5 (one third life size). Slightly more expensive than other wide-to-tele zooms. If you buy a 35-210mm you may never need another lens – but you'll always be saddled with a very large mass of glass on the front of your camera.

### 70 - 200mm *f*4 ~ 5.6 F

*Minimum aperture: f22 ~ 32*
*Closest focus: 1.1m*
*Filter thread: 49mm*

The basic autofocus zoom is very similar to the Pentax-A series lens of the same specification. Unless you intend to buy an AF series body, it offers no advantages in price or performance.

**70 - 210mm $f4$ ~ 4.5 SMC Pentax-F**
*Minimum aperture: f22 ~ 28*
*Closest focus: 1.1m*
*Dimensions: 99 x 71mm*
*Weight: 542g*
*Filter thread: 49mm*

A superior design optically, the SMC Pentax-F lens also has an extra 10mm of range at the long end – not of great significance. Once again, a lens to consider only if you firmly intend to change to AF cameras. As the aperture only changes by half a stop across the zoom range, this is also a good lens for manual use (most of the time this shift can be ignored).

**250 - 600mm $f5.6$ ED (IF) SMC Pentax-F**
*Minimum aperture: f32*
*Cloesest focus: 3.5m*
*Dimensions: 149 x 439mm*
*Weight: 5,400g*
*Filter thread: 43mm (rear) or 112mm (front)*

A high performance zoom for sports and action work, natural history and landscape – strictly for tripod use, and very substantial! Internal focusing, extra-low dispersion glass and the latest optical design contribute to the quality and cost of this lens alike.

## Teleconverters

Telephoto converters or multipliers fit between the camera body and lens, and increase the focal length optically. A converter usually has between four and seven elements, and retains all the couplings and functions of the camera and lens combination.

There are two strengths available – 1.4x and 2x. The reason for 1.4x is that this exact figure involves one *f*-stop in light loss, which is penalty you pay when a teleconverter is fitted. A 2x converter means 2 *f*-stops in light is lost. If you fit a 1.4x converter to a 50mm *f*2 lens, it becomes a 70mm *f*2.8; use a 2x, and you get a 100mm *f*4.

The 1.4x converter is of most use if you own fixed focal length lenses. These are often fast to start off with, so retaining as much of maximum aperture as possible will help. A 135mm *f*2.8 lens becomes a 190mm *f*4, which is a very useful combination. The 1.4x converter is not much use with zooms, because no zoom in the Pentax range has a range of less than 2:1 (a 35-70mm zoom is a 2:1 ratio zoom). If you fit a 1.4x converter to a 35-70mm zoom, you get a 50-100mm zoom, so all the focal lengths from 50 to 70 obtained with the converter are wasted – you get much better results and a faster working aperture with the zoom on its own at these settings.

A 2x converter is an ideal addition to a zoom. The 28-80mm becomes a 56-160mm, the 35-70mm becomes a 70-150mm, and the 70-210mm becomes a 140-420mm. In most cases there is some overlap, but not as much as you would get with a 1.4x.

It is worth buying the genuine Pentax converters, and matching the type of converter to the lens you intend to use it with. Independent converters often produce inferior results, as they are not optically matched to any range of lenses, and have to be a general compromise.

**Takumar A 2x**

This is a budget-priced 2x converter in the A-mount, under the Takumar brand name. It is the same price as most independent converters, and is matched to the Pentax lens range generally. An excellent all-round choice as a standby converter for any of your lenses.

**Rear Converter A 1.4X-S**

A high quality Pentax-A series converter specifically intended for lenses under 200mm (including the 70-210mm zoom). This converter is the correct choice for the 50mm, 85mm, 100mm 135mm and 200mm prime lenses.

**Rear Converter A 2X-S**

Similar to the 1.4X-S, but 2x power. Matched, as above, to the shorter focal length lenses and zooms.

**Rear Converter A 1.4X-L**

The L indicates matching to longer lenses – from the 300mm prime telephotos up to the mirror lenses.

**Rear Converter A 2X-L**

As above, but a 2x version for the longer lenses. Ideal in combination with the 300mm *f*4.5, 400mm *f*2.8 and similar fast long telephotos.

Be warned that the telephoto converters are surprisingly expensive, the Takumar-A excepted. A single converter will cost the same as the average zoom lens. For the K1000 or P30n owner, therefore, the Takumar-A converter seems a sensible standard choice, at a quarter of the price of the other converters.

If you see a 1.7x converter offered for Pentax, do not buy this for your K1000 or P30n. It is an autofocus converter which allows you to use most A series lenses with autofocus on the SFX/SF7 SLRs.

# Accessories and beyond

The advantage of owning an SLR is that you can expand the system in many ways. Pentax offer a range of accessories compatible with the K1000 and P30n, including the flashguns and lenses already mentioned. You can use any independent K or KA-mount lenses, and any independent flash units which are guaranteed to be correctly dedicated to the P30n.

It is often better to keep to genuine Pentax items, especially as far as flash and A-type lenses go. There is some risk of jamming non-Pentax lenses on the mount of either the K1000 or P30n – more so with the latter. This advice mainly applies to older items such as early independent K-mount lenses.

You can use screw-thread Pentax lenses from the original Takumar, auto Takumar, Super Takumar, SMC Takumar and SMC-Pentax ranges. This requires **Mount Adaptor K**, a small ring which you first screw on to the old lens. The lens can then be mounted, and used with manual stop-down metering only. A small sliding switch on most screw-thread lenses allows rapid closing down to the working aperture from full viewing aperture, but if you forget to do this you picture will be seriously overexposed.

To remove the adaptor/lens from the camera, you must unscrew the lens first, then remove the Adaptor K using a finger-nail or small pointed object to release a catch. This is rather tricky. The normal bayonet lens release is disabled when using the Adaptor K. If you don't remove the adaptor, different screw thread lenses can be fitted, as the body is temporarily converted to a screw thread body.

Watch out for some older Pentax lenses labelled *SMC Pentax F*. There are new lenses with the same designation – autofocus lenses. The early "F" lenses were for full-aperture metering with the Spotmatic F mount. Don't buy one by mistake under the impression that it's a new AF-mount type!

## Close-up attachments

There are several ways of making a standard 50mm lens focus much closer, which also work with other prime lenses. They are most successful with the 35mm, 100mm and 135mm. If you move the lens away from the camera body, it will focus closer. So inserting a spacing ring between the body and lens can extend the focus range.

There are two sets of extension rings or tubes – the **Auto-Extension Tube Set K**, and the **Extension Tube Set K**. The difference is in the coupling. The auto set allows full aperture metering (K1000 and P30n)

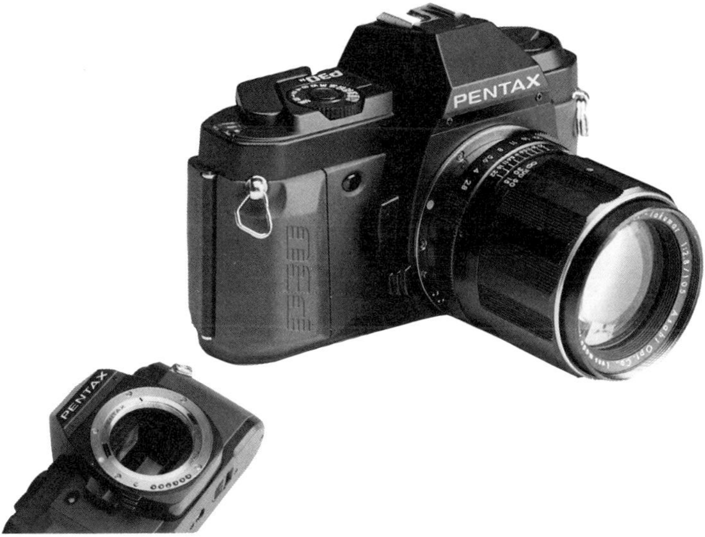


*Above: Mount Adaptor K fitted to a P30n body, with the author's 105mm screw-mount Super Takumer lens attached. To remove the lens and mount, it is necessary to first unscrew the lens, then detach the mount using a sharp point to release its catch.*

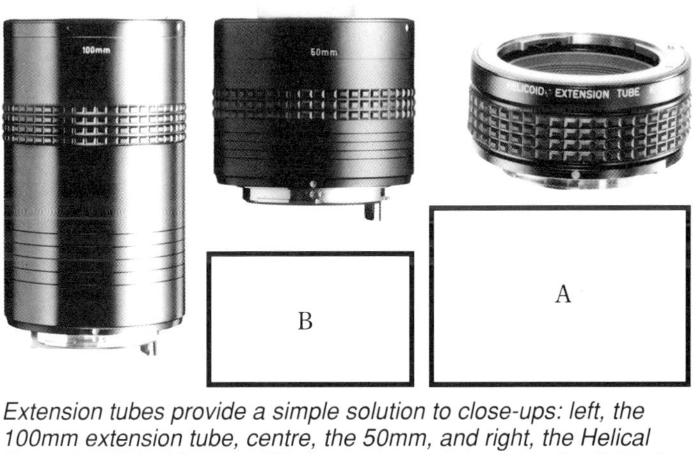


*Extension tubes provide a simple solution to close-ups: left, the 100mm extension tube, centre, the 50mm, and right, the Helical Extension Tube K. Area "A" shows precisely how small a field of view will be obtained with the standard 50mm lens and 50mm tube; Area "B" shows the field covered when using the 100mm tube.*

and aperture priority auto exposure (P30n); the plain set requires manual stop-down and metering, with no auto exposure coupling. The Auto set is to be recommended in preference.

Each tube in the set is progressively longer, and with the standard 50mm *f*2 or *f*1.7 you can obtain a continuous focusing range with minimal gaps. All three tubes used together will permit an image slightly larger than life-size with the 50mm. It is very important to read the instructions fully, as many close-ups are taken using flash, and the marked aperture on the lens is no longer applicable when tubes are added. With 50mm of extension tubes behind a 50mm lens, each aperture becomes equivalent to two stops less – a marked *f*4 is a true *f*8, and so on. Exposure metering through the camera compensates for this, but for flash you must be sure to look up the required correction in the Extension Tubes instruction manual, and apply it.

You can use extension tubes with zooms, but zooming will result in loss of sharp focus. Handling is more acceptable if the zoom if left on a fixed focal length, and only the focus control of the lens is adjusted.

There are two further close-up devices which go between the camera and lens – the **Helicoid Extension Tube K**, and the **Auto Bellows A**. Both offer continuous adjustable extension. In the case of the Helicoid Tube, this covers a limited range compared to the Extension Tube sets, favouring higher magnification. The helicoid (screw-thread) variable tube can be used with the Bellows Macro 100mm for focusing between infinity and close-up, and exposure is entirely manual.

The Auto Bellows A gives a much longer range, allowing high magnifications such as 4:1 (four times life size). With the 100mm macro lens head, focusing from infinity to beyond life size is possible; with a 50mm standard lens, the closest focus is already around half life size. The Auto Bellows provides auto stop-down for exposure using a twin cable release, but there is no linkage for the full aperture metering, so metered manual at stopped-down aperture has to be employed.

A **reversing ring** allows you to attach wide-angle lenses, reversed, on to the front mount of the bellows. This optical arrangement provides superior results at higher magnifications with the 28mm and 24mm lenses.

## Copy Stands

Unique to the Pentax system, the copy stand or legs consists of a short extension tube fitted with four adjustable legs. The tube works with the standard 50mm lens, and the legs automatically position the camera the correct distance from the flat object (such as a map or book page) to be copied. Be careful to light this evenly, and avoid the shadows cast by the legs, which are as thin as stability will permit. The **Copy Stand K** provides a quick, reliable method of making accurate photographic

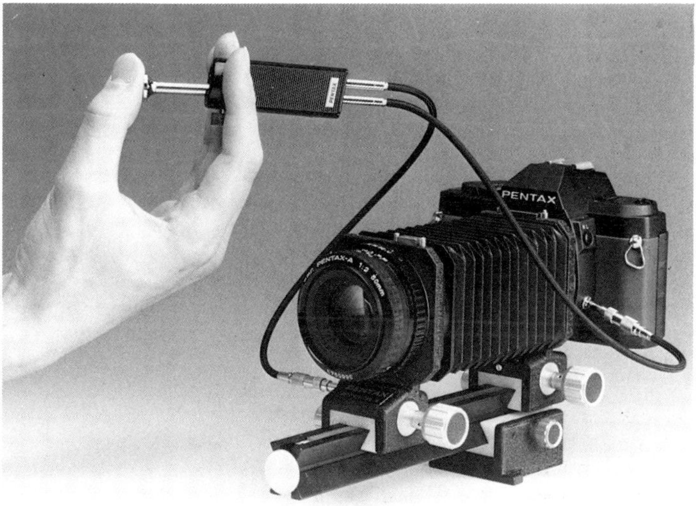


*Above: Auto Bellows K set up for use with the standard 50mm lens. Below: the Pentax Macro copy stand, illuminator and accessories for slide copying and high-magnification shots.*

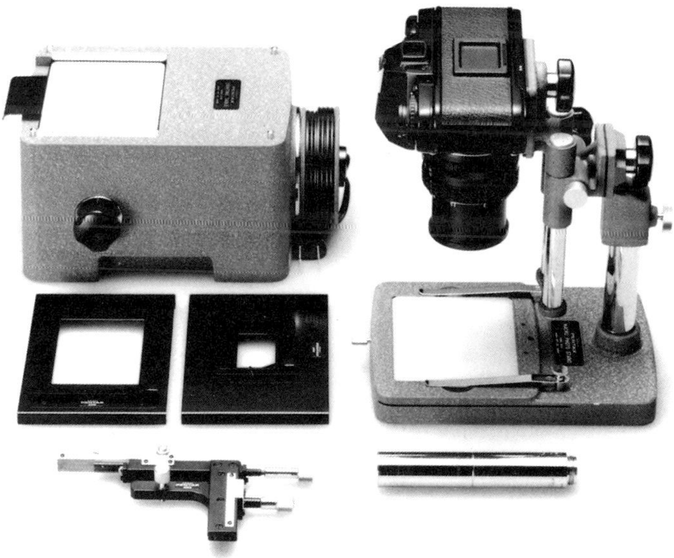

copies from pictures and photographing small objects such as jewellery, medals, stamps and coins. The Macro Photo Stand and macro Lighting Table are both ideal accessories for very detailed close-ups at ratios from quarter life size to high magnification.

## Microscope adaptor

The Pentax K **microscope adaptor** is an adjustable tube, which fits the standard eyepiece tube of most optical microscopes. Remove the microscope eyepiece, and ensuring that the microscope has been securely locked after focusing and aligning on the specimen, attach the camera with the adaptor ready fitted. Some adjustment to focus may be needed, and the screen image will be dim; you may need to put extra light through the microscope to view comfortably. Exposures can be made by daylight via a condensor mirror, or by flash on an extension cable (you need to experiment to establish the correct distance). Do not try to make exposures in colour using the built-in illuminator of the microscope; the results will be very yellow. You can take black and white pictures this way.

## Telescope adaptor

The same adaptor will attach the Pentax K-mount body to many telescopes, both terrestrial and astronomical. You may need two tripods, carefully adjusted, to ensure stability – one for the telescope and a second for the camera. Some telescopes such as the Questar and Celestron can be ordered with a camera adaptor ready-fitted and collimated for correct focusing. Your Pentax can also be used to take photographs through telescopes and binoculars with eyepiece lenses fitted. In this case, a special adaptor has to be made up, or your camera positioned on a tripod just behind the telescope.

Early Asahi (Pentax) telescopes often had a camera cradle to hold a Pentax SLR close to the eyepiece. The camera's standard lens is used in the normal eye position, and simply views through the telescope. This method produces lower sharpness and may cut off the corners of the image.

## Telescope lens eyepiece

An independent accessory, a telescopic lens eyepiece attaches to the mount of any suitable Pentax-K lens (the 70-210mm zoom is ideal) and converts it to a monocular telescope. In this way, your Pentax tele lenses can double as high quality telescopes ideal for wilderness expeditions and bird-spotting. With a tripod-mounted telephoto, you can use such an attachment for prior sighting before fitting the camera.

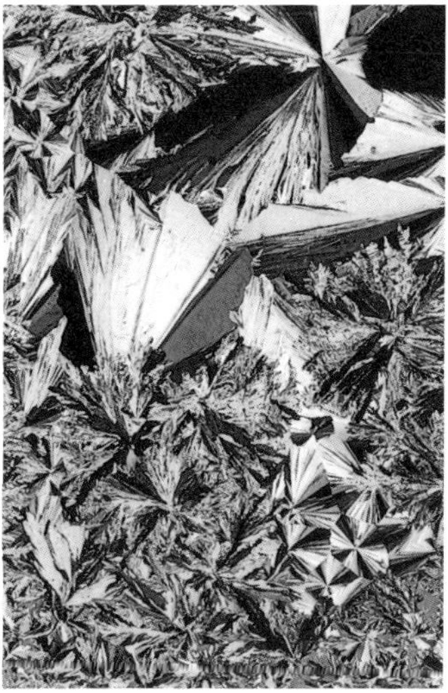

*Above: a 35mm photomicrograph by Mike Travers*

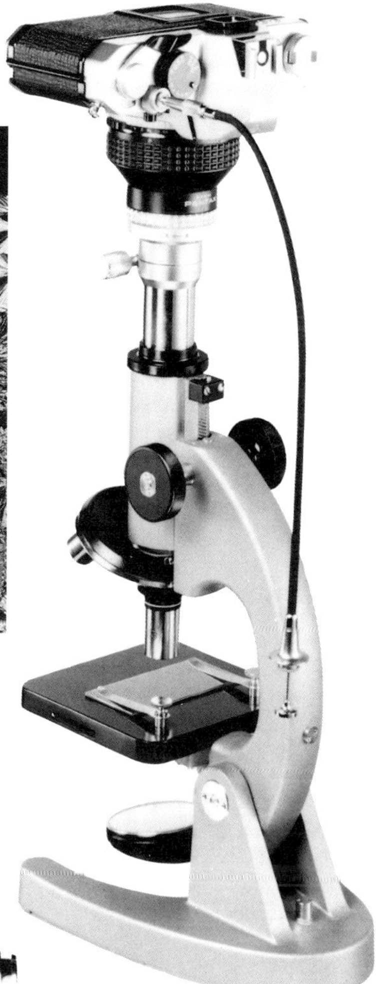

*Right: an optical microscope showing the camera mounted in position after first setting-up the specimen by eye*

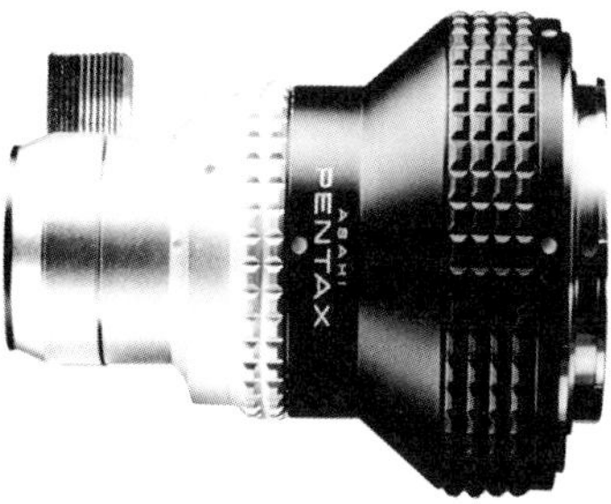


*Left: the Pentax microscope adaptor allows you to connect a K1000 or P30n to almost any microscope*

## Viewfinder accessories

A rubber cup can be fitted to the grooves on either side of the eyepiece, providing a better light-seal and increased comfort. These grooves also accept various other accessories. The camera instruction manual explains how to use the eyepiece cap supplied with the P30n to ensure that stray light does not affect auto exposure when using a tripod. With the K1000, the rubber cup serves the same purpose – take the meter reading with your eye sealed all round, and no stray light can enter. This is important when using stopped-down reading with the Auto Bellows and similar set-ups.

When making copies using a copy stand, you view down into the camera vertically, and overhead light can have a strong effect. Be certain to use the cap on the P30n under these conditions. With the camera mounted for ground-level close-ups, viewing can be very difficult, so a Right-Angle Finder is attached to the eyepiece. This 90° "tube with a bend" incorporates a prism to keep the image the right way round, and an eyesight correction adjustment. It can be rotated to cope with different camera positions.

For critical focusing, the Focusing Magnifier should be used. This attaches in the same way and enlarges the central part of the focusing screen to twice the normal magnification. You cannot see all the screen, so the Magnifier is hinged to flip out of the way for composition. It, too, has eyesight adjustment.

The viewfinder itself has a fixed -1 (one dioptre of short sight) correction, which suits most European users up to middle age. If you have very short sight, long sight or astigmatism, you may need either an off-the-shelf dioptric correction lens (from Pentax) or a prescription lens (made by your optician to fit the Pentax slide-on correction frame). Either type will attach to the eyepiece in the normal way.

## Close-up lenses

Pentax make close-up lenses in three strengths to fit the main filter thread sizes in the system (49mm, 52mm and 58mm). These lenses are pocketable, inexpensive and very easy to use. They are ideal for zoom lenses, as they have no effect on the zooming action and also retain all auto functions in full. A +1 dioptre lens, for example, can be used with the 70-210mm zoom which normally focuses down to 1.1 metres. With

*The effect of filters: top, without a filter this black and white picture shows very few clouds and a pale white sky. Bottom, with an orange filter fitted, the response of the film is changed so that the sky records as the right shade of grey and the clouds can be seen.*

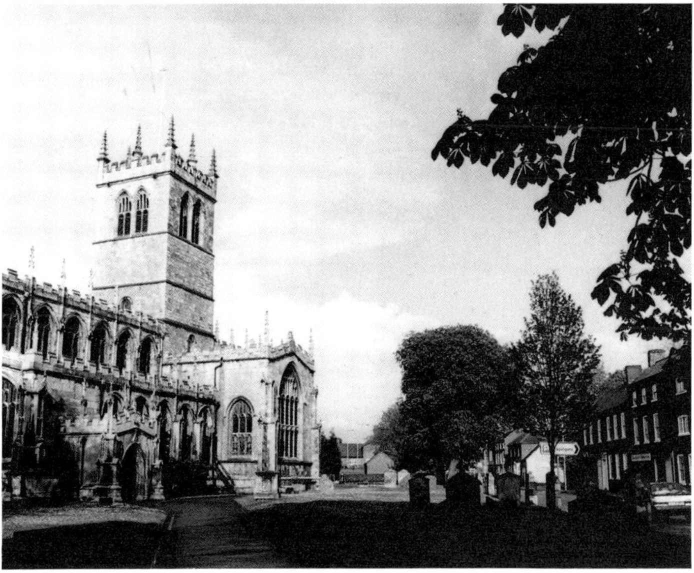

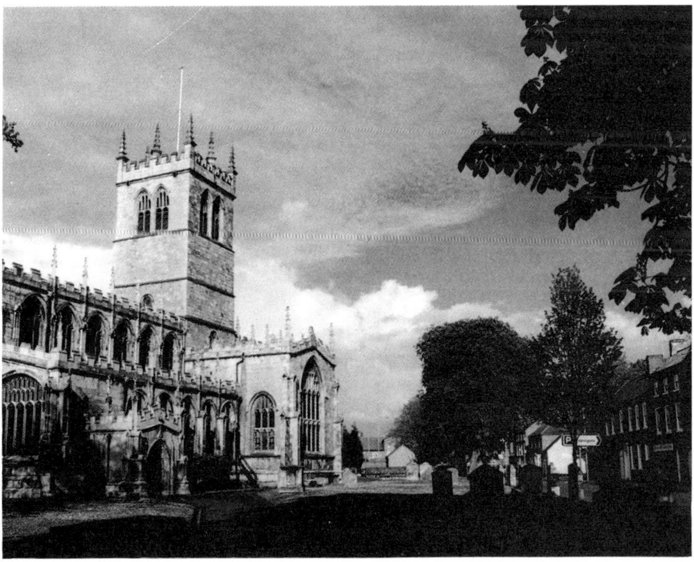

a 1 dioptre lens in place, the zoom focuses between one metre and 55cm. You cannot focus on infinity when a close-up lens it attached.

The +2 close-up brings the focus to 50cm or less, and the +3 to 30cm or closer. With the 210mm end of the zoom range this allows true macro shots. The pocketability and convenience of these lenses makes them ideal for travel, mountaineering, and natural history photography where small flowers or insects can be recorded at frame-filling size without having to fit extension tubes.

## Filters

Your dealer should have advised you to purchase a haze, skylight or ultra-violet filter to fit permanently to each lens you own. These filters are essentially clear, and are used for protecting the lens from damage. The haze and skylight filters have a very slight warm tint which cuts out excessive blue from distant views. Pentax filters are super-multi-coated to improve contrast.

For colour or black and white, a polarizing filter is a useful all-round accessory. The polarizer can be used to deepen light blue skies, cut reflections off water or wet streets, eliminate glare from foliage and thus improve spring and autumn colours, or eliminate reflections in plate glass and polished non-metallic surfaces. The exposure system of your camera will compensate automatically for the neutral grey colour of the filter.

A soft-focus filter improves portraits, but needs using with care. Only buy one if you need it. You can achieve some interesting soft effects simply by breathing on the front of the lens or UV filter (no harm is done) just before taking a shot, or stretching a bit of gauze or net fabric over the lens.

Coloured filters are used for black and white as well as for colour film. Those for colour film include the 80A, a blue filter which removes the yellow cast from tungsten lighting, and 82A, a warm-colour filter for using special tungsten films in daylight. The 80A is the only one you are ever likely to need. Of more use might be an FL-D or fluorescent-to-daylight filter, which helps eliminate the unpleasant green effect given by lighting tubes. An 81A is good on dull winter days, as this filter warms up the colours a little so that things look a little more sunny!

Black and white filters include yellow, yellow-green, orange and red. All four are used to control the way that the sky, in particular, records in black and white. Without a filter, blue skies may come out plain white. A yellow filter brings them back in; a yellow-green improves foliage as well, and can also be kinder to faces if people are in the picture; orange deepens the sky to emphasize white clouds; red turns the sky nearly black and increases overall contrast. All these filters can also be used with colour for a strong single-colour effect.

## Hoods, caps and cases

Most Pentax lenses come with a lens hood or shade, or have an extending hood built-in. The basic advice is: if you have a hood, use it – if you don't, buy one and use that. There is NO circumstance where a lens shade can fail to improve a picture, or reduce the risk of flare from stray light. Just make sure the hood matches the lens and does not cut off the corners of the image.

Lens caps are essential, to keep your equipment in good condition. Always re-fit the lens cap before putting your camera away. If you remove the lens from the body for storage, fit the lens rear cap and the camera body cap too.

Cases are available with normal front parts (for the standard 50mm lens) or extended fronts (to fit the 28-80mm zoom). Using a fitted ever-ready case may slow down film changing, but it does keep the camera in good condition and protected against slight knocks. Soft pouches or hard cases for your lenses, and a good holdall to carry everything (preferably each item in its own pouch or case) will make life easier. Don't be a walking Christmas-tree!

## Insurance and care

Finally, remember that unlike other items of value, your Pentax has to be with you to take good pictures. If you want a shot from a mountain-top, you have to take the camera there. Your whole outfit might be worth a fair amount, and you would never consider walking round a tourist resort with a few watches hanging round your neck on straps. Yet photographers do this every day, and to a thief the camera is no different from a bundle of notes on a string waiting to be cut free.

So, insure your Pentax properly, and always return your warranty cards or keep dealer receipts. Use a security marker to put your post or zip-code on the camera baseplate invisibly. Buy a camera bag which has a zip as well as a flap on the top, and avoid large aluminium cases with "Pentax" written all over them!

Keep a pouch of lens-wipes and a blower in your case, and keep the camera clean – especially the filter in front of your lens.

*Looked after, your Pentax will outlast this millenium (comfortably!) just as my own original Pentax equipment remains just as usable in 1990 as it was in 1963, when at the age of 11 I was first allowed to try out what was then my father's much-prized S3. Although the only item from such an early date which I still own is my 105mm f2.8 Super-Takumar, all the other cameras and lenses have kept going for decades rather than years.*

*The K1000 is built in the same way, and the P30n, though relying on batteries and new technology, should prove to be no different.*

# Index